Law in American Meetinghouses

Law in American Meetinghouses

Church Discipline and Civil Authority in Kentucky, 1780–1845

JEFFREY THOMAS PERRY

Johns Hopkins University Press
Baltimore

Printed in the United States of America on acid-free paper
2 4 6 8 9 7 5 3 1

Johns Hopkins University Press
2715 North Charles Street
Baltimore, Maryland 21218-4363
www.press.jhu.edu

Library of Congress Cataloging-in-Publication Data

Names: Perry, Jeffrey Thomas, 1984– author.
Title: Law in American meetinghouses : church discipline and civil authority in Kentucky, 1780–1845 / Jeffrey Thomas Perry.
Description: Baltimore : Johns Hopkins University Press, 2022. | Includes bibliographical references and index.
Identifiers: LCCN 2021018616 | ISBN 9781421443072 (hardcover) | ISBN 9781421443089 (ebook)
Subjects: LCSH: Faith-based dispute resolution—United States—History—19th century. | Ecclesiastical courts—United States—History—19th century. | Baptists—Legal status, laws, etc.—United States—History—19th century. | United States—Church History—19th century. | Baptists—United States—Discipline—History—19th century. | Church and state—United States—History—19th century. | Faith-based dispute resolution—Kentucky—History—19th century.
Classification: LCC KF4868.F34 P47 2022 | DDC 347.769/0909034—dc23
LC record available at https://lccn.loc.gov/2021018616

A catalog record for this book is available from the British Library.

For my parents, Thomas and Deborah Perry

CONTENTS

A NOTE ON SOURCES

For the sake of clarity, I have corrected or updated spelling from primary sources throughout the book, but I have not altered the original authors' intentions.

Law in American Meetinghouses

INTRODUCTION

> If I was in the neighborhood, I would live and die out of religious society, before I would trust my character and property with [the church] again.
>
> —Jacob Creath Jr., referring to the David's Fork Reformed Church, 1840

In December 1803, members of the Mount Pleasant Baptist Church in Jessamine County met at a congregant's home to determine whether Brother Singleton had disregarded his guardianship duties. Singleton allegedly held "seventy-five pounds in bonds and property," as well as a 30-year-old enslaved man named Mingo. The property belonged to Singleton's servant, "an active and good fellow" named Edmund Mason. Witnesses claimed that Singleton had made a contract "to keep [Mason] as a gentleman for his estate so long as he" lived. One witness asserted that far from keeping Mason as a "gentleman," Singleton had failed to properly provide for him, dressing the young man in "common negroes' clothing." Another, Brother George Smith, claimed to have known Singleton since 1781, when they lived at a nearby frontier station. One night in the fall of 1782, Smith said he had been awakened by a cry of "Murder!" which he later "learned [was] Br. Singleton beating Edmund Mason." Over the next seven years, young Mason continued to confide in Smith. Often malnourished while serving in Singleton's household, Mason feared death by "Cholic." After a full investigation, the church ruled that Mason's term of service to Singleton was over and that Singleton owed Mason $526.10 in principal and interest for the property of Mason's that he had been holding. Just over a year after its decree, however, the church learned that Singleton had failed to comply and had "suffered himself to be sued."[1]

Most Americans today would not think of their local church as a site for arbitration and would likely be hesitant to bring their property disputes, moral failings, or personal squabbles to their kin and neighbors for judgment. Perhaps fewer would expect a fair hearing. But from the Revolutionary era through the mid-nineteenth century, many Protestants endowed local churches with immense authority and were willing to subject their private and public actions to congregational scrutiny. Churches insisted that brethren refrain from suing each other before "infidels" at local civil courts, and they assumed jurisdiction over a range of disputes typically considered matters for common law, equity, and criminal tribunals. As one might expect, charges of immorality—swearing, drunkenness, adultery—dominated disciplinary sessions, but church records are also peppered with disputes over trespassing, landholdings, probate, slave warranty, and theft. Church members expected disciplinary decisions to arise from impartial consensus and to be authoritative. When church discipline failed, the wronged often pushed back, and their responses highlight the various forces—religious, economic, and legal—that shaped the "law" of the church and ultimately hindered that venue's ability to arbitrate member disputes effectively.

Historians of American religion have grappled with church discipline for nearly a century. In his 1933 article in *Church History*, the Turnerian religious scholar William Warren Sweet proclaimed that churches were the "moral courts of the frontier." A simple "random turning of the pages of any of the old [church] record books," Sweet said, should convince anyone that churches "fought the battle for decency and order," saving "the west from semi-barbarism."[2] Other mid-twentieth-century historians latched onto Sweet's heroic characterization of church discipline.[3] By the late 1970s, however, historian Donald Mathews lamented that church record books remained an underused archival source, with those who had simply "looked" at them claiming they had found nothing.[4] Since then, many scholars have taken up his call. With the historical profession's turn to social and cultural history, church disciplinary records, and church record books in general, have come to be regarded as valuable resources through which to examine the social relations of post-Revolutionary America. Over the past twenty-five years, scholars have used disciplinary records to look at racial and gender relations, among other things, and they disagree on whether discipline served as a form of social control. These works, which count charges, excommunications, and acquittals while mining the language surrounding disciplinary proceedings for prevailing "cultural attitudes," do not firmly posit church discipline within the wider legal landscape. Nor do they fully consider the causes of the decline in church discipline and its relationship to the repositioning of religious institutions in the early republic.[5]

Legal scholars, likewise, have been hesitant to seriously consider church discipline as constituting "law" and have not recognized that its persistence and decline during the first half of the nineteenth century was entwined with the process of separating church and state. Historians during the past two generations have argued that soon after the Revolutionary War, if not before, New Englanders had embraced the courthouse over the meetinghouse for matters of dispute resolution. They have not considered the persistence of church discipline in the South and West well into the nineteenth century. Scholars of American church-state relations have also encouraged us to think about the separation of church and state not simply as a constitutional matter but as a cultural reconceptualization of churches as private institutions set apart from roles of civil governance. These scholars rely on court rulings and legislative actions to highlight the gradual process of disestablishment but have ignored church discipline.[6]

This book recovers how ordinary Americans, Black and white, enslaved and free, understood and created law in their local communities, specifically at their houses of worship. Though civil authority loomed in the background, individuals and groups made choices about which institution—church or state—could best serve their immediate needs. Disciplinary rates fell gradually during the early nineteenth century, a decline that quickened after 1830, and this process affected religious organizations' social roles in their communities and ultimately helped reposition religion and the state in American society. More than through legislative statutes and constitutional enactments, it was through what James Madison concluded were the inevitable "collisions" between "religious and Civil Authority" that Americans redefined churches' power alongside that of the state.[7] As this volume shows, important and heretofore overlooked collisions occurred when churches took up disputes, weighed evidence, and passed judgment. It demonstrates how those collisions, compounded by social transformations and religious controversy, led one prominent Baptist-turned-reformer to eschew church authority and exclaim that he would "live and die out of religious society" before trusting his "character and property with [the church] again."[8]

In this book, I focus on three questions: What role did Protestants' practice of church discipline serve within their communities from 1780 through 1845? What forces, religious and otherwise, led to the noted decline in disciplinary activities—in effect a reformulation of church ritual—over that period? And finally, what did this decline of once-prominent sites for the production of local law mean for broader legal developments and the relationship between civil and religious authority? Pursuing these questions, this book examines the ways ordinary individuals understood "law" in their local contexts, whether in a neighborhood meetinghouse or a county courthouse. A key arena in which the line between civil and religious authority became murky was in the practice of local law and in the often messy realm of dispute resolution. Though this book draws on evidence from other states and various Protestant denominations, it concentrates on Kentucky's Baptists from that state's frontier origins during the Revolutionary War through 1845.

Kentucky's experience during this period is a microcosm of the internal struggles and divisive anxieties that gripped the United States during the tumultuous decades of Western expansion and state building. At the time of the 1783 Paris Peace Treaty, "Kentucke"—then Virginia's westernmost county—was part of the far West, the United States' "first frontier," which was undergoing a violent, chaotic settlement. Nonetheless, uncertain governing authority, bloody battles with Natives, and contentious land disputes did not slow migration west of the Appalachian Mountains. Kentucky's settlers played out the ideals of the American Revolution in a place largely free of colonial-era institutions and social hierarchies, and many ordinary Americans trekked west aspiring to achieve their own version of republican independence. All migrants were not free, and Kentucky's growth unleashed disputes over slavery's righteousness and its future in the state. Debates over the slave institution animated the 1792 state constitutional convention and propelled a subsequent convention in 1799. Kentucky remained a slave state, but strains of antislavery, emancipationist, and abolitionist sentiments persisted through the antebellum era.[9] The slave question split local churches during the first decade of the 1800s, subsided for nearly three decades as the state's racial hierarchy solidified, and exploded once again during the late 1830s and early 1840s as major Protestant institutions split at the national level. Moreover, Kentucky's settlement and development occurred amid the integration of a market economy that altered the economic and social relations of Americans across much of the republic. The white men who migrated west hoping to find self-sufficiency and a family farm instead often found landlessness and economic exploitation as absentee speculators bought up land titles and an emerging elite class of merchants and entrepreneurs implanted a liberal economic order devoted to capitalistic development. During the early nineteenth century, Lexington and the Bluegrass region witnessed the beginnings of economic diversification, which historians have termed the "market revolution."[10] Across much of the Union, as in the Bluegrass, economic diversification, capitalistic investment, and new notions of acquisitiveness radiated outward from urban centers, stressing local forms of authority, including churches—institutions central in maintaining early Kentucky's social order. Once-marginal and dissenting sects such as the Baptists flourished on Kentucky's frontier, attracting large numbers of converts at the very time that most states and the federal government separated church from state and provided for religious liberty. This new religious marketplace set the stage for decades of evangelical revival and acrimonious competition between religious groups. Kentucky was home to both, witnessing some of the first camp meeting revivals that would help initiate the Second Great Awakening as well as sectarian squabbles that split churches and neighborhoods along doctrinal lines. Kentucky, then, while serving as a model for subsequent westward expansion, was also a testing ground for the Revolutionary ideals of liberty and equality. Kentuckians negotiated the growing pains of the young republic, and studying their travails provides an entry point into broader debates about the role of religious groups in post-Revolutionary American society.[11]

Baptist churches, owing to their early arrival in Kentucky, their congregational form of governance, and their extensive record keeping, are valuable institutions through which to study how individuals understood local authority.[12] They were the first local institutions of any kind in the trans-Appalachian West, appearing along with sustained Euro-American settlements in the 1770s and 1780s. The local church served as Baptists' highest earthly authority, an "enclosed garden" theoretically set off from the secular world. Its flourishing demanded the cooperation and subjection of all members, whether Black or white, enslaved or free. A church majority determined most matters—from reception of new members and disciplinary actions to doctrinal changes or a minister's ordination. Though governing associations united often-remote congregations, they had no binding authority over individual churches, and their scriptural basis and function proved a constant source of disagreement. Many Baptists guarded their congregational independence and feared its usurpation by ecclesiastical councils at the state or regional level. Thus, there were no appeals up to a synod of church elders or requirements to square a decision with a distant judicial council. Disciplinary cases stayed local.

Church record books from the period provide glimpses of communities navigating extensive social, economic, and religious transformation. This book adopts a cultural-legal approach and views disciplinary records as commentary on governance, windows through which we can grasp subtle changes in how individuals both envisioned and engaged with authority.[13] Qualitatively, it relies on religious periodicals, local and state court records, a variety of publications relating to church discipline, and a deep reading of over thirty church record books from Upper South states—mostly Kentucky but also Tennessee and Virginia. Seven of these books are from churches located in Kentucky's Bluegrass region and span the period from the late 1780s and early 1790s to 1845. Their disciplinary records serve as the foundation for my coded database, which includes more than 2,600 charges.[14] Examining changes in Baptists' disciplinary activities over time illuminates how individuals on the ground understood law in their local communities as they redefined the place of religious organizations in the new republic.

Churches served as important sites for the production of localized law during the half-century following the War of Independence. At least monthly, sometimes more often, members gathered at the neighborhood house of worship for a Saturday business meeting. After prayer and reception of new members, the moderator inquired of the congregation's "peace." When he did so, the assembled brethren transformed from a community of worshippers to a gathering of law-producing actors in pursuit of a harmonious social order. Transgressors defended or repented for their actions, while members empowered as jurors interrogated witnesses and dispensed punishments. Charges of immorality or disorderly conduct abounded at the monthly meetings, but so too did causes we would typically imagine being pled at local common-law or chancery courts. Discipline was at once a moral sword aimed at eliciting repentance from sinners and an arbitration tool used to resolve neighborhood disputes.

Historian Laura Edwards argues that localized law in the post-Revolutionary South "recognized multiple sources and sites of legal authority." Between 1787 and 1840, in refined statehouses, lawyers and jurists fashioned formalist state legal systems that uplifted abstract rights of liberalism circumscribed to white men. At the local level, however, ordinary people—even those, such as women and Blacks, who often lacked legal personhood in the eyes of the state—crafted law to maintain their social order, at times infringing on individual rights in order to protect their communities' "peace." Rooted in an Anglo-American concept of "the ideal order of the metaphorical public body," the notion of the peace guided the legal process and clung to a different logic than that espoused by elites at the state level. Local courts looked primarily to custom for guidance and relied on community gossip for background on cases, for information on litigants' character, and for indications of witnesses' reliability. "Impersonal, prescriptive markers of status"—race, gender, age, class—remained front and center, engendering inconsistent and unequal outcomes. Nonetheless, subordinate groups influenced law in their local communities. Idiosyncratic and rooted in social relations rather than formal jurisprudence, localized law produced no precedent, only options for resolution. Individuals initiated the legal process, and "law"—not simply a disengaged body of ideas to be consulted but an organism cut through with the potential contradictions and unpredictability of life—emerged from their interactions. It occurred in magistrates' offices, taverns, fields, and meetinghouses. "Law was," Edwards concludes, "everywhere and nowhere."[15]

Like Edwards, this book adopts an expansive view of law but recovers churches' roles as vital sites of law making. The primary goal of church discipline was to obtain sinners' repentance and thus purify the fellowship. In other cases, such as business- or property-related disputes, churches aimed to resolve the matter fairly. They also sought to maintain harmonious relations within the church and extended neighborhood. Civil suits between members at the courthouse risked "cross swearing among the members of the church" or heightened tensions within the congregation.[16] So, when confronted with a member's rumored theft, adultery, indulgence in "spirituous liquors," breach of contract, fighting, or fornication, churches deployed investigative committees to speak with witnesses and the accused. Committees served citations at private homes and on street corners. They traveled long distances to chase down estranged members delinquent in attendance or subscription monies. The practice of localized law seeped beyond the meetinghouse's gates to members' homes, where interested parties met to broker deals and, after a breach of contract, where member-appointed committees returned to hash out the specifics with all those involved. Law emanated from slave quarters when an enslaved church member accused another of stealing his provender or perhaps his wife, or when an enslaved female accused her master of abuse. If Americans during the early republican period embraced law as the "modality of rule," as legal scholar Christopher Tomlins argues, Edwards reminds us that at the local level, the people "still saw it as *their* 'modality of rule'" and entrenched in local institutions.[17]

Though individual churches included rules of discipline along with their founding documents (covenants and constitutions), Baptists looked generally to Matthew 18:15–17 to structure disciplinary procedures. There, Jesus instructed early Christians to deal with sin first in private, with the offenders, and to take the matter to the church only when they refused to listen. If they remained unrepentant, then the church should deal with them as they would with "pagans" and "tax collectors": by excluding them from religious society. Through written reports to regional associations, religious periodicals, and word of mouth, churches in Kentucky and elsewhere publicized excommunications. They also encouraged members to refrain from interacting socially and economically with excluded persons. Churches did not possess the power to corporally punish the guilty, but their actions in local regulation force us to reconsider law's location in America from the Revolutionary era through the mid-nineteenth century.

The focus and rigor of discipline changed over time, reflecting a broader reconceptualization of local governance during the first decades of the nineteenth century. In the early 1840s, anxious religious leaders lamented the "almost entire neglect of Discipline in many churches."[18] My database shows not only an overall decline in discipline after 1830 but a shift in focus toward "internal" matters such as non-attendance at meetings or failure in church duties. Charges against white members for household disputes, theft, and business- or property-related disagreements become sparse, in some cases nonexistent. Scholars have noted a decline in discipline beginning after 1830 but have not adequately accounted for this phenomenon.[19] This book posits the confluence of three factors that hindered churches' ability to dispense discipline: the solidification of Kentucky's gender and racial hierarchies, the expansion of a market economy, and the rise of an innovative and competitive religious marketplace between 1780 and 1845.

Although the first permanent settlements in eighteenth-century Kentucky were made up largely of white men, Blacks and a small number of women did migrate west during the late 1770s and early 1780s. Kentucky's fluid frontier environment provided them unique opportunities to assume roles denied them in the more settled areas of the East. Both groups took up arms alongside white men to help thwart Native attacks and played key parts in maintaining the social order. Many Revolutionary era Baptist churches also granted degrees of power to women and Blacks, allowing them, for instance, to vote on matters of church governance and discipline. Yet by the 1810s, as evangelicals shed their more iconoclast views on racial and gender relations, and as the gentry and their values spread throughout Kentucky, churches gradually redefined full membership as the province of white males. Still, churches remained important venues through which wives challenged husbands' patriarchal rule. Enslaved people, too, relied on churches to secure their belongings or settle disputes with one another. Churches even on occasion reprimanded slaveholders for selling enslaved people "down river" or for excessive abuse.[20]

Despite these slivers of recognition for Blacks and women, churches played an important role in solidifying the state's social hierarchy. During the first three decades of settlement, anti-slavery Baptists percolated through the state, denounced their slaveholding brethren, and in some cases incited church schisms. The controversy largely receded by the 1810s, however, as church unity trumped the moral question of slavery.[21] Baptists and other evangelicals fell in line with the state, acknowledging its jurisdiction over the matter, as Kentuckians strengthened the institution of slavery and increased their policing of free Blacks. They constructed watch houses and employed slave patrols, and, as this book shows, Baptist churches emerged as important sites for the disciplining of Blacks. By the 1830s churches in the greater Lexington area were witnessing a rise in charges against Black members while whites were becoming less likely to face discipline. This increased role in regulation of Blacks was a central part of churchgoers' reformulation of their local legal culture. White members may have no longer envisioned their churches as authorities for regulating themselves in matters other than church duty, but the churches still had a role to play in helping state authorities maintain Kentucky's race relations.

Kentuckians also negotiated dynamic economic transformations that reformulated their social relations and weakened churches' authority. As a political economy emphasizing liberal values eclipsed the settlement period's moral economy, which was more attuned to communitarian ideals, churches' role in arbitrating the property-related disputes of their brethren receded. Not only did members' civil disputes hold the potential to drive wedges in the church fellowship, but the sin of covetousness, long denounced by Baptists and other religious groups, simply became harder to pinpoint in the speculative, acquisitive cultural milieu. Americans had also reconfigured debt from a moral failing to a near requisite of doing business in the expanding capitalist system, and sinful economic behavior became harder to identify. Meanwhile, gentry values heralding both material acquisition and family privacy radiated from urban centers such as Lexington. Churches, in turn, slowly lost power—and in some cases ceded it—over their members' economic matters. Economic and business-related disputes could not be properly adjudicated without the coercive powers of the state. One Kentucky Baptist, hinting at the subtle ways the market had ruptured his church community, lamented his brethren's handling of a disputed hemp deal, insisting "I have lost little in being excluded from their fellowship and communion."[22]

While they searched for legal certainty in the new economic landscape of boom and bust, Kentucky Baptists faced other challenges, from within and without, to their churches' stability. Historians of American religion have rightly characterized the post-Revolutionary period as "one of the most dynamic and creative periods in the history of Christianity."[23] The separation of church and state across much of the republic ushered in a competitive religious marketplace, and evangelical culture soon moved from the margins to the mainstream of American life. The turn-of-the-century revivals in the West fueled the latter process but also laid the seeds of dissension within religious groups. Between 1800 and 1845, Kentucky Baptists and their counterparts throughout the republic argued among themselves over the power of regional governing associations and the justification for missionary societies and other centralized institutions (often based in the Northeast) aimed at reforming society. While doctrinal disagreements appeared as soon as Americans planted churches in the region, by the 1820s the trans-Appalachian religious landscape burned with dissension as the influence of Alexander Campbell, Barton Stone, and other "reformers" spread through Protestant churches. Schisms pervaded Western churches, with Kentucky Baptists facing the brunt of Campbell's insurgency—which by 1832 had joined ranks with Stone's followers to form the Christian Church. Hoping to avoid further discord, governing associations turned away queries over doctrine from member congregations, expelled churches adhering to unorthodox beliefs, and insisted that their affiliated churches exclude "Campbellites" from their fellowships. Some churches witnessed an initial increase in excommunications. But gradually the dissension and schisms hindered churches' disciplinary power, and many churches affected by the insurgency went years without a recorded disciplinary action. Religious controversy altered member relations to the point that many no longer viewed their churches as impartial tribunals, or as one group remonstrated after their church trial in 1831, "If this is the way you dispose of business in your courts of Conscience; we do not wish to have any more cases in the Court."[24]

This book shows how the combination of these factors led Americans to reimagine the power and place of their local churches. Its goal is to understand why, in the introduction's opening anecdote, members of the Mount Pleasant Church believed they could rightly determine whether Singleton was a proper guardian for the ward Mason. The members assumed that collectively as a spiritual body, their authority should hold sway in such a case. They went to great lengths to establish Singleton's history of neglect despite promises to provide, and even levied a financial judgment, declaring Mason's time with Singleton done. But as we also saw, Singleton did not agree with his former brethren. After failing to pay Mason what he owed, Singleton found himself embroiled in a lawsuit. Each party's actions reflect a collision of civil and religious authority. Constructing state authority in the early United States was more than the physical process of building courthouses, passing local regulations, or enforcing legislation. It entailed an ideological transformation in which individuals constructed the boundaries of the secular and the religious through concrete choices. Ultimately, the diminishing discipline rates alongside critiques of the practice signaled Americans' broader reconceptualization of local governance. Law rooted in state institutions emerged as *the* "modality of rule" and not simply *a* modality of rule competing with and at times complementing churches in maintaining the local peace. But religious ideas and motivations continued to influence "secular" matters in a variety of ways, and vice versa.

This is not a teleological tale of secularization, one in which rational modernity, with its scientific and formal legal system, replaced superstitious and backward religious practices. Rather, it looks to the myriad ways Protestants pursued their communities' "peace" in the absence of state-established churches. The "religious" and the "secular" are conceptual tools created by scholars. In trying to make sense of the past, we apply labels to fashion dialectical categories. Their boundaries are permeable, however, with lines blurring in often unexpected or inexact ways. The categories also depend on one another. They are formed, reinforced, or redefined in relation to the other.[25] Like scholars, historical actors defined some matters as religious and others as secular (or "worldly"), but the lines between these two categories were also insecure. Legal discourse permeated church disciplinary actions. Disputants compared church procedures with those of the state and at times even contrasted church decisions with state precedent in similar cases. This book contends that declining discipline signaled one way Americans reconfigured the boundaries of religious and secular authority, yet it also demonstrates how they used instruments of the state to pursue their social reform initiatives and secure their church property in the competitive religious landscape.

Churchgoers' reconceptualization of local religious authority can be seen beyond diminished disciplinary activity. While by the 1830s and 1840s many churches may have lost enthusiasm for disciplining their own, religious actors turned to missionary and reform movements. With strict Calvinist notions of salvation waning, the distinctions between the saved and the potentially saved became less discernable. Albeit with some controversy, Baptists and other Protestants in the Bluegrass—like religious men and women across the Northern states—embraced numerous reform efforts, including female education, anti-gambling and temperance societies, and domestic and foreign missionary organizations. Discussion of such endeavors dominated churches' business meetings. Members' funds trickled upward to state-level and even more distant organizations. Religious authority, the focus of which had been once directed locally through discipline, was now funneled through centralized institutions. Some of these efforts were denomination based, others ecumenical. At times, too, individuals and churches turned to state authority and petitioned legislators to bring about their reform goals. Perfecting the "peace" became churchgoers' far-reaching pursuit to reform their states, nation, and the world in order to usher in Christ's return.

So much religious innovation, institutional and doctrinal, led churchgoers to seek out state authority to secure their meetinghouses. Although historian Nathan Hatch's 1989 book, *The Democratization of American Christianity,* depicts a freewheeling marketplace of democratic religion, characterized by ordinary people assuming the reins of their spiritual destiny, property concerns animated the new religious landscape.[26] In post-Revolutionary Virginia, the state assembly and Episcopal Church leaders battled over glebe properties, and in Massachusetts and Vermont, churches turned to litigation to secure their property rights as emerging sects such as the Methodists, Unitarians, and Universalists combated with Congregationalists for adherents and control of church meetinghouses.[27] In the West, well before the first schisms of the 1820s arising from the Stone-Campbell movement, communities looked to state instruments to exclude what they believed to be dangerous doctrines (usually Catholicism and Shakerism) from common worship spaces dubbed "republican meetinghouses." During the early 1800s, many churches built their own private houses of worship. To secure their properties, donors of land and money wove doctrinal beliefs into the land deeds, attaching reversionary clauses that guarded against potential theological divergence from the church's articles of faith. These stipulations could be highly specific, spelling out points of religious doctrine from which the church could not deviate and still retain the property. As Baptist church majorities determined the theological course of their fellowship, such land deeds leveraged material consequences against theological innovation. At times they empowered minority factions to claim church property when the majority voted to support missionary endeavors or to embrace the doctrines of the Stone-Campbell movement. When that happened, churchgoers turned to courts and insisted that judges determine which faction constituted the "true" church.

Scholarly attention has been focused overwhelmingly on church property suits arising from the sectional schisms, but a handful of similar cases reached

Kentucky's Court of Appeals, the state's highest court, during the 1830s and 1840s.[28] The outcomes of these cases often hinged on an 1814 Kentucky statute that provided for shared use of church meetinghouses in case of schism. Indeed, the 1814 act encouraged church factions to turn to state authority, and when they did, abstruse theological debates filled testimonies and flummoxed judges, who voiced uneasiness about wading through religious matters. Yet many still did, designating churches' sectarian identity or ordering churches to revisit internal votes. While legal historians have looked to the appellate decrees as precedent for later U.S. Supreme Court cases, they have not examined the case files from local chancery courts. These documents illuminate how acrimonious doctrinal schisms really were—even for neighborhood residents unaffiliated with the church property in question—and are rich with evidence of individuals' conceptions of authority, property, and the role of the state in buttressing religious society.

This book begins in Virginia in the 1780s. It follows the movement of Euro-Americans into the contested ground of "Kentucke." Professing Baptists, among the first convoys into the wilderness, quickly set about establishing churches and pursuing their neighborhood peace through the ritual practice of discipline. Churches grew in number and membership during the turn-of-the-century revivals, bringing even more Kentuckians into the nexus of church discipline. The middle chapters examine how societal changes affected church discipline, focusing, respectively, on household relations, economic transformation, and religious controversy. By the 1830s Baptists were simply unable or unwilling to pursue discipline as rigorously as they had previously. The inability to contain divisive internal conflict led churchgoers to turn to civil authorities to help arbitrate messy disputes that implicated church property.

"The Want of Discipline"

Baptist Churches and Local Law in Frontier Kentucky

> Look, as free voluntary consent, and mutual engagement are absolutely necessary to constitute any civil society, or corporation; so they seem as necessary to constitute that which is sacred, such as is a church of Christ.
>
> —Robert Bragge, *Church Discipline: According to Its Ancient Standard* (1768)

> It is the duty of a Church to attend to and take up the complaint of any aggrieved member and so to administer justice and judgment as to make peace if possible.
>
> —Bryan's Station Baptist Church, August 1806

In January 1786, after years of concerted opposition by marginal religious groups and sympathetic politicians, Virginia's legislature passed "A Bill for Establishing Religious Freedom." Authored by Thomas Jefferson, the statute clearly endorsed freedom of individual conscience and insisted upon church-state separation. Jefferson denied the power of civil and ecclesiastical authorities to impose their beliefs on any person. He labeled forced taxation for religion's benefit "sinful and tyrannical" and maintained that people's beliefs should not prevent them from "being called to [an] office of trust and emolument." To do so was to deny a citizen's "natural right" and pervert "the very religion" such measures sought to protect. Religious belief was a private matter: "The opinions of men are not the object of civil government, nor under its jurisdiction." And with that, no longer could dissenting religious groups like the Baptists be "restrained, molested, or burthened" by state authorities "on account of [their] religious opinions or belief."[1] James Madison, a member of Virginia's House of Delegates—and one of the religious dissenters' key allies in their quest to abolish the establishment of a state church—quipped soon after to Jefferson, "I flatter myself" that "in this Country extinguished forever [is] the ambitious hope of making laws for the human mind."[2] Although the statute did not disentangle the Protestant Episcopal Church from state government immediately or completely, it did transform religious adherence from a public to a private matter, redefining churches as voluntary associations of like-minded members.

Just three months later, as Madison, Jefferson, and the dissenters basked in the bill's passage, Baptists at Bryan's Station, about five miles northeast of present-day Lexington, Kentucky, considering "their scattered state and the want of discipline among themselves," constituted a church.[3] Their "scattered state" may have persisted from the settlement's near destruction less than four years earlier. The four Bryan brothers from North Carolina had established Bryan's Station in 1779. Native Americans soon killed one of the brothers, and the others, pestered by rumors of their Tory sympathies, returned east. The fortified station endured, and by 1782 it provided security and community for a small number of pioneers. In August of that year, a band of Natives three hundred strong attacked the station. The fort held for two days until the confederation of Shawnees, Mingos, Wyandots, and Lenni Lenapes retreated. A makeshift army of pioneers pursued their attackers north along the old buffalo trace (the path later connecting Maysville and Lexington), eventually engaging the Native coalition at a hill overlooking the Licking River, not far from a spring and salt lick known as the Lower Blue Licks. A disastrous encounter for the pioneers, the Battle of Blue Licks left seventy-seven whites dead. Others scampered back to Bryan's Station as Natives "stripped and scalped the corpses of those who had fallen," torturing the few prisoners who remained alive. In the context of increased Euro-American migration to the region, the defeat at Blue Licks reminded pioneers of their still-tenuous position in "Kentucke." Still, the station survived, Easterners continued to pour in, and the search for social and moral order remained. The Baptist minister Lewis Craig had arrived in north-central Kentucky from Virginia in late 1781 with much of his congregation in tow, hoping to find or perhaps create their western "Canaan." It was he and Augustine Eastin, another recently arrived preacher, who organized the small church at Bryan's Station, one of many established by Craig and his fellow travelers.[4]

Like other Baptists in the region, the eight men and women who constituted the Bryan's Station Baptist Church bound themselves together through a church covenant that, among other things, denoted the obligations entailed in church discipline and the congregation's subjection to it. Rooted in scripture, church discipline served to maintain order within the fellowship, address and repair members' wrongdoings, and if necessary cast out the unrepentant. Its goal, whether the punishment was rebuke, suspension, or exclusion, centered on "the purity of the church; the warning of all, and the recovery of the sinner," one Revolutionary era Baptist minister reminded his brethren.[5] Disciplinary actions fill church record books. Soon after the founding of the Bryan's Station Church, members excommunicated William Peyton for drunkenness and use of profane language. It was not long either before members considered discipline's role within the wider community. In July 1787 a member asked about "the expediency or inexpediency of Church meetings for Discipline being in private or public." Members agreed that such meetings should "be altogether in private." Thus, accusations of personal wrongdoings, arbitration of member disputes, and confessions of moral transgressions—all part of church discipline—would take place in front of member-only gatherings, away from the gaze of those who were not full church members.[6] They, and Baptists throughout the new United States, saw their churches as "enclosed gardens"—regulated corporate communities, intent on the spiritual salvation and worldly welfare of the whole fellowship.[7]

Because church gatherings often drew many neighborhood residents who, for whatever reason, never became full members, church discipline also played a role in the wider social regulation of the post-Revolutionary United States. This was especially true in the rural and frontier areas, which often lacked convenient or consistent access to state-based courts of justice and where inhabitants crafted and participated in a fluid marketplace of authority. Virginia's governing authority in the backcountry proved weak during the eighteenth century.[8] The combination of this decentralized, distant governing authority and the all-too-close Native threat, which made excursions far from station, village, or town less appealing, meant that much "law-making" was left to those on the ground. The initial accommodations between pioneers and Indians had dissipated by 1780. Even as this process played out, settlers turned to extralegal and informal governing associations, such as Kentucky settlers' Boonesborough Covenant (1775) or the Watauga Association of Tennessee (1772). These rudimentary governing institutions were themselves displaced by the appearance of county governments and a more formal court system. But the early arrival of Baptists and other religious groups allowed local meetinghouses to fill part of the initial authoritative vacuum.

In June 1792, after years of increased migration to Virginia's westernmost county, Kentucky became a state. Its new constitution, like that of its mother state, delineated the boundaries between church and state. While some of the more informal and customary legalities that had regulated pioneer life fell by the wayside, the new constitution did not, and could not, dictate completely how Kentuckians pursued their social order. It could not tell Brother Ashurd of the Mount Pleasant Baptist Church in Franklin County to forgo his church and take his land dispute with Brother Chilton to the local courthouse—that the only authority to settle such a matter was vested in the state.[9] Indeed, during the 1790s Kentucky churches heard cases on issues ranging from an enslaved woman's alleged fornication to whether Brother White of the Buffalo Lick Baptist Church had "knowingly and willingly smuggled and kept" a hog for which another member had paid.[10] And so throughout the 1780s and 1790s Baptists gradually developed an institutional structure. They plied their discipline alongside their spiritual worship in hopes of transforming the "dark and bloody" ground of Kentucky to the Edenic paradise they believed awaited them.

Within six years of founding their church in 1786, Baptists at Bryan's Station heard charges ranging from fighting and drunkenness to adultery and slave insubordination. Their vote of July 1787 may have signaled members' desire to contain discipline behind closed doors, to keep their garden enclosed, but word of their excommunication of John Rogers's enslaved woman, Cate, in August 1792 for "setting fire to a house and absconding herself from her master's business" surely spread through the community. Moreover, questions lingered about the church's role in the community. In late 1793 the church responded to a member's query related to the power and place of their fellowship in the new commonwealth. "The design of a church," the clerk recorded, was not only for the "Glory of God" and advancement of his kingdom across the world, but "secondly her power extends, to make any rule for her own government consistent with the word of God, and to exercise her power in the Discipline of her members agreeable thereto."[11] Despite the state's constitution, which defined religious organizations as voluntary institutions removed from roles of civil governance, members still imbued their local churches with immense authority over their public and private lives. Disciplinary rates increased during the first decade of the nineteenth century as religious fervor enveloped thousands of Kentuckians. In the shadow of state institutions, a vibrant marketplace of authority reigned, with "law" percolating through local meetinghouses.

"... the rich and illimitable acres of a western Canaan."

A throng of men, women, and children, including enslaved people, congregated at an isolated meetinghouse near Fredericksburg, Virginia, in September 1781. With Cornwallis's surrender to George Washington at Yorktown still over a month away, those gathered at the Upper Spotsylvania Church prepared for an arduous, wartime journey west. They agreed to leave the following morning, and on this "farewell Sunday," as cattle grazed between packed wagons, the large congregation overflowed into the field outside the house, many gatherers finding shade and a seat under trees. Their pastor, Lewis Craig, spoke from a temporary pulpit. Perhaps hoping to calm what must have been an anxious group, Craig—described as "stoop shouldered" with black hair "thick set, and somewhat curled"—discussed the Baptists' experience in Virginia over the previous two decades. He insisted that "though [they were] already worn and weary from the long campaign" against religious persecution, God would lead them to "the rich and illimitable acres of a western Canaan." Virginia's established Anglican Church had weakened in the decades leading up to Craig's sermon, with Baptists and other evangelicals chipping away at the links between church and state. But for Craig and his followers on that late summer day, with "the country [still] scorched and wasted and impoverished by the war," Kentucky appeared to be their Canaan in the wilderness.[12]

Craig knew firsthand the religious persecution that by the 1780s had helped to attract thousands of adherents and supporters to the Baptist cause. Some of those assembled beneath the trees, envisioning the Promised Land of "Kentucke," surely remembered 1768, when colonial authorities had seized Craig, John Waller, and James Childs for preaching without licenses at the same Spotsylvania meetinghouse where they now convened.[13] Some also probably watched two days later when a lawyer labeled Craig and his associates "great disturbers of the peace," so set on their religious views that they could not "meet a man upon the road" without ramming "a text of scripture down his throat." When Craig refused the court's request to cease preaching in the county for one year and a day, his congregants might have been among those following along as the sheriff transported him to the Fredericksburg jail—where he remained for four weeks—and listening as the incarcerated preacher exhorted through his cell's iron-barred window.[14] Three years later authorities in Caroline County again arrested Craig for preaching without a license and imprisoned him for three months.[15]

Craig, whose brothers Joseph and Elijah would also become notable Kentucky Baptists, came to the faith during the late years of what historians have categorized as the First Great Awakening, a period of religious revival and contention that witnessed the growth of the Baptists in Virginia and the Carolinas. Born in the late 1730s in Orange County, Virginia, Craig was raised on a farm and had little formal education. He awoke to his "sense of guilt and condemnation" while listening to Samuel Harris preach in 1765. More than a decade older than Craig, Harris was also a Virginian but had been born into a more respectable family. As a young man Harris moved to Pittsylvania County and soon impressed his new neighbors. He held many local offices, serving as a churchwarden, sheriff, justice of the peace, and militia colonel, but he remained restless, becoming "serious and melancholy without knowing why." Harris concluded eventually that guilt over his sinfulness had caused his gloomy state. Sometime around 1758 he experienced a conversion and was baptized. Ordained as a ruling elder in the church, he began preaching in parts of Virginia and North Carolina. Like his disciple Craig, Harris experienced run-ins with colonial authorities—perhaps exacerbated by his former role in the established church—and on separate occasions was arrested for disturbing the peace, dragged from the pulpit by his hair, and accosted by a mob opposed to his preaching to soldiers near Fort Mayo.[16]

It is easy to lump all eighteenth-century Baptists into one category, but divisions over doctrine and church practice permeated the ranks of Virginia Baptists, and these distinctions migrated with Craig's church and others into Kentucky. Baptists' progress in Virginia derived primarily from three sources. Robert Norden, a missionary from England's Assembly of General Baptists, arrived in the colony in 1714 and formed a church in Prince George County in southeastern Virginia. Sporadic Baptist activity in that area continued until 1750, when General (non-Calvinist) Baptists from Maryland moved into the colony's Northern Neck. Numbers of General Baptists remained small into the 1760s. Regular (Calvinist) Baptists arrived in Virginia from Pennsylvania in the early 1750s. Members of the Philadelphia Baptist Association, the Regular Baptists established churches throughout the Northern Neck and Virginia's Southside through the 1760s. Around the same time, a Baptist sect known as the "Separates"—who embraced more emotional forms of worship and stricter discipline than their Regular counterparts—made forays into Virginia's Southside. The Separates arose in New England, emerging from the schisms of the 1740s, and by the early 1750s had found success in North Carolina before spreading their message throughout Virginia. Although for many at the time and since, the significance of doctrinal subtleties between these three groups was very real, Baptists themselves have not always been clear on the differences, and neither have their opponents. Many Separates, including Lewis Craig, for reasons that are not entirely clear, abandoned that position upon arriving in Kentucky and adopted the Philadelphia Confession of Faith. In 1787 the distinction between Regular and Separate in Virginia vanished as Baptists united with the organization of the Baptist General Committee. Still, in Kentucky, divisions between Regulars and Separate Baptists persisted until 1801, when they agreed to a union.[17]

Distinctions aside, preachers like Harris and Craig faced social and legal persecution because the Baptists' doctrine threatened the fabric of the colonial social order. The Separates, in particular, aroused condemnation. Often refusing to obtain licenses to preach, their emotional, impulsive worship style proved a stark contrast to the established church's structured religious forms rooted in the Anglican *Book of Common Prayer*. Baptists directly challenged Anglican doctrinal beliefs and practices, speaking out against the practice of infant baptism. Moreover, their insistence on strict norms of social behavior and their success in converting enslaved people spurred on their persecutors. Especially at the local level, Baptists faced various forms of harassment, from simple inconvenience to fines, whippings, and incarceration. With an arrest warrant in hand, for example, authorities once interrupted Lewis Craig's brother, Joseph, as he preached. Joseph slipped out the back door into a swamp, only to be chased down by dogs and pulled from a tree. On his way to court, he flung himself from the horse and, in a peaceful act of civil disobedience, refused to ride or walk any farther. The magistrate reportedly let him go. Others, like the layman Thomas Waford, were not as lucky. Traveling with a group of preachers in August 1771, Waford had his personal effects searched and was whipped by a magistrate. Waford allegedly carried a scar on his face for years after.[18]

Although dissenting groups struggled for recognition within Virginia's legal-religious landscape for much of the eighteenth century, the War of Independence helped disseminate ideas of freedom of conscience. By the time armed conflict commenced between colonists and redcoats in 1775, Presbyterians, Baptists, Quakers, and Mennonites had all petitioned Virginia's House of Burgesses for some aspect of religious toleration: the ability to itinerate and worship freely, to acquire legal incorporation, or to be exempt from swearing oaths. Their pleas were at least partially successful. As Virginia legislators met to draw up a new state constitution and declaration of rights in the summer of 1775, James Madison introduced an amendment to guarantee "the full and free exercise" of religion and to end the many civil privileges granted on account of one's religion. Patrick Henry tried to move Madison's amendment, which would have in effect abolished the established church, through the convention. The measure failed, and delegates accepted instead a watered-down amendment that called for the free exercise of religion but said nothing about the privileges Madison had evoked in the first draft. For the establishment's supporters, "free exercise of religion" provided simply legal toleration and nothing else. But the war had weakened the established church. When the colony split from Britain, so too did the church, which abandoned "Anglican" for the appellation "Episcopalian." Many ministers remained loyal to the crown and returned to England. Others found themselves hard pressed to collect their salaries, in conflict with vestries, or overworked owing to ministerial resignations or deaths. Dissenting ministers like Craig still faced discrimination, but as petitions flooded the General Assembly, it was clear the tide was turning in their favor.[19]

Jefferson first drafted his "Bill for Establishing Religious Freedom" in 1778 while a member of a committee charged with revising Virginia's laws so they better reflected the new state's republican character. Many legislators balked at the thought of disentangling the established church and the state government completely. Pressing the issue, dissenters continued their petition campaign through the early 1780s, decrying proposed legislation for a general assessment (requiring Virginians to pay taxes to the religious group they belonged to). Virginia Baptists funneled much of their political action through the General Committee, an organization that first met in October 1784. It represented four regional associations, and its delegates included some of the most influential Baptist ministers in the state. The General Committee circulated petitions against assessment throughout eastern Virginia, organized support for the passage of Jefferson's statute, and sent delegates to lobby the state legislature. Such direct action made an impression. Madison later reported to Jefferson that "the steps taken throughout the Country to defeat the Genl. Assessment, had produced all the effect that could have been wished. The table was loaded with petitions and remonstrances from all parts against the interposition of the Legislature in matters of Religion."[20] The opposition campaign successfully derailed the assessment bill, and in January 1786 the assembly passed Jefferson's "Bill for Establishing Religious Freedom."[21]

All this remained on the horizon as Craig and his followers gathered outside the Spotsylvania meetinghouse in September 1781. The day after Craig's "farewell Sunday" speech, nearly 200 members of the Upper Spotsylvania Church departed in a convoy along with another 300–400 migrants. Captain William Ellis, a former Continental Army officer, and several soldiers also traveled with the group. Ellis had already ventured to Kentucky once, helping to organize Grant's Station (just five miles from Bryan's Station) in 1779, only to return to Virginia when Native attacks led to the station's abandonment. Moving west, Craig's group passed through Charlottesville, where earlier that summer the British lieutenant colonel Banastre Tarleton and his raiders had chased then-governor Thomas Jefferson from his home at Monticello. In mid-September, the convoy crossed the Blue Ridge Mountains at Buford's Gap, eventually making it to Fort Chiswell, a small trading outpost where a state militia guarded a deposit of lead used to make bullets. There, the convoy heard rumors that outlaw Tories and Natives allied with the British were roaming the region, and the row of solitary graves along the road as they continued westward did nothing to calm their fears. Craig's church members had planned their departure from Virginia in September to avoid the hardships of traveling and settling during the winter. Yet the persistent threat of Native attack forced them to bivouac for a month in Abingdon. Not until early November did the migrants begin their route west on the Wilderness Road—Daniel Boone's path through the Cumberland Gap. On the second Sunday in December, Craig, in hopes of reinvigorating his flock, again preached about their "promised land" beyond the wilds. That night Natives attacked the migrants' camp. Return fire from Captain Ellis and his riflemen scattered the assailants, but daylight brought news that one of Ellis's men had been killed. The man's scalped corpse surely reminded all that their Canaan was not empty, even if they wished it to be.[22]

Their relocation west of the Appalachian Mountains had thrust Craig and his followers into Virginia's backcountry borderland, a juncture where European and Native cultures collided.[23] The area that came to be known as Kentucky had been a hunting ground for prehistoric peoples dating back twelve millennia. Around AD 1000, the Fort Ancient culture developed in the Ohio Valley. Though the Fort Ancients—which over time gave rise to the Shawnee culture—made use of agriculture and foraging, they depended largely on meat acquired by long-distance hunting parties and thus lived a more nomadic existence, with more inchoate political and religious structures, than their Mississippian counterparts. Between the fifteenth and seventeenth centuries, climate change and European intrusions into their lands splintered Mississippians' traditional cultures. For the Fort Ancients, shifting-field agriculture and the long hunt remained crucial. With Shawnee villages located north of the Ohio River and hunting camps moving through the lands to the south, the Shawnees, like their Fort Ancient ancestors, did not develop centralized political institutions. They were divided into autonomous units under village chiefs whose primary responsibilities were to resolve disputes and form alliances for defense or trade with other villages. By the eighteenth century, while its trails served as arteries of trade for Natives and European powers, Kentucke served primarily as a winter hunting ground for the Shawnees and other groups from the surrounding region, such as the Miami, Chickasaw, and Lenni Lenape.[24]

The trails that facilitated Indian-Indian and Indian-European trade also trafficked in diseases and encouraged further European intrusions into Native lands. In exchange for valuable furs and deerskins, Europeans inundated Indian country with iron pots, kettles, pewter plates, glassware, and alcohol. While Indian hunters depleted the deer and beaver populations, European traders settled small outposts in Indian villages. Others, like the Virginians Thomas Batts and Robert Fallam, claimed vast tracts of trans-Appalachia for their royal governor and King James II as early as the late 1600s. Expanding trade networks and spurious land claims coincided with an increased effort by the Iroquois, coming from the northeast, to acquire the Ohio River valley. Continued warfare and the effects of disease weakened the Shawnee, splitting them into four factions. Over time, two factions relocated to the Shawnee River valley, just west of the lower Appalachians and Cherokee territory. A third moved east into southern Pennsylvania, while the fourth settled along the upper Savannah River. The tenuous peace between the Cherokee and their new Shawnee neighbors dissipated by the 1710s, however, and Shawnee from both river valleys wound up in southern Pennsylvania. Now allied with the Lenni Lenapes, the Shawnee were at odds with the dominant alliance in the region: the Iroquois and the Covenant Chain's Six Nations.[25]

This Indian "frontier" might be better characterized as a "borderland," as various Native groups sought trade and military alliances with the European powers who cordoned the region. In the 1740s the British formed two land companies to explore and claim the Ohio Valley, and before long they became suspicious of French influence in the region. Instructed by Virginia's governor to ward off their competition, a young George Washington attacked a small French force and soon after, in July 1754, suffered a defeat at his makeshift Fort Necessity near Pittsburgh. Within a year, Britain and France were at war. Each side formed alliances with Native groups. The French lost control of the Ohio River valley during the late 1750s, and the 1763 Treaty of Paris removed them from the continent. King George III's Proclamation Line of 1763 circumscribed colonists' settlements to east of the Appalachian Mountains, much to the consternation of British veterans, who had been promised land grants in the West. For Ohio Valley Natives, it appeared from the Proclamation Line, as well as from previous agreements with the British, that the new imperial power in the region sought to protect them from continued settler colonialism. Not as adept as the French at negotiating, however, the British soon aroused Native resentment in the Ohio River valley, and Shawnee, Mingo, and Lenni Lenape warriors joined Pontiac's rebellion. Though short lived, the rebellion terrorized English backcountry settlements and probably did a better job, temporarily, of holding off trans-Appalachian English colonialism than did King George III's imaginary line.[26]

With Pontiac's uprising quelled by the start of 1765, small groups of long hunters, whose hunting expeditions could last for months, with land companies from Virginia and the Carolinas on their heels, began to explore the region more fully. At Fort Stanwix in 1768, the Iroquois, who had negotiated for the Ohio River valley in the 1740s, ceded their claims to the British. Subsequent treaties (of Hard Labor in 1768 and of Lochaber in 1770) with the Cherokees convinced many colonists that Native territorial boundaries were negotiable. Hunting parties pushed deeper into Kentucke. John Findley and Daniel Boone passed through the Cumberland Gap in the summer of 1769, set up camp, and hunted for meat and furs for six months. Along with the furs and tales of masculine exploits, rumors of fertile lands, immense bison herds, and a plethora of smaller game filtered east, piquing colonists' interest. Land companies, including those that had first sent agents into the West during the 1740s, followed Boone and the long hunters and, in defiance of the 1763 Proclamation Line, began selling titles to speculators. Though most speculators intended to remain absentee, by the early 1770s their agents had begun tramping into the backcountry to secure their investments, as did war veterans seeking lands they had been promised. In March 1774 James Harrod led fifty pioneers into Kentucke and began constructing Harrodstown. As other pioneers, inspired by the initial success of Harrodstown, traipsed into the Native lands, Shawnee and Cherokee militants attacked western settlements, and Harrod's men abandoned their station. Colonists retaliated, defeating a Shawnee war party and massacring a group of Mingos. Pressed by land speculators, the governor of Virginia, Lord Dunmore, sent militiamen into the Ohio country to secure the colony's authority. In October the militias met a party of 1,000 Shawnee, sent them fleeing north of the Ohio River, and through the Treaty of Camp Charlotte convinced the Shawnee to abide by the 1768 treaty at Fort Stanwix.[27]

In early spring of 1775, James Harrod returned to his destroyed settlement and began to rebuild, and by May Boone and a party of thirty pioneers had chopped their way through the Cumberland Gap and formed Boonesborough, a frontier "station" along the Kentucky River. Stations, collections of log houses connected by a high wooden wall that acted as fortified structures, served as pioneers' primary defense against Native attack. Over the next five years thousands more poured into the Bluegrass region and constructed stations like the ones at Fort Harrod and Boonesborough. Much more than defensive structures, stations were the center of settler life for nearly a decade after the first Euro-Americans arrived in Kentucke. They were often made up of families and single men hailing from the same neighborhoods back East. Mutual protection and a steady food supply required communal effort, and all inhabitants, including women and enslaved people, played important roles in the stations' survival. Residence in the stations, which were dirty, cramped, and in most cases unsanitary, was meant to be temporary but could stretch on for years until the area beyond the wooden walls became safe enough for families to claim their own land. By 1782 Euro-Americans had constructed more than a hundred forts and stations in Kentucky.[28]

The liminal and at times prolonged station existence slowed the growth of formal institutions, including churches, and much of the social order stemmed not only from the kinship and neighborly relations of station inhabitants but from a common worldview. Even as Kentucke's demographics diversified, historian Craig Thompson Friend notes that all migrants understood that their journey west redirected them from "the beaten path of American society." And though certainly not all migrants practiced their faith, most shared a common spirituality rooted in Judeo-Christian traditions. For them, the West was an Edenic garden, its wilderness in need of appropriation. Most migrants, including those with Craig's Travelling Church, envisioned the West as a Promised Land where they could obtain plots of "virgin" land that would provide a high yield and secure their agrarian independence. Individual rights could be guaranteed only through a shared moral economy that stressed community values of peace and harmony. Mutual respect and obligation, along with the meting out of justice to transgressors of the social order, helped ensure that pioneers' stable cosmic order, their garden, did not deteriorate.[29]

For their part, the Shawnee and Delaware tried to control the influx of the new arrivals. Some Native leaders, like Cornstalk, initially sought accommodation with the pioneers, one that would make the Ohio River a permanent frontier between the two cultures. Younger Natives, however, believed that by forming a pan-Indian confederation and an alliance with the British, they could quell the migration and regain control over their hunting grounds south of the Ohio River. Divisions between the accommodationist and militant bands persisted through 1777, and the latter continued their attacks on frontier stations and migrants bound for Kentucky. White pioneers rarely distinguished between those Natives who sought accommodation and those who did not and killed adherents of both strategies indiscriminately. Accommodationist sentiment virtually disappeared among Natives after whites, having lured him and his party to Fort Randolph under the pretense of friendship, assassinated Cornstalk. Further accommodation between Natives and settlers appeared hopeless as the 1770s came to a close, and violence continued. Some Shawnee went west to Missouri, others south to the Tennessee River. Those who remained behind continued their hit-and-run tactics against white intruders. The end of the Revolutionary War and waning of British support also led many Shawnee and Wyandot leaders to rethink their goal of preserving the hunting grounds south of the Ohio River.[30]

The persistent Native threat through the 1780s convinced many settlers that they needed more responsive, perhaps forceful, governance. Virginia claimed the Kentucky region, and as its population swelled, legislators sought to secure their authority over the sprawling backcountry settlements by creating new county governments. Settlers had begun constructing their own extralegal governing associations soon after their arrival. Judge Richard Henderson and his associates at the Transylvania Land Company negotiated with local Natives in the mid-1770s to acquire much of present-day Kentucky. Boone had worked briefly for Henderson, clearing paths and leading migrants into the region. As frontier stations multiplied in the Bluegrass region, their representatives gathered at Boonesborough in 1775, forming a rudimentary government, which, among other things, established courts and set punishments for criminal activity. The short-lived Boonesborough Covenant focused primarily on issues such as clarifying how courts would operate, regulating the militia, and setting fees for local officials. It did little to regulate morality but did pass a measure entitled "An Act to Prevent Profane Swearing and Sabbath Breaking."[31] Many settlers, displeased with the speculator Henderson's high land prices and believing their titles would be better protected under Virginia's authority, asked the state legislature for assistance. The General Assembly agreed to step in. In December 1776 legislators sliced out the territory west of the Alleghenies and designated it Kentucky County. With governing authority now emanating from Williamsburg (and after 1779, from Richmond), the legislature created by the Boonesborough Covenant never reconvened.[32]

The creation of new counties went a long way toward bringing local government to the growing transmontane populace and signaled settlers' desire for more effective governing institutions. Responding to a population influx in the late 1770s, the Virginia General Assembly laid out three new counties in 1780: Fayette, Jefferson, and Lincoln. County courts recorded everything from property transfers to powers of attorney. They also regulated local roads, riparian rights, and probate actions involving wills, guardians, and executors. Local justices of the peace handled most public and private legal matters, overseeing ferry operations, taverns, and mills. They appointed road supervisors, registered livestock marks, and even created a basic public welfare program to assist orphans, the mentally incapable, and the poor. Local courts, for the most part, proved effective during the 1780s at handling economic matters. Indeed, although some may have packed up and continued moving west when a courthouse appeared in their neighborhood, wanting, as one observer noted "to have nothing to do with justice," Kentuckians' consistent pleas for more responsive government demonstrated that most desired more, not less, local government.[33]

Although by 1780 the power balance between Natives and white settlers had shifted in favor of the latter, venturing into Kentucky in 1781, even for a large group like the Upper Spotsylvania Church, remained a dangerous endeavor. The nine months leading up to Craig's departure had witnessed the killing of 131 people by Natives in the Jefferson County area alone.[34] In early December, Craig's convoy finally crossed through the Cumberland Gap into Kentucky and over the next two weeks slowly continued north. The group settled on a site that would become the town of Lancaster in Garrard County and established Craig's Station. Upon arrival, the church members gathered to worship around the Bible brought with them from the Spotsylvania meetinghouse. They also remained on guard. Members attended meetings with their rifles and stationed armed sentries outside the building.[35] Others described similar experiences. The Baptist minister William Hickman recalled churchgoers traveling in groups to Sunday services in the 1780s, with the men acting as armed escorts. Native attacks endangered the very survival of small congregations—Cooper's Run Baptist Church had five of its members killed in its first year of existence.[36]

At the beginning of 1782, only three Baptist churches existed in Kentucky. In the years after their arrival in December 1781, members of the Travelling Church—and others who had gathered at the Spotsylvania meetinghouse to wish them luck and followed soon after—dispersed through central Kentucky and organized churches. Much of the congregation relocated their church to South Elkhorn, near Lexington, in 1783. That same year, Joseph Bledsoe, father of the future jurist and Kentucky senator Jesse Bledsoe, established the Gilbert's Creek Church of Separate Baptists. The "eccentric and zealous" Joseph Craig, who had flung himself from the magistrate's horse, would go on to form another Separatist church at Boone's Creek in 1785.[37] Fellow traveler William Cave was an early member of the Big Crossing Baptist Church and an elder in the Bullittsburg Baptist Church. Lewis Craig assisted in the organization of the Bryan's Station Baptist Church and its arm at David's Fork in Fayette County. Captain Ellis was a founding member of the church at Bryan's Station.

". . . with their meetinghouse in a central place."

At about the time that Craig and members of his Travelling Church began dispersing through central Kentucky, the Baptist preacher John Taylor prepared for his own mission into the wilderness. Born in 1752 in Fauquier County, Virginia, Taylor was baptized in the early 1770s and preached at the South River Baptist Church. When he told his congregation of his plans to move to Kentucky, they warned he was going to "a country of strangers, and Savage rage." Upon arrival, Taylor quickly embarked on extending the Baptists' institutional network, converting migrating strangers into settled neighbors. He joined the church on Gilbert's Creek before moving on to the South Elkhorn Baptist Church pastored by Lewis Craig. Within a year of his arrival, he helped Craig organize the Great Crossing's Church before moving to Woodford County and constituting the Clear Creek Baptist Church in 1785.[38] Over the next nine years, Taylor traveled and preached throughout Kentucky. He baptized scores of converts and delighted in any advance in the Baptists' cause.

In June 1794 Taylor helped organize the Bullittsburg Church "on the margin of the Ohio River" in what was then Campbell County.[39] "This little new church in the wilderness," Taylor gushed, "was far from any establishment of the kind," and no one, including the church's eight original members, was "free from Indian danger." The Bullittsburg Church soon joined the Elkhorn Association of Baptists, a regional governing body founded in 1785 by, among others, Taylor and Lewis Craig. Taylor and his family became full members of the church in 1795, bringing the membership up to thirteen, "all of whom,"

Taylor recalled, "I was well acquainted with."[40] Despite its small size, the church flexed its disciplinary muscles in October 1795, excluding Benjamin Bryan for disorder, lying, and "keeping persons out of their property."[41] In a small frontier town like Bullittsburg, excommunication from the church could have serious consequences for one's social or economic standing.

Baptists' growth in Kentucky developed alongside increased migration to the region. Most migrants to Kentucky in the late 1770s and 1780s came from the Chesapeake backcountry and the contested borderlands between Natives and European settlers in Pennsylvania and the Carolinas. They often had little connection with the mythic cavalier world of coastal Virginia. Primarily Scots-Irish, Scottish, and Irish, these early settlers created a backcountry culture in Kentucky of communal cooperation and neighborhood justice for those who transgressed the social order. By 1790, however, on the eve of statehood, the pioneer world of the 1780s seemed to be slipping away as migrants of various cultural backgrounds flooded into Kentucky. Individuals of Welsh heritage from New Jersey trekked the old buffalo trace in the 1790s alongside New England Yankees and poor Englishmen from the Mid-Atlantic, a diverse group of European immigrants, and African Americans from the Carolinas and Georgia. Moreover, the arrival of the gentry class from Virginia's Tidewater and Piedmont regions brought a certain degree of refinement, or at least an impetus to refine, that distinguished Kentucky's future from the frontier conditions of the previous two decades. The gentry transformed the trails leading into central Kentucky from roughshod paths into reliable trade routes, conduits that brought not only commercial goods, news, and people but also greater connections to the social and cultural landscape of the Eastern states.[42]

Increased migration west of the Appalachians led to calls for statehood. In the spring of 1792, delegates met in Danville for a constitutional convention. Contentious debates over full manhood suffrage and the future of slavery preceded the gathering, though James Madison's friend and leading delegate George Nicholas helped shepherd the suffrage proposal with little resistance once the delegates met. Slavery proved more divisive, and church leaders led the resistance. The Presbyterian minister David Price and antislavery Baptists pressed for an unconditional end to slavery in the new state. Slavery's proponents managed to prevail, arguing that the institution, though immoral, was the foundation of Kentucky's economic prosperity.[43] The new state constitution, which would be revised in 1799, forbade establishment of a church but did not articulate notions of free thought or religious equality. Instead, it incorporated provisions that favored Protestant Christianity over other faiths and required religious oaths for office and court testimony. Baptists and other Protestant groups were free to form churches, incorporate themselves into legal entities, and pursue discipline.

Although Baptist churches grew slowly during the 1790s, they benefited from increased migration and greater security. Taylor's Bullittsburg Church expanded and continued to regularly discipline members. By 1797 Taylor was gratified that several new arrivals, many of them "Baptists of the first class," had settled in the area and joined the church. Before long the church claimed "about sixty members," many of whom Taylor praised as "good old peaceable disciplinarians." The church continued to grow as the decade closed—and revivalism began bubbling through the region—eventually claiming "about two hundred members," all "very compactly settled with their meetinghouse in a central place." Only a few members, Taylor remembered, "were a little scattered off," leading the dispersed members "to contemplate a new constitution" for a church of their own. They petitioned their Bullittsburg brethren for assistance in organizing a new church, and in no time Taylor reported that the new church was "perhaps equal in strength" in both "number" and "property."[44]

Churches claiming authority over both the secular and spiritual were nothing new in the Upper South during the eighteenth century. Virginia's established Anglican Church had often assumed civil functions; the church and the local courthouse served "as twin centers of power and authority."[45] Because parish boundaries usually aligned with those of the county, the church played an important role in maintaining the social order. Church leaders worked to identify disorderly behavior and assisted in providing care for the poor and the orphaned. The church even helped settle disputes over property boundaries. By the time Craig, Taylor, and others had relocated to Kentucky, though, the established church's role in daily life had been transformed. In the 1740s and 1750s, county courts assumed jurisdiction over civil matters, and grand juries rather than church leaders presented criminal charges. Virginia's state assembly initiated much of this change, a process accelerated by Revolutionary era disestablishment. County governments centralized their authority over temporal matters, and churches—now considered private, voluntary institutions—focused on matters deemed "religious."[46] Although the close relationship between church and state may have been disintegrating during the post-Revolutionary period in Virginia and other Eastern states, evangelical sects did not shy away from civil roles. Indeed, the same evangelicals who pushed for an end to disestablishment clung to the belief that Christian churches were central to the social order and should inform legislation. Baptists envisioned their churches as important sites of governance. Congregations continued to relieve the poor by organizing member contributions of food, cash, or labor. Through their practice of discipline, they persisted in regulating various aspects of members' lives, arbitrating civil disputes, and charging members with moral transgressions. Although men of the enlightenment such as Jefferson and Madison may have wished to draw a line between the "civil" and the "religious," their former allies in the disestablishment cause envisioned a much different relation between the two spheres.

A congregational sect, Baptists viewed local churches as the highest earthly authority. Unlike their Methodist and Presbyterian counterparts—who constructed hierarchical structures made up of circuits, synods, or state and regional governing assemblies—Baptists typically left decisions about doctrine, form of governance, and disciplinary activity to church majorities. Baptist churches, especially those of the "Regular" order, constituted their fellowship according to written confessions of faith. These documents articulated a range of theological positions and member obligations, from the belief in predestination to the protocol for speaking in monthly business meetings.[47] Written church covenants maintained the fellowship's purity, for, as the preacher Silas Noel remarked, "A nuncupative creed is not calculated to quiet disturbances, or to exclude corruption."[48] Converts who sought baptism, and thus full membership in the fellowship, had to accept the covenant's expressed terms. Many churches even required the founding documents to be read at their monthly gatherings to remind members of their commitments to one another and the collective. John Taylor recollected that before joining the Baptists in the early 1770s, he had heard a church covenant read aloud at a group baptism and concluded "that no man on earth could comply with it." Taylor, of course, eventually subscribed to the faith and like any other convert—white or Black, enslaved or free—accepted that adherence to the group's covenant was all part of being a "legal" member of the church.[49]

If one desired a voice in the church community—whether about doctrine, use of the meetinghouse, or discipline—membership mattered. In the wake of the Great Awakening along the East Coast, Baptists placed more weight on the differences between membership and nonmembership than they did on distinctions of gender, race, or social status. One reason for their immense success in the decades preceding and following the War of Independence was this very inclusivity, at times extending full membership privileges to groups such as women and enslaved people, who generally lacked personhood in the eyes of state law. Membership did not come easily. Whereas Presbyterians, Anglicans, and other congregational churches accepted infant baptism, Baptists sought to build churches of true believers, visible saints baptized only after they had publicly related their conversion experience. Those who demonstrated God's favor claimed the appellations of "brother" and "sister," regardless of social status. This practice stemmed in part from Baptist theology, which celebrated the equality of all baptized souls. And during the settlement period the same frontier conditions that created more fluid gender roles and unstable race relations also infiltrated meetinghouse walls, providing women, free Blacks, and the enslaved with authority in church matters, including discipline.[50]

For many settlers in Kentucky, social and religious life revolved around local church gatherings. Merchants, budding entrepreneurs, and farmers brokered deals on meetinghouse lawns as their congregations assembled for Saturday business meetings. In some areas the church connected all neighborhood residents. John Taylor noted that in the 1790s everyone within "a circle from a center of three miles" radiating from his Clear Creek Baptist Church were members, and that one could stride through town addressing each passerby with the title "brother."[51] Churches continued to serve as vital centers of activity well into the nineteenth century. Pastor James Fishback insisted that his church at Mount Vernon, Kentucky, proved so central to the community that "scarcely one family in the neighborhood" did not have "one or more members of the Church in it." Thanks to the church, Fishback concluded, "no neighborhood enjoyed more uninterrupted peace, kind feelings and good order & happiness, than did the one about Mt. Vernon."[52]

Churches' centrality in community life—for members and nonmembers—helped to enforce disciplinary decrees and ensured that actions taken at the meetinghouse spread through the area. Many of the more than 200 members of the Bullittsburg Church, along with numerous nonmembers, probably watched in September 1800 as Lewis Connor answered a charge of trespassing into a neighbor's orchard and stealing apples. Some served on the investigative committee, and all full members would have served as the jury, which, after his recantation, voted to maintain Connor in the fellowship. Five months later the same members acquitted John Murfey for "having an affray with a Certain man."[53] Church members at Bryan's Station may have voted to hold disciplinary sessions in private, but it is likely that word of Brother John Hancock's 1794 exclusion from the church for refusing to pay a debt, "unjustly holding money in his hands," filtered through the neighborhood. It perhaps even led some to think twice before doing business with him.[54]

Effective church discipline relied on communal supervision of individuals' conduct, which Baptists considered keeping "watchcare." A key aspect of their church ritual, discipline derived its authority from the New Testament—primarily the Gospel of Matthew and Paul's letters to the Corinthians. Baptists' insistence that members bring their disputes to the church held the irony that such disputes at the meetinghouse could sow rifts within the fellowship. So, pointing to the "gospel steps" laid out in scripture, Baptists distinguished between private and public offenses. Following Matthew 18:15–17, members were not to divulge private disputes. Instead, churches instructed them "to go to the offender, and endeavor in a tender, friendly manner, to convince and reclaim" the transgressing member. If the matter could not be resolved between the two of them, the offending brother refusing to show repentance, then "the offended brother is to take one or two [other] brethren with him" in a second attempt to gain repentance through private consultation. Only if this second visit failed should the matter be brought to the church. Once before the church, if the transgressing member continued to deny his sin, the minister admonished him. "Should this prove ineffectual," the minister Samuel Jones wrote in his 1805 *Treatise of Church Discipline*, "and the offender continue obstinate and impenitent," the church should "proceed to higher acts of censure," which included both suspension and excommunication.[55]

Excommunication was the most drastic punishment dispensed by churches. Suspension, though discussed by various ministers as a useful tool in reclaiming straying brethren, does not appear as often as an admonishment or exclusion from the church body. Jones dismissed suspension in his 1805 tract, claiming suspensions were "rather a delay, or a postponement" of punishment. Church tribunals did not have the authority, of course, to corporally punish their offending brethren, but their decrees carried social weight. Especially in the early days of settlement, when local and state courts remained distant or were seldom convened, church discipline provided an impetus for individuals to practice restraint while far removed from traditional institutions of control, such as the family or local government. Social ramifications arising from a church's decision, one historian recently asserted, "carried enough moral suasion to change actions and attitudes."[56]

Protestants in England and North America had long advocated cutting off all interaction with their excluded brethren. Pointing to Matthew, chapter 18, Thomas Hooker noted in 1648 that excommunication or exclusion (as later Baptists often termed it) was the "*cutting off*" of unrepentant sinners "from all

Church-communion." Whatever rights admission to the fellowship had bestowed upon him were "now disannulled by his Excommunication." Though Hooker denied that excommunication could "*take away a man's civil rights*," he did advocate that members treat those excluded as "heathens."[57] Even well after Kentucky achieved statehood, which brought with it more responsive governing institutions, exclusion from church fellowship could affect one's standing in the wider community. One church leader reminded Baptists of their duty to follow strict "*avoidance of free and familiar*" interaction with the excommunicated. Those cast out "should be made to feel the amazing weight of the solemn sentence," the writer continued, "by a corresponding conduct, on the part of *every* member of the church," even "*every* member of *every* church."[58] News of disciplinary activities often spread beyond the confines of meetinghouse walls and could affect one's business transactions and personal reputation. Hemp dealer William Collins, after being excluded from the Elizabeth Baptist Church in Bourbon County, Kentucky, discovered that news of his contract dispute and excommunication had dispersed into surrounding counties well before he took the matter to local courts.[59]

Though congregationally structured, with much greater autonomy than many of their other Protestant counterparts, most Baptist churches linked to "sister churches" through regional governing associations. Associations were the nexus for intercongregational relationships, serving as sites of information and socialization. Especially in the early years of settlement, associations also connected geographically remote congregations. Member churches elected delegates to their association's annual meeting—typically held over a weekend in August or early September—and supplied them with a letter detailing their church's physical and spiritual condition. Free to separate from associations as they pleased, some churches corresponded with more than one association or with none, or attended association meetings sparingly. As one Kentucky church insisted, a congregation "may be in one association today & tomorrow in another." This fluid nature of associational affiliation, however, does not mean that these bodies had no influence on church practice. Association meetings often revolved around questions of theological doctrine, proper forms of church government, and even discipline.[60]

If an association deemed a church's doctrine unsound or its practices unbiblical, it possessed the power to remove the offending church from the fellowship. This was not a small matter, as excluding one church could lead to division not only within that congregation but in the association as well. In 1823, for instance, the Long Run Association, composed of churches in the greater Louisville area, excluded the Drennin's Creek Baptist Church for "forming a union with a body of Separate Baptists distinct from and not in union with us." Other churches weighed in, asking if the scriptures prohibited churches from corresponding with others outside their "union," to which the Long Run Association answered that it was "unadvisable" and "unscriptural" for a church "to commune with other Christian Societies," even if they were "orderly according to their views—yet, differing from us in faith and the administration of ordinance." The association's decision appeared to perpetuate tensions within the excluded congregation at Drennin's Creek: delegates to Long Run encouraged the church minority to apply for membership in the association in 1825.[61] By that time, however, the first traces of discord and eventual schism arising from Alexander Campbell's Reformation Movement had begun to filter through the association and its member churches. For the next decade Kentucky Baptists wrestled with internal dissension, and association delegates spent much of their time fielding questions over the association's scriptural authority or examining churches' doctrinal leanings and excluding schismatic factions. In a time of increased religious competition, with adherents shopping around for their best fit in the religious marketplace, an unstable association could be further weakened if one church's exclusion grew into a larger exodus. Thus, if a central responsibility of associations was to cultivate harmonious relations between isolated congregations of like mind, their failure to do so could potentially disrupt or alter the ritual of individual churches.

Disciplinary decisions, and the authority or necessity of associations to infringe on church autonomy, proved a constant source of tension. Baptists heralded their congregational freedom, yet as the Baptist historian Albert Wardin Jr. notes, "for all practical purposes," an association could act as an "ecclesiastical court," hearing appeals from disgruntled individuals caught on the wrong side of their churches' tribunal. Some associations did not shy away from this role. At their 1803 meeting, for instance, delegates to the Long Run Association heard charges that "the Arian System of Faith" was prevalent among members of the Fox Run Baptist Church. The accuser, William Marshall, had been excommunicated by members of Fox Run "for refusing to sit with [the congregation] in a Church capacity on account of said heresy." After an investigation the association announced at its next meeting, in September 1804, that although Fox Run had sufficiently dealt with Marshall's charges of heresy, the church should not have excluded him from the fellowship. The matter did not rest, and the following year two member churches lodged complaints against the Long Run Association for meddling in church affairs. A committee from the Six Mile Baptist Church insisted that "we think no Excommunicated person has a right to Appeal to an Association."[62]

From settlement through the antebellum period, the justification for associations remained a source of contention. Jacob Creath Jr., a member of a prominent family of Kentucky Baptists, insisted that associations "are unknown to the New Testament and to the purest and best days of Christianity."[63] Even John Taylor, who had been instrumental in founding the Elkhorn Association of Baptists in 1785, later warned that associations could usurp the disciplinary powers of autonomous congregations. Taylor's critique, however, came in the 1820s, amid discord emanating from Campbell's challenge and a missionary impulse that many Kentucky Baptists feared. Associations understood this tension and the fear experienced by Baptists who were jealous of their congregational independence, and at times they tried to reassure their member churches that they did not mean to overstep their authority. When the Goshen Association of Virginia Baptists disbursed "Help for the Churches"—a short pamphlet devoted to church government—the delegates declared "that we assume no power to impose this, or any of our proceedings as an Association, on your consciences." Its only purpose was to "to offer, and to recommend" some tips for church constitution and discipline.[64]

Baptists relied on a network of sister churches for information on potential converts and often sought help from nearby congregations in arbitrating difficult disputes. One could not pick up and depart unannounced, planning to easily join another church. Churches required members to alert the congregation of their intention to move, gain letters of "dismission," and settle any standing grievances or debts. Kentucky churches examined dismission letters closely. If much time had passed since an individual's former church had vouched for his or her conduct, or if a new arrival claimed to be Baptist but possessed no letter, the prospective church inquired into the person's recent doings. Churches looked to the past conduct of all members, enslaved or free. In Tennessee, Nashville's First Baptist Church, for instance, ordered the clerk to "write the church on Mill Swamp, Isle of Wight County, Virginia, concerning Anthony, a servant formerly a member of said church." Some churches placed expiration dates on their dismission letters and reminded departing brethren that the letter could be revoked if they did not speedily join another church. The Franklin Association of central Kentucky insisted that dismission letters should "be considered as credentials for one year only." If more than a year had lapsed and the dismissed had not joined "some sister Church in the vicinity of their residence, they [should] be considered as having violated covenant obligations" and at risk of suspension or exclusion from the Baptist order.[65]

This network of sister churches worked to spread godly discipline across a mobile region, holding members accountable for their actions even when they strayed far from their home congregation. Of course, this supervision was rooted in Baptists' system of watchcare and their hope that effective discipline would reform transgressors. When Sister R. Jones of the Indiana Creek Baptist Church spent time in the neighborhood of the David's Fork Church in 1804, the latter congregation sent word of her misconduct back to her Indiana brethren, "in order that it may be settled among themselves." Likewise, when John Hansborough visited Knox County, Indiana Territory, in 1814, his brethren at the Flat Rock Baptist Church back in Kentucky excluded him from their fellowship after they received word "by Christian proof" that he "had been guilty of profane secularizing and other profane conduct."[66]

Associations remained an important part of the Baptists' institutional structure, with numerous such bodies organized in the two decades following the arrival of Craig's Travelling Church. As they did in Virginia, doctrinal differences divided Kentucky Baptists during the late eighteenth century. Regular Baptists, Calvinists who adhered to the Philadelphia Confession of Faith, predominated in Kentucky's Bluegrass region in and around Lexington. Separate Baptists rejected all creeds, placed faith in the scripture alone, and tended to settle south of the Kentucky River. These geographical and theological considerations led Regular Baptists to organize the Elkhorn and Salem Associations, while Separates coalesced in the South Kentucky Association in 1787—the same year that Virginia's Regular and Separate Baptists reconciled their doctrinal differences—though it was not until 1801 that the Regular and Separate Baptists united as one. By 1785 there were eighteen Baptist churches in Kentucky, many of them belonging to one of the three associations. In 1790, two years before statehood, 3,105 Baptists worshipped in forty-two churches. Though the pace of growth was slow in the 1780s, after statehood and the subsequent pacification of local Natives in 1794, the number of religious congregations rose through the end of the century. By 1800, Kentucky Baptists had organized six associations made up of just over one hundred churches with a total membership of 5,110. The spread of churches reached the point where, as historian Ellen Eslinger notes, "most neighborhoods, particularly in the Bluegrass region where settlement was most advanced, enjoyed reasonable access to public worship by the time of the Great Revival in 1800."[67]

"will the church approbate a Bro. to go to law . . ."

As purveyors of good order, Baptists and their religious counterparts throughout the region envisioned churches as law-producing sites and the practice of discipline as a viable alternative to local and state courts. Baptists certainly perceived a difference between state-based law and church practices, but the latter emerged from the immediate social relations of the congregation and could be a more responsive, familiar legal venue. Their conception of churches' law-making powers can be seen in how they discussed disciplinary procedures. In June 1808, for example, the preacher Carter Tarrant explained to the Mount Gilead Baptist Church that witnesses on his behalf would not appear "without [being] legally called for by the Church."[68] John Taylor reminisced about a period of peace within his former congregation at Buck Run, claiming that only "one legal complaint" had appeared before the church.[69] Some complainants introduced cases they had prepared "legally for the church," while others referred routinely to discipline as "ecclesiastical law" or "Baptist jurisprudence."[70]

Baptists hoped to contain member disputes within the fellowship, both to promote order among the brethren and to protect a church's reputation within the surrounding area. Demanding that members refrain from "going to law"—suing one's brother before infidels—proved one way to maintain harmonious member relations and avoid potential "cross swearing among the members of the church" at court.[71] Citing Corinthians, one manual on discipline reminded churchgoers that, although the injunction against recourse to state courts had emerged when the law had been administered by "heathen judges"—something the writer hinted was no longer the case—"arbitration in a friendly way" by church brethren "is still the proper and preferable mode."[72] Although churches did at times approve members' recourse to the courts, members suing each other in local and state courts risked airing dirty laundry in a public setting and held the potential to exacerbate conflict or provoke a schism within the congregation. It also undercut the church's authority over members' affairs.

Churches charged disputing members who sought state authority without approval. This practice continued well after statehood. In July 1825, for example, Brother John Sturgeon of the Flat Rock Baptist Church in Shelby County, Kentucky, asked his brethren, "Will the church approbate a Bro. to go to law with [another] Bro. in any case or not[?]" When the church denied the request, Sturgeon, feeling pangs of guilt over his legal doings, entered a charge against himself for "going to law with Bro. Isaac Keller." Sturgeon's query and admission opened an investigation into members' courthouse actions. The church formed a committee of "six Brethren" to investigate "Sister Deborah Bohannon in defending a lawsuit against Bro. James Bartlett." The church ruled that both Bohannon and Bartlett (even though the latter was answering a charge) had "erred in going to law." Bohannon made satisfaction for her transgression. The church clerk did not record Bartlett's fate in this particular case.[73] Flat Rock Baptist Church's insistence, however, that members rely on its authority for dispute resolution rather than the local courts serves as a clear example of the continued importance of the meetinghouse as a site for legal production, a place where members and nonmembers ordered their communities.

Although disciplinary actions revolved primarily around member transgressions or disputes, some outsiders looked to the neighborhood meetinghouse for resolution. Nonmembers' requests for arbitration by church majorities highlight the varied character and location of law in post-Revolutionary America. In September 1808 a Tennessee church heard a complaint from a nonmember who "desired [the] church to take into consideration & try to settle" a dispute between himself and a church member. The young lawyer and future lieutenant governor of Kentucky, Robert McAfee, reported in 1803 that he had visited "the Holeman's [B]aptist Meeting House, to settle a dispute between two men." Although he concluded that "nothing was done," McAfee saw little unusual in arbitration at the meetinghouse—mentioning this case as casually as those he pled in the local court—or in the church's seeking a lawyer for guidance in the matter. Local and state judges also made their opinions of church procedures known, sometimes at the disputants' request, and nonmembers could testify in cases heard by church tribunals. Judge Adam Beatty, for example, was highly skeptical of actions taken by the Mayslick Baptist Church against its pastor Reverend Gilbert Mason, and four individuals, "not members of any church," testified on the minister's behalf.[74]

Post-Revolutionary Baptists did not shun the secular legal system. Indeed, they could not if they wanted to secure title to their land or file a will. Baptists played integral roles in the civil government. James Garrard arrived in Kentucky in 1783 and two years later returned to Virginia to serve as Fayette County's new representative in the state assembly. Garrard later became justice of the peace in Bourbon County, as did at least five other Baptists who had migrated with him to Kentucky.[75] Leonard Young, a member of the Bryan's Station Baptist Church, also served as Fayette County's justice of the peace and as such pursued social order through both legal venues. In 1803 he entered a charge of rape against Richard Tomlinson at the November church meeting, charges that he had been informed of by the victim in his role as county magistrate. The church excluded Richard Tomlinson, as well as his kin, Elijah, for having "broken the laws of our Country."[76] Yet tensions persisted between an evangelical culture rooted in a communitarian ethos and a burgeoning state-based legal regime devoted to perpetuating a liberal economic order. As historian Stephen Aron notes of Kentucky at the turn of the century, "lawyers jeered evangelicals" and "evangelicals scorned lawyers." Church discipline was a way for churches to "maintain order" without the assistance of lawyers—though as McAfee's account shows, not all evangelicals shunned lawyers' participation in church arbitration. The accuser and accused acted as arbitrators, and full members as jurors. Churches served as important legal sites because local courts in the 1790s and first decade of the nineteenth century were "clogged by land litigation" and seemingly governed by greed. Church tribunals, "swift, simple, and seemingly democratic," Aron continues, were "everything disheartened Kentuckians wished their legal system to be."[77]

Historians have characterized the decade and a half following the Revolutionary War, before the frontier revivals of the turn of the century, as a period of religious doubt, one in which preachers across the new United States espoused fears of atheists and deists to their increasingly empty pews.[78] Professors of faith in Kentucky and elsewhere were vocal about the rise in infidelity, especially among the nation's youth. The Philadelphia Baptist Association reminded its member churches in 1796 that liberty of conscience in some cases proved dangerous. The "wicked" had prevailed, the circular letter declared, "as we observe crowds of unreflecting youths, pressing on to ruin, fascinated with systems which, though congenial with depravity, are at an infinite remove from holiness and truth."[79] In Kentucky, observers voiced similar ruminations on the state's religiosity. The anti-slavery Baptist preacher David Barrow wrote in his journal in 1795 that of all the denominations in Kentucky, "the Deists, Nothingarians and anythingarians are the most numerous." That same year, the Methodist minister James Smith passed through the state, noting that infidelity had "given Christianity a deadly stab."[80] By the end of 1801, Kentuckians had witnessed the first outpouring of religious fervor that would continue through 1803. The revival—the first rumblings of the Second Great Awakening—swelled the ranks of Kentucky Baptists. The church at Bryan's Station, for example, baptized 420 new converts. The congregation became so large that its arm at David's Fork, which had been a part of the Bryan's Station Church since its founding in 1786, broke off in 1801 and constituted its own church. A member of the Elkhorn Association, it claimed 297 members in 1802. Over the next three years, the religious fervor more than doubled the number of churches to 219 in Kentucky and tripled the number of Baptists to 15,495. Churches continued to expand in the coming decades, with 31,689 Kentuckians claiming membership in a Baptist church by 1820. Fifteen years later, after the most divisive schisms and the exodus of members resulting from the Stone-Campbell movement had subsided, Baptist churches claimed close to 40,000 members.[81]

From 1800 to 1830, Baptists pursued discipline regularly, exerting church authority to regulate various aspects of members' lives. Those years witnessed dramatic growth in membership rolls, and discipline was regularly pursued.[82] Yet throughout the period from 1800 to 1830—the high point of disciplinary efforts—some Kentucky Baptists expressed uneasiness about church authority within the context of shifting household relations, economic transformation, and religious insurgency. It remained common for churches to arbitrate domestic or property-related disputes, and in some cases, the two matters were intertwined. In 1809, Brother Boyce asked the church at Bryan's Station, "If a member of the Baptist order have a claim on two persons jointly bound by a written contract," and one of them was a Baptist and the other was "under no church government," but both "refuse[d] to comply with their contract, to what tribunal" should the aggrieved party seek recourse? Boyce's query at once illuminated his expansive vision of law—that the church should be a legitimate arbiter—as well as a gnawing uncertainty that the church's legal authority could in fact resolve the conflict.[83] The next three chapters examine the causes of that uncertainty among Baptists and how their choices ultimately helped reposition the authority of their churches alongside that of the state.

Churches' "Perplexing Difficulties"

Race, Gender, and Household Relations

> Oh, that the church could be freed from such perplexing difficulties . . .
>
> —John Williamson, clerk of the Pleasant Grove Baptist Church, December 1845

By 1823, when he published his *History of Ten Baptist Churches,* the preacher John Taylor had been laboring to convert souls and establish churches in Kentucky for more than forty years. Taylor helped constitute the Elkhorn Association of Baptists in 1785. He organized the Clear Creek Baptist Church, the Bullittsburg Baptist Church, and others, claiming that to be a member of a Baptist church was one of the "greatest pleasures on earth." In his 1823 *History,* Taylor delighted in the progress of the Baptist cause and the growth of the churches he founded. Discussing the Clear Creek Church in Woodford County, he highlighted the Castleman family. "Old Brother Castleman" and his wife had been married "perhaps fifty years." The two were baptized together not long after marrying and "raised children, a number of them" professing Baptists. Their grandchildren, too, were attached to Baptist churches "in different parts of [the] Commonwealth." Indeed, Taylor reported, "[t]he family at home, is a pretty respectable church among themselves." But the family at home included more than Castleman's children and grandchildren. The family owned "many black people," and several of them had also been baptized. In January 1823 two enslaved boys, one "about ten years old, the other about eight," were received by experience into the Clear Creek Church. Despite their age, "what they related to the church could not be objected to," and the boys followed in the path of their fourteen-year-old sister, who had obtained membership in the church the previous month. Two other men belonging to Castleman were even licensed preachers. Castleman also "long kept a great Tannery," where he trained "numerous" apprentices, many of whom had become "professors of religion." This extended household of children, grandchildren, apprentices, and enslaved people, Taylor concluded, "has been a great nursery to the Baptist church for near a half of century."[1]

When the Castlemans were baptized in the early 1770s, many of their kin and neighbors may have lamented the couple's newfound religious affiliation. During the Revolutionary era, many Southerners viewed evangelical culture as a threat to the household, not a nursery of piety and good order. Evangelical sects too closely resembled marginal religious groups such as the Quakers and Shakers. They appeared to lure individuals away from family connections and extended power within churches to women and Blacks. These features, along with their questioning of slavery, their cultivation of the spiritual family based upon church membership, and their intrusive disciplinary methods, convinced many that evangelicals were a threat to the entire society.[2]

Yet Baptists posited a clear linkage between the household, the church, and the social order. Their initial understanding of family was not the traditional unit formed by bloodlines and marriage but rather a more encompassing view that stressed acceptance of Protestant values and included enslaved people, free Blacks, and white women as spiritual equals. Similar to John Locke's contractual theory stipulating that individuals voluntarily submit to the state, giving up some rights in exchange for protection, Baptists entered religious society willingly, relinquishing some "worldly" affairs in exchange for spiritual shelter. Baptists valued church membership and a commitment to the church's communal goals over "earthly," socially prescribed markers based on race, class, or gender.[3] Their use of "brother" and "sister" when addressing fellow members signified the ability to construct family bonds without bloodlines, and by extending these appellations to subordinate groups, Baptists and other evangelicals endeavored "to extend orderly moral community into both farmhouses and slave quarters."[4] The household relations of all members, Black and white, enslaved and free, fell under the jurisdiction of the local church. No matter their race or gender, all Baptists were "children of the same Father," just as Jesus Christ "was the head of his family, and his apostles [members of] his household."[5]

Joining a Baptist church entailed individuals' submission to church authority over all matters, including those of the household. Churches sought to regulate anything that threatened domestic peace and that, if not quelled, could damage the fellowship's harmonious relations. Members punished instances of verbal and physical abuse, marital separation and divorce, drunkenness, extravagance, sexual deviance, and slave disobedience.[6] They encouraged mothers and fathers to avoid "sending [their children] into all the gay fashionable and often vicious scenes of amusement and dissipation."[7] They reminded enslaved brethren to "be obedient unto their own masters," to not steal or talk back, and to display "good fidelity" in all things.[8] At the same time, churches served as authoritative sites through which those denied legal personhood in the eyes of state law, such as women and the enslaved, could find resolution for their disputes. Wives charged husbands with cruelty and infidelity. The enslaved charged their masters with abuse and charged one another with a range of transgressions from adultery and disobedience to drunkenness and theft.

Despite these broad actions to regulate household relations, antebellum observers often lamented churches' decreased authority over familial matters. By the 1830s church leaders in the slave states began to disseminate Northern ideals of domesticity more enthusiastically. Like Castleman's nursery of piety, the home became a church, "a sanctuary tended by wives and mothers." Most important, it restored moral authority to the home. This, historian Christine Heyrman notes, led to a "withering of congregational discipline" as many families sought greater privacy in domestic matters.[9] In Kentucky, Baptists' retreat from disciplining the household was not total. Churches became increasingly reticent to punish white members for private matters but continued to discipline Black members—though even in this sphere discipline slowed over the course of the 1830s. As Kentucky developed from a frontier region to a state, from a place in which gender and racial relations were contested to one in which the socially prescribed roles of an Old South slave state prevailed, community intrusions on household privacy diminished. Over the same period, the state enacted a variety of divorce laws that clashed with Baptists' view of the marriage contract as inviolable and perpetual. Baptists decried the ease with which spouses could acquire a legal separation and largely ceased arbitrating cases of quarreling or estranged spouses. As the region's slave system and racial hierarchy hardened in the two decades after the War of 1812, Kentucky Baptists followed suit, their local meetinghouses emerging as sites through which to police the state's growing enslaved population. The focus of discipline applied to white members gradually turned to matters more clearly within the church's authoritative scope: transgressions related to members' failure in their church or Christian duty. Meanwhile, more disciplinary attention shifted to enslaved members, who were disproportionately punished for sexual offenses and theft.

". . . keeping a disorderly house."

Sometime before the fall of 1809, Eliza Bainbridge had taken up residence with Captain Norborne Beall in Spring Station, her children in tow. In August Eliza's husband, Absalom, sent a letter to their daughter, Juliet, demanding that she return home immediately lest he had to "whip [her] home." Juliet's mother might have been satisfied with "going to hell herself," but Absalom was determined that the rest of his family would not follow her. "Do not you know," he implored Juliet, that "I am by the Laws of God & man Lord & master of my Family & that I have a right [to] Chastise everyone in it if they do not obey me in all things reasonable?" Bainbridge assured his daughter that Captain Beall probably wished he had never meddled with her mother.[10] Yet the following month Absalom sent Beall a formal notice accusing him of "harboring and detaining my wife Elizabeth Bainbridge contrary" to his consent. "Unless [Eliza] speedily returns home, Absalom asserted, he would "resort to legal redress" against Beall and apply for a divorce from his wife.[11] Eliza apparently did not speedily return, for in December Absalom sent a letter to her at Spring Station, cryptically warning that he would spend all the money he could raise "& every drop of blood in my body" to obtain satisfaction from Beall. "Should I die before him if God will permit me, I will haunt him & every white person on the plantation." Beall, Bainbridge concluded, was "a target I shall always keep my eye on."[12] In 1809, with Kentucky arriving at the threshold of Old South values, Bainbridge interpreted his rights as a father and husband through both the laws of God and man, insisting he held broad authority in all matters "reasonable."[13] State law did grant Bainbridge the right to demand the obedience of all his dependents. Yet Eliza Bainbridge's actions demonstrated her own willingness to buck his authority and find succor elsewhere.

Patriarchy in law and practice was not firmly entrenched during the first decades of trans-Appalachian settlement. Most settlers carried with them legal traditions from the Carolinas and Virginia. Marriage in the established colonies was viewed as a contractual relationship between man and woman, with the husband serving as household head, responsible for and sovereign over his wife, children, servants, and enslaved people.[14] In the Western regions, frontier conditions led to more tenuous kinship networks and a less solidified patriarchal order. The continued threat of Native attack spawned fluid gender identities and provided white women with greater opportunities than were customarily available in the older coastal societies. Frontier stations relied on women to complete their traditional duties but also to pick up a rifle and defend the settlement. Moreover, men were more likely to venture from the stations' walls and thus faced a greater likelihood of death in Native skirmishes. This left a large number of widows in frontier Kentucky with immense responsibilities, from providing for their families to protecting and maintaining property. Before statehood, too, Kentucky's legal system remained weak, and enforcement of and engagement with Virginia law was lax. "It was not uncommon in the 1780s," historian Craig Thompson Friend writes, "to see a woman filing a warrant at the land office or attending court as an administrator of her husband's estate."[15] With the gentry's arrival in the region during the 1790s, such autonomy for women and other dependents weakened.[16] Although increased immigration brought gentry values regarding the proper place of women (specifically, a wife should be her husband's emotional partner), many whites welcomed some cultural prescriptions and rejected others. Frontier women generally accepted the legal strictures of marriage but often saw themselves as vocal partners rather than submissive dependents, at times even asserting their property rights after marriage.[17] This stance eroded over the course of the 1790s, however; historian Honor Sachs has shown that during the "crucible of Kentucky statehood," lawmakers forged a society that solidified white men's patriarchal powers over their households and dependents.[18]

Even after statehood, the household head did not operate as an absolute monarch who could dispense justice without outside supervision or repercussions. Local courts were generally not dependents' first stop when seeking protection from an abusive patriarch. When disputes arose within the household, husband and wife could seek outside assistance from the church, friends, neighbors, and kin before pursuing the authority of civil courts. In the more formal legal settings of local courtrooms, gossip networks proved important in establishing the credibility of witnesses or the personal character of disputing parties.[19] Neighborhood churches were central sites in a community's gossip network, and these churches, much like local courts, sought to enshrine their own conceptions of domestic relations within members' households.

In some cases, churches strayed from secular society's prescribed gender roles. In the decades following the Revolution, historian Linda Kerber insists, civil society relied upon "righteous mothers . . . to raise the virtuous male citizens on whom the health of the Republic depended."[20] Although surely Baptists expected wives and mothers to inculcate republican virtue in their young, they also articulated a vision of the household in which each spouse was dependent upon the other and both created a family unit of shared responsibility. This was especially true in promoting the cause of religion within the household. In 1803 David's Fork Baptist Church in Lexington appointed three members to labor with Brother Lewis Berry "in order to show him his duty in family worship night."[21] In 1831 leading Baptists in Kentucky reminded "heads of families," to bring their "children up, in the nurture and admonition of the Lord," reading them scripture and providing them with "good advice." The following year, the Elkhorn Association's circular letter warned "we fear [prayer] is too much neglected by heads of families."[22] At least one Baptist governing association referred to both spouses as "'heads of households' with responsibility for maintaining religion within the family and household."[23]

In their effort to watch over their brethren and maintain familial relations, churches extended their authority into the household. Heads of households should be benevolent patriarchs, not the tyrants of their hearth. If they strayed from the reciprocal duties of their marriage contract or failed to adequately provide for their dependents, they faced admonishment or exclusion from their local church. Such was the case for Brother Joseph McCarly, whom the Flat Rock Baptist Church of Shelby County excluded for attempting suicide and "mistreating children that [were] under his care."[24] Churches heard accusations against patriarchs for overstepping their authoritative role, but such instances appear only occasionally in church record books and did not always work out in the dependents' favor. The Elk Lick Primitive Baptist Church leveled a series of charges against Brother Farier in August 1812, including wife abuse, intoxication, and profane swearing. Farier admitted that he abused his wife and drank too much but denied that he ever used coarse language, in response to which the church voted satisfaction and retained him in fellowship.[25] Similarly, in 1823 J. Gardner admitted to the Red River Baptist Church that while out of town on business he had drunk to excess. His wife claimed that upon his return "he abused her & one of the children, and made use of foul language." In response, Gardner said "he did not remember it" but "did not deny it, not knowing what he did or said." The alcohol had "made him almost beside himself." He apologized for his alleged, though unrecalled, behavior, and the church restored him to fellowship.[26] Neither Sister Farier nor Sister Gardner found protection from their abusive spouses at their local churches.

Yet women did use church discipline to settle disputes, bringing charges against one another as well as against white men and enslaved members. Churches gave women, who were often denied legal personhood in the eyes of state law, an authoritative venue through which to resolve disagreements.

Sister Walton, a member of the Licking Locust Baptist Church, traveled to the Mayslick meetinghouse in 1799 and charged a member there, Brother William Markwell, with wrongfully accusing her of false statements.[27] Sister Polly Lehew related to the Bullittsburg Baptist Church in 1812 that she was having difficulties with Nancy Horseley, who in turn had used "abuseful [*sic*] language" toward her. A committee of two male members was sent to reconcile the sisters.[28] Likewise, when in 1831 Sister Laton accused Milly, an enslaved woman belonging to a nonmember, of theft, the Mount Pleasant Baptist Church formed a committee of three men to visit Milly's owner and obtain the facts of the case.[29]

Although churches could provide women with recourse to settle their disputes, even to challenge their husband or household head, Baptists also elevated wives' dependence and subjection to their husbands. In 1806 Sister Polly Frost of the Mount Pleasant Baptist Church confessed that "she had frequently gone to Frolics" but insisted it was only "in obedience to her Husband." The church, believing it "criminal" for "members to attend Balls and Frolics," advised Frost "to take the Scripture," not her husband, "as her guide."[30] Such an instruction—to buck the authority of one's husband—was rare. In Polly Frost's case, it stemmed from the insistence of Mr. Frost—who was apparently not a member of the church—that she act contrary to the gospel and church rules. Churches more often pressed wives to obey their husbands. The Long Run Baptist Church leveled charges against Sisters Esther Casey and her daughter Evelin for "keeping a disorderly house," appointing a committee of ten men to investigate. The committee, "after a short retirement," called for the women's exclusion from the fellowship.[31] In 1820 the Harrod's Creek Baptist Church charged Nancy Carder with "quarreling with a neighbor" and "disobedience to her husband" and later heard allegations against Eliza Dunnagin for "neglecting her family concerns" and "for not being in Subjection to her own husband." Two years later the church excluded Sister Edmons "for threatening to whip her husband and afterwards putting her threats into circulation."[32] Moreover, when in 1828 Sister Hannah Morton composed and sent a letter of grievances against her pastor to the Bryan's Station Baptist Church, she did so only with the "sanction" of her husband.[33]

Baptists, like Americans across the republic, viewed the marriage compact as central to maintaining order within households and the wider neighborhood. Well after statehood and the enactment of the state's first divorce law, the local community remained an effective disciplinary outlet for regulating marriages, and neighborhood churches emerged as key institutions through which communities policed spousal relations.[34] Kentucky Baptists often dealt swiftly with charges pertaining to divorce or separation. The Flat Rock Baptist Church noted in April 1813 that Peter Young and his wife, Polly, had separated, "and each of them being talked to express that they have no idea of living together again." Such expressions earned their immediate exclusion from the fellowship. In other cases, churches refused to accept prospective members because of their domestic situation. George Nation attempted to join the Tick Creek Baptist Church of Shelby County in 1810, but objections arose "in consequence of his first wife's leaving him and refusing to live with him." He had since married another woman, and the church declined to accept him. Nation remained outside of the fellowship.[35]

When Kentucky churches disciplined members for transgressions related to household relations, they focused primarily on white male members. Of the 54 charges between 1780 and 1845 related to spousal quarreling or separation, mistreatment of family, or "meddling" with another's family, 27 went against white male members. The churches heard another 12 similar charges against white women, at times disciplining both spouses. The David's Fork Baptist Church charged Stephen Franklin and "his wife for quarreling and fighting, and drinking too much." It did not help their case that they maligned the preacher. Yet upon obtaining satisfaction, the church "acquitted" the Franklins.[36] Two quarreling spouses did not always meet the same fate within meetinghouse walls. In 1825 the Old Mill Creek Baptist Church heard reports that Brother and Sister Draper had been quarreling. The couple appeared and pled guilty before the church. Upon Sister Draper's acknowledgment that she had also drunk to intoxication, members excluded her but retained her husband.[37]

Baptists, unsurprisingly, did not take sexual offenses such as adultery and fornication lightly and pried into members' private lives to rid the fellowship of such transgressors. Within the churches of the dataset, adultery and other sexual transgressions made up just over 9% of all allegations heard between 1780 and 1845. The Flat Rock Baptist Church, for instance, excluded Sister Jane Carl for adultery in August 1822, saying little about the details of the case. Similarly, the Bullittsburg Baptist Church excluded Sister Polly Ryle in 1813 with no commentary.[38] Other charges brought up specific actions taken by the accused. In September 1804 Sister Mary Blackford testified to the church that she saw Sister Sally Burnnell "on the bed with a man not her husband," talking and "kicking about" until "ten or eleven o'clock at night." Brother Levi Vancamp and Sister Priscilla Shotwell faced charges of abandoning an infant child in 1821. The Mayslick Baptist Church determined that they had "secretly convey[ed] an infant child into the state of Ohio and left it in the nighttime exposed." The church excluded the two but retained Brother John Shotwell, who "was also privy to the plan." Less than a year later, after hearing "reports of a public nature in circulation prejudicial to her religious character," the Mayslick church excluded Sister Bernetta B. Weddell for having a "child at about 5 months after her marriage."[39]

Adultery was a break in the very marital contract that churches sought to uphold. Between 1780 and 1845, the churches from the data set heard 142 cases of adultery. Of those, 30 (21%) were leveled at white members. An overwhelming 111 (78%) were alleged against Black members. The disparity became more pronounced over time. After 1830 the churches showed little interest in whites' sexual dalliances outside of marriage. Between 1831 and 1845, 91% of the 35 adultery charges were leveled against Black members, with the churches recording only 3 such charges against white brethren. This same pattern played out in relation to other sexual offenses such as fornication, seduction, and lewd or "unchaste conduct." Between 1780 and 1845, the churches in the data set took up 99 allegations of sexual misconduct. Like adultery charges, a disproportionate number of these allegations were directed against Black members: 62% compared with 37%.[40]

Baptists and other Protestants encouraged enslaved people to marry, holding them to the same standards of marital fidelity as their white brethren.[41] Charges against enslaved members for fornication and adultery fill church minute books. For instance, the Harrod's Creek Baptist Church quickly excluded "Sister Fanny belonging to Br. Evins for the sin of fornication" in August 1820.[42] At other times, the church court became a venue in which to punish large numbers of enslaved members at one time, as in November 1804, when Asa Tompson, a member of the Bryan's Station Baptist Church and future sheriff of Fayette County, Kentucky, charged five "black members for the sin of adultery." Three of the accused belonged to Asa Tompson, one to Clifton Tompson, and another to a "Tandy"; it is unclear whether Tandy was a church member. Asa and Clifton Tompson insisted that they had "dealt with" the accused, who had "all confessed the fact." Despite the alleged confession, not one of the accused adulterers answered the church's citation, and all were excluded from church fellowship, which may signal that some enslaved members did not welcome church authority over their sexual lives.[43] Ultimately, however, membership in a church and its institutional recognition of enslaved people's marriages were conditional and seen as a privilege by church bodies, perhaps more so for enslaved members, who had been deemed by the wider society as inherently immoral and unfit for the marital compact. To become a church member was to fall under the jurisdiction of a higher authority. The Harrod's Creek Baptist Church succinctly relayed this vision in 1820, when its brethren excluded enslaved member Milly for her alleged adultery, not only from the church fellowship but from "the privileges of the Laws of God."[44]

Free and enslaved Blacks used church discipline to articulate their own visions of marriage. More than simply a tool for social control or a way of disseminating Baptist values to the enslaved, church discipline served as a mechanism for enslaved people to police their own communities. In October 1814 Brother Austin, a member of the Red River Baptist Church and the property of Josiah Fork, "made known to the church" a difficulty between him and a female member. After an investigation, it appeared that Austin was dissatisfied with Sister Rachel because he thought her "conduct toward her husband did not comport with that of a Christian." Two enslaved men testified to the same, and the church body excluded Rachel in April 1815.[45] Likewise, in 1824, John, an enslaved member of the David's Fork Baptist Church, entered adultery charges against Polly and Condorus, the property of a nonmember. The church excluded both the following month.[46] John's charges against the enslaved members of another master's household and Brother Austin's accusations against Rachel show the enslaved taking advantage of their churches' governing authority to regulate the familial relations of their fellow enslaved people. Slave neighborhoods' gossip networks could prove as central to instilling godly discipline as whites' accusations.

Although Baptists stressed the importance of faithful marriage for their Black members and placed much weight on charges brought by enslaved people against one another, church bodies were intimately involved in regulating these members' marital relations and did not tolerate their acting without the authority of the church body. When James, the property of a nonmember, "exercised a gift contrary" to the order of the Bryan's Station Baptist Church and had "likewise undertaken to marry Negroes," a committee was formed to investigate. The case was set aside for nearly a year until July 1792, when James confessed to holding "public meetings" and "marrying black people." The church acquitted him after he agreed to cease his transgressions. James explicitly challenged the authority of the church by preaching without its authorization, and the fact that he married Black people compounded the offense. In a similar October 1795 case, Sam, also enslaved and a member of the Bryan's Station Church, was charged for holding "disorderly" meetings and "marrying black people." The members of the church were not opposed to marriages of enslaved people. Indeed, their support for such marriages can be witnessed in the charges of adultery continually leveled against their enslaved members. From its founding in 1786 until 1860, the Bryan's Station Baptist Church heard thirty-two charges of adultery against Black brethren and only one charge against a white member for the same transgression.[47]

While members at Bryan's Station focused primarily on the sexual offenses of their enslaved brethren, charges related to divorce, abandonment, and sexual offenses dwindled alongside disciplinary rates in all the churches after 1830. Though divorce cases were a small part of discipline, they disappear after 1820. Churches' responsibility, even prerogative, to regulate white members' private relations especially began to lag. Early on, not long after statehood, clashes with civil law arose. In 1805 the Mayslick Baptist Church took up and then dismissed a member's query about whether it was "consistent with the laws of Christ for a person to marry a second time after being divorced from their companion according to the Law of the country."[48] With civil authority looming in the background, members proved unwilling to make a declarative statement regarding remarriage after divorce, even though the scriptures—such as Matthew 19:9—forbid doing so unless for specific reasons, like adultery. Many Baptists still decried the ease of civil divorce. At their 1825 gathering, the Long Run Association of Baptists, one of Kentucky's largest such bodies, received a query on whether "a man who puts away his wife," or vice versa, was an adulterer if he then married another. The association responded that according to the scriptures, any man who put away his wife, except for the cause of her adultery, himself committed adultery. "And we came of opinion," the body concluded, "that an act of the Legislature of the State cannot justify a course of conduct" that God condemned. Anyone, then—even with a legal divorce from the state—who married a second time was guilty of adultery and should be subject to the discipline of his or her church.[49] More than two decades later, area Baptists still lamented the law of the land regarding divorce. In the late 1840s the *Baptist Banner* exclaimed that Kentucky's law of marriage was "not a bit more binding upon the parties than jumping over the broomstick." Virtually "any pretense," the paper insisted, could be brought up by husband or wife, and the "Legislature and courts" would find it sufficient for a divorce decree. More than a blemish upon the marriage institution, such practices were "destructive to the morals and purity of society, a disgrace to the parties" and their extended families, and "a foul stain upon the escutcheons of the Commonwealth."[50]

Members of the Long Run Association were reacting to a series of marriage laws enacted by Kentucky's legislature. In 1798 the state's first alimony law took effect. While not providing for a legal divorce, the law acknowledged that in instances of prolonged separation, adultery, and "cruel, inhuman and barbarous treatment," circumstances arose in which it was better for the woman to have her legal identity restored and for her estranged husband to provide for her.[51] "An Act Regulating Divorces in this Commonwealth," enacted in 1809, provided both spouses with paths to legal separation. It granted circuit courts the authority to decree a divorce to a husband if his wife was living in open adultery, had been convicted of a felony in the United States, or had abandoned him for three years or more. Women could attain a divorce if their husband was living in open adultery, had abandoned her for more than two years, or had been convicted of a felony anywhere in the country, "or where his treatment of her [was] so cruel, barbarous and inhuman as actually to endanger her life." An 1843 law broadened the terms necessary for a divorce. It shortened the requisite length of a husband's abandonment from two years to one and provided for divorce in cases of a husband's impotence, his habitual drunkenness, and his cruel treatment meant to "destroy her peace and happiness."[52]

Even state judges expressed misgivings when hearing divorce suits as they tried to reconcile the sanctity of the marital contract with the states' liberalizing divorce laws. Judge George Robertson, in *Logan v. Logan* (1841), expounded his view of the marriage contract as well as the power of state courts to dissolve the marital relation. Both parties to a marriage, he averred, needed to understand that having bound themselves together "in the most sacred and endearing of all earthly relations," they were bound by both "human and divine law" treat each other with kindness. "If this cannot be done," Robertson continued, then both parties "'must suffer in silence.'" Courts were not forums through which individuals found the "cures for all the miseries of life," and unless there was evidence of cruelty, a Kentucky court did not have the authority to separate "those whom '*God* hath joined together.'"[53] Couples seeking a divorce in the post-Revolutionary and antebellum United States understood that by breaking the terms of their mutual contract, they offended "the larger community, the law, and the state, as much as offending" each other.[54]

Baptists and other evangelicals did not deny the state's importance in regulating the marriage contract; rather, like many of their judicial counterparts, they saw it as both a religious and a secular compact. As such, evangelicals agreed that marriage necessitated the backing of civil authority. "Marriage is a civil as well as a religious institution," Baptist reformer Alexander Campbell wrote in 1828. "It is, therefore, a proper subject of civil legislation."[55] The issue of property transmission certainly played a major role in this understanding, but so too did moral issues. One Tennessee Baptist, referring to a couple who had been married by someone who was not a magistrate or a licensed minister, asked rhetorically, "Could their children, by the old English law, inherit the property? By no means." In "the eyes of the law," he stated, "no marriage existed." If such "informal marriages" were pronounced lawful, the writer concluded, then "all order would be abolished, and the greatest immorality and libertinism [would] succeed" throughout society.[56]

Still, churches became less willing to involve the fellowship in household matters for fear that such contentious, maybe even scandalous, cases could damage member relations. In January 1828 the Frankfort Baptist Church heard allegations against Sister Owen dealing with separation from her husband, Robert, a nonmember. An investigative committee reported in March that the separation had occurred before Owens became a member, and the "committee of the church [did not] have cognizance of the acts of persons anterior to the time of becoming members." They did claim, however, that they believed the "marriage contract . . . was nothing more than a mere nullity, and that [Owens] was not bound" to it. One committee member dissented from the report, and many others appeared upset. Although "some members may feel wounded with [Owens] for her course she has pursued," the committee expressed "the hope that they will be disposed to forgive Owens" for her "aberration from the path and duty." Immediately thereafter, Owens accepted a letter of dismission.[57]

At other times, when churches heard cases of domestic strife, they were likely to find that the interested parties did not appreciate the intrusion. Church cases revolving around domestic relations held the potential to cause a larger fissure in a church's social fabric as individuals grew weary with their neighbors' and fellow brethren's intrusions into their private affairs. The Elk Lick Primitive Baptist Church in Scott County excluded James Neale for adultery in August 1846. Five members, however, voted against exclusion, and two of them, Jacob Neale and Penelope Jones, refused to fall in line with the church majority on the matter. A committee was formed to labor with the dissenters. They reported in September that Neale and Jones remained unreconciled with the church's actions. When a vote was taken whether to continue them in fellowship, a majority voted for their excommunication. Five more dissenters voted against this action, which led the majority to call for their exclusion as well. In all, the charges against James Neale for adultery led to eight exclusions and months of intra-church strife.[58]

". . . having his wife taken from him and removed to a distant part"

Enslaved members' sexual relations remained an area of disciplinary focus throughout the period of study. Charges did slow after 1830 as Kentucky Baptists grappled with the circumstances slavery posed to their own authority. Churches did not always exclude enslaved people convicted of adultery, and at times they implicitly recognized the difficulties the slave institution created for maintaining marital relations. To preserve the peace of the fellowship, some churches simply acquitted enslaved members in adultery cases, avoiding the need to rectify slavery with notions of Christian monogamy.[59] In July 1810 the Tick Creek Baptist Church of Shelby County cleared "Henrey belonging to Brother Dupey and Rose belonging to Brother Hansborough" of adultery. Although Henrey and Rose already had spouses, the church thought that "they had better live together as husband and wife than to part." The church clerk did not record the details of the case. Perhaps both of their spouses had been sold off to distant regions, and Tick Creek members realized that any familial stability for its enslaved members was better than isolation. Or, just as likely, Brother Dupey and Brother Hansborough worked out the particulars themselves and encouraged the rest of the church to let the matter rest. Just two months later, however, the Baptists of Tick Creek resolved that it was "contrary to scripture and good Order for Masters who have Servants to part them from their Husbands and wives" but insisted that enslaved people so separated should not "marry again whilst their former companion is living."[60]

Churches' quest to regulate slave marriages proved even more difficult when marriages crossed the line between enslaved and free. Such cases illuminate the tension between the marriage contract, the slave system, and church authority. When Caleb, a free Black man, was charged by the Fox Run Baptist Church with adultery in October 1824, he claimed that he had married another woman only because his first wife was "in [the] possession of Br. Oswald Thomas" and Thomas had forbidden Caleb from seeing her. "After a thorough investigation," the Fox Run Church agreed "on a view of the whole circumstances of the case" to acquit him.[61] Even as a free Black man, Caleb could not assume the patriarchal responsibilities of a husband, could not even visit her, as his wife already fell under the authority of Thomas. The forced separation of married Black church members occurred often enough that

Baptist governing associations received queries from affiliated churches on the matter. As early as 1786, Kentucky's first association received a query asking whether it was "lawful for a slave being an orderly member and compelled to leave his wife and move with his master about five hundred miles, then to take another wife?"[62] In 1812 the Long Run Baptist Association urged its member churches to "act prudently and tenderly toward that afflicted people" when "a black member, having his wife taken from him and removed to a distant part" married another. The association said nothing of how to deal with an enslaved woman if the roles were reversed.[63]

Similar debates appeared in the religious press as Christians sought to delineate churches' role in recognizing and maintaining slave marriages. An anonymous writer, Onesimus, insisted in an 1830 editorial that God had "placed the essential principles of marriage within [enslaved people's] power." Being "human" and thus "rational creatures," the enslaved were fully capable of understanding the "obligations of a voluntary pledge." An enslaved person was "on equal ground with his master" in regard to marital responsibilities and was "equally bound to fulfil his engagement." The church had "nothing to do with it," even when enslaved people were forcibly separated from their partners. "The guilt," Onesimus insisted, resided with "the man" who separated the spouses and brought "the misfortune to the slaves." Churches had the right to punish masters who sold enslaved people for covetousness or "cupidity." But even so, masters should "sympathize with the suffering party, and encourage his submission" to his contractual obligations. Separation did not end the marital contract, Onesimus concluded, claiming there was "just cause to doubt [an enslaved person's] religion" if he or she "violate[d] a pledge of this solemn kind for a temporary gratification."[64] Onesimus, though holding the enslaved accountable for marital fidelity, believed that owners were central parties in their enslaved people's marriage contracts and thus could also be punished by the church for separating spouses.

Unsurprisingly, this was not a universal view. Corinthinus, responding to Onesimus in early 1831, disagreed and pointed to state law's failure to recognize slave marriages. If "there be no legal marriage with our slaves, there is no marriage at all," and "consequently, [slave marriages] are not under the letter of the gospel discipline." Indeed, the "orderly or disorderly" conduct of enslaved members should be subject to church discipline, but to insist that their marriages were lawful was an attempt "to change the original order and design" of the marriage institution. Onesimus may have wished to recognize slave marriages based upon consent or affection, but forbidding enslaved people who had been separated from their spouses from finding other partners was not within the church's jurisdiction.[65] Too much focus had "been laid upon masters who separate slaves from their companions." Corinthinus did not hold such masters blameless but rather asserted that blame was "divided" among any number of people depending upon the situation. Key to Corinthinus's argument, however, was his deference to state authority over slave relations. The workings of church tribunals in regard to slave marriages were subject to the jurisdiction of civil law. Since there was "no legal way to marry" enslaved people, churches could not punish those enslaved for adultery or masters for forced separations; "there can be no true evidence of crime," he concluded, in circumstances where a crime "could not be committed."[66]

Churches nonetheless continued to view enslaved people's family life, and marriage in particular, as "under the letter of gospel discipline." For instance, like its sister church at Bryan's Station (which leveled thirty-two charges against Black members for adultery and only one against a white member from 1786 to 1860), the David's Fork Baptist Church focused its discipline on its Black members. From 1803 to 1860, church members took up fifty-seven adultery charges. An overwhelming fifty-five of those were against Black members. Likewise, of ten fornication charges, seven were leveled against Blacks. In other household matters, too, the church exerted greater authority over Black members than white. The church recorded charges of spousal separation or abandonment against three Blacks and only two whites, while seven Blacks and three whites faced charges of mistreatment of family.[67] This disciplinary focus became even more disproportionate over time. After 1830, 100% of adultery charges within the church were directed toward Black members, who were also the only ones to be accused of mistreating their family through the late antebellum period.

Kentucky Baptists' disproportionate focus on the sexual activity of enslaved people was just one part of their conflicted relationship with slavery. Church discipline provided Black members, free and enslaved, a forum through which they could settle disputes among themselves. At times, discipline even provided communal refuge for mistreated Black members. After the turn of the century, however, as Kentucky embraced the values of the Old South and as Baptists shed their more radical views on equality, instead of finding authoritative recourse for their own injuries, Black members found themselves singled out for charges seldom leveled against their white brethren. Many cases involved with slavery highlighted the contradiction of preaching spiritual equality at the meetinghouse while accepting the civil classification of the enslaved as chattel property.

"[*Is*] Involuntary Hereditary Slavery . . . supported by the word of God or not?"

On May 7, 1818, William Allen informed his brethren at the Mayslick Baptist Church in Mason County "of certain reports in circulation prejudicial to the character of Bro. Arron Mitchell." He said it related to the purchase of an enslaved female from "a Mr. Whitehead near the mouth of the Beaver [River]." The church then appointed Allen and another member to visit Whitehead, to take Mitchell with them, and to report at their next meeting. Five weeks later the committee submitted their statement. Brother Mitchell had desired to purchase a "black woman for his own use" at home and "occasionally in the factory." Whitehead named his price, and when Mitchell retorted the number was too high, the seller reminded Mitchell "that he could get more from an Orleans trader, but that he would not sell her to that market." Mitchell proceeded with the purchase and, according to the committee, shaved two years off the woman's age in the bill of sale. He also promised to come back two weeks later to buy the woman's child "if he liked its mother." Crossing the river after the deal, Mitchell asked the ferryman if he knew anything about Mitchell's new property. The ferryman replied only that he had heard "that she was not a good house wench." Perhaps dismayed, Mitchell said he "heard that before." Once at shore, the ferryman asked for his pay, and Mitchell, feeling duped, responded "that Mr. Whitehead was to pay it." Upon hearing the report, the church members excluded Mitchell.[68]

The clerk did not specify the church's reasoning for Mitchell's exclusion. Participation in a slave sale was not the issue. The Mayslick Church had debated the righteousness of slavery for well over a decade by the time of Mitchell's case. In 1805 a member asked whether "Involuntary Hereditary Slavery is supported by the word of God or not." A "large majority" of the church resolved that it was not. The church's ruling failed to satisfy the whole congregation and did not quell members' anxieties over slavery's righteousness. In March 1806 fifteen members declared nonfellowship on account of slavery, and three years later Brother John Johnson withdrew from the church, claiming that "he could not live [happily] in the church on account of her fellowship with slave holders."[69] Over the next decade, however, many of these departed members returned to the church. The actions of the Mayslick Church between 1805 and the end of the next decade mirror broader developments among Kentucky Baptists, developments that, at least for the time, ended the most divisive debates over slavery in the state.

The Baptists who trekked across the Appalachian Mountains in the late eighteenth century hoped to build covenanted communities based on spiritual equality, and for some, that vision necessitated an end to slavery. Baptists and other evangelicals were at the forefront of the emancipation movement during debates over the first state constitution in the early 1790s. The Elkhorn Association of Baptists even sent a memorial to the convention pushing for a constitution barring slavery. Notable antislavery Baptists such as Carter Tarrant, William Hickman, and David Barrow nevertheless encountered many who saw slavery as integral to their financial success and the state's future, and as Kentucky entered the Union in 1792, slavery prevailed. But when, just a few years later, calls for a new state constitution began circulating, slavery's future in the commonwealth once again took center stage. Ministers such as the Presbyterian David Rice pressed the state to reconsider its constitutional sanction of slavery. The opposing forces were too great. The new 1799 constitution retained slavery. Many Kentucky Baptists fell in line with the state, insisting that slavery was a civil issue, not a religious one. Even the Elkhorn Association, which had sent a memorial opposing slavery to the first state constitutional convention, joined sister associations in declaring slavery a political matter beyond the authority of churches.[70]

A determined cohort of emancipationist Baptists in Kentucky continued to question slavery's morality. Carter Tarrant and John Sutton helped establish the antislavery New Hope Baptist Church in Woodford County.[71] Meanwhile, Tarrant and Barrow denounced slavery from their pulpits, engendering vocal reactions from their opponents. Baptists against emancipation now claimed that antislavery, not proslavery, positions should be subject to church discipline. The controversy came to a head at North District Association's 1805 meeting, when delegates heard charges against Barrow for "meddling with emancipation." Five ministers presided over Barrow's trial and, finding the minister unrepentant, excluded him from the association. Barrow was a respected Baptist leader, having served in the Revolutionary War and faced extensive religious persecution in Virginia during the late eighteenth century. His expulsion from the North District Association set off controversy in the region's churches. Proslavery Baptists expelled their emancipationist opponents. As divisions over slavery's righteousness percolated through Bluegrass congregations, emancipationists organized their own churches and, in 1807, their own governing body, the Licking-Locust Association.[72]

This persistent emancipationist impulse among a small number of Kentucky Baptists dimmed to a flicker over the next few years. Many emancipationists picked up and moved to Ohio or Illinois, continuing their activism in areas free of slavery. Carter Tarrant died in 1816, and the formidable Barrow followed four years later. The struggling Licking-Locust Association disbanded soon after. Throughout the 1810s many onetime emancipationists returned to their former churches. For instance, in 1813 the Mayslick Church welcomed back two members who had "formerly joined an emancipating Church, which [has] since dissolved."[73] As historian Monica Najar notes, after 1810 Kentucky Baptists hoped to stem division in their churches by surrendering "any authority over slavery as an institution."[74]

This shift did not stop Baptists in Kentucky and across the slaveholding states from adjudicating cases dealing with relations between masters and enslaved persons. Indeed, as the case of Bro. Mitchell that opened this section demonstrates, Kentucky Baptists continued their role in disciplining one another and did not shy away from cases dealing with slavery. Mitchell's transgressions appear to have been related to his forgery on the bill of slave—shaving two years off the slave's age—and his failure to return two weeks later to purchase the enslaved woman's child. As members such as those at Mayslick sparred over this peculiar form of property, their local meetinghouses transformed into venues through which slaveholders and nonslaveholders confronted enslaved people's "double character" as both persons and property, brothers and sisters in Christ *and* expendable commodities.[75] These disputes not only highlighted the racial hierarchy hardening within trans-Appalachian churches during the early republican period but also reflected how masters' religious and social reputations were intimately bound up with the actions of enslaved people in their households.[76]

In March 1798, for instance, the Red River Baptist Church charged Brother James Waddleton with making false representations about a slave woman he had sold to fellow member Thomas Finch. The church investigated the matter, noting that the dispute between the two brethren "appears to be precarious." Initially Waddleton welcomed the church's investigation, reporting "by Bro. Brown that he was willing that the Church should take his affair into consideration." Mary Finch, Thomas's wife, testified that Waddleton had claimed "that the negro girl was set for any business & to go on errands." After purchasing the girl, however, the Finches grew dissatisfied with her and believed that Waddleton had swindled them. The church, "after deliberation," declared Waddleton guilty and ordered him to appear. With his character questioned in the front of the church body, he refused to appear as directed and "expressed his intentions to withdraw from the Church."[77] Without doubt, the ruling percolated throughout the neighborhood, informing members and nonmembers alike of Waddleton's less-than-upright business practices. The fact that the case stretched on for more than a year—Waddleton ignored numerous church summonses—also ensured that the gossip networks of the surrounding region caught wind of and spread the matter. Perhaps even worse, beyond the enslaved woman's inability (or perhaps unwillingness) to live up to her former owner's representations, a white woman had pointed out his failings.

The question of whether a member should use force against the enslaved people in his household, especially if they were members of the church, bedeviled Kentucky Baptists. In 1792 the Bryan's Station Baptist Church heard allegations against one of their own for "raising a stick against" a Black brother, Arch. A member also asked "whether Church members are at liberty to chastise their children or servants who are members with them in Christian society." Though the offending brother came forward and gave satisfaction for his actions against Brother Arch, members also decided to lay the query about chastisement "aside and not decide on it."[78] Baptists did punish members for mistreating their enslaved people, as the Mount Gomer Baptist Church did in 1797, excluding William Bledsoe for "abusing his Negro unmercifully."[79] The enslaved did not always find refuge from abusive masters within church walls, however. In 1809, for instance, the Buffalo Lick Baptist Church heard reports "spread by a negro woman" that Brother Thomas Baskett had gotten into a "violent passion," made "at her with a knife," and chastised her with a cowhide. Baskett came forward and made "some acknowledgements" of his conduct, and the church voted to bear with him.[80]

As Kentucky Baptists largely ceded their authority over slavery as an institution after 1810, the tension between Black members' dual status as spiritual equals but social inferiors may be best represented by two actions taken at Shelby County's Buffalo Lick Baptist Church in late 1810 and early 1811. Since its constitution in 1805, the only case members heard involving an enslaved person had been the abuse charge against Thomas Baskett. Soon after that case Brother Rucker sought clarification on enslaved members' use of discipline. In December 1810 he asked whether "it is the Opinion of this Church that slaves have the same privileges of Gospel dealing and Discipline as free members," to which the church "answered they have." As members, the enslaved were expected to practice watchcare and subject themselves to communal regulation. This was where their equality stopped. The church made that clear during the following months. In January 1811 it excluded Brother W. Rice for leaving the fellowship "on account of slavery and his having joined the Emancipators." Over the next six months, members excluded two Black members, Mike for theft and Hannah for adultery. In October, when a member complained against Br. Webber for "using the rod on a black brother instead of taking the Gospel steps," a majority of the church voted that Webber had not "violated the rules of the Church [or] the word of God."[81]

Like members of the Buffalo Lick Church, Baptists throughout the region did not take accusations of theft by enslaved people lightly. Masters and other community members often took advantage of church tribunals to punish enslaved persons for theft. Such charges not only illuminate whites' anxieties over what they believed were Blacks' furtive natures but also betray a grudging recognition that slaves worked together in accumulating property. The Tick Creek Baptist Church recorded charges against Wiggin, the property of Brother Ned Larkin, in the fall of 1814 and excluded him with his owner's apparent blessing.[82] Thomas Graves charged his slave, Harry, at a central Kentucky church in 1801 for stealing his "stockings." Six months later the same church heard charges against an enslaved woman, Letty, for "stealing from her mistress."[83] In 1826 the Beech Creek Baptist Church charged enslaved member Adam with making a contradiction in saying that Brother Farmer had "given him a dictionary." At the same meeting the accusation of a contradiction was converted to a charge of theft, and the church excluded Adam for "having a book that was not his."[84] Rose, belonging to Sister Willis, was charged "for concealing stolen money" by the Little Cedar Lick Church in 1842.[85] The following year Pastor Thomas Dudley watched as the Bryan's Station Baptist Church excluded his bondswoman, Cealey, for "concealing stolen property."[86] The charge of "concealing stolen property" hints at the underground economy of slave life in the trans-Appalachian West. If Cealey and Rose had been the actual perpetrators of the theft, rather than accomplices, the clerk would surely have made that delineation. Their actions as accomplices, however, severed them from the privileges of church membership and much of the social interaction that came with it.

Although church tribunals could potentially cut off an enslaved person from his or her site of religious and social community, they had no power to corporeally punish transgressors and thus may have served as more lenient venues of punishment than county courts. Take for example the enslaved men Sam and Humphrey, who in April 1813 were charged at the Fayette Circuit Court for stealing four shirts, three waistcoats, one pound of sugar, and "sundry other articles." A fellow slave, Dick, testified in the case, but at some point he too was implicated in the thievery. The Fayette County jury dismissed the charges against Sam, sentenced Humphrey to ten lashes at the whipping post, and Dick to twenty strikes with the whip.[87] Across town and less than a year later, the David's Fork Baptist Church charged an enslaved member, Ned, with theft and excluded him from the church fellowship.[88] Punishing enslaved members in church courts also held potential monetary benefits for slaveholders, for local courts often levied court fees upon owners if an enslaved person was found guilty of theft. A jury for the Fayette County Circuit Court convicted Jim, the property of Elijah W. Craig, for the theft of "a sorrel horse," which he rode for "several days by which the horse was greatly impaired." The court decided "that Jim shall be taken to the public whipping post and there receive thirty-nine lashes on his bare back." Furthermore, the court ordered Craig to pay the legal costs.[89] In cases when it was an option, recourse through the church could save slaveholders money and avoid the risk of bodily punishment—representing potential lost labor—to their bondsmen.

More than the passive subjects of discipline, the enslaved used church tribunals to punish thieves and legitimize their own property claims. In the eyes of state law, enslaved persons could not own property. Yet as legal historian Dylan Penningroth has demonstrated, the enslaved—though considered by state law to be chattel property themselves—claimed rights to various forms of property, often with the tacit or outright consent of their masters. Between 1800 and 1880, he contends, "an extralegal economy took shape in the South," one whose traces barely made it into statute books or local courts but that operated "in yards, cities, and back roads across the South." This economy—though whites tolerated and at times took part in it—was controlled largely by members of the Black community.[90] Using public ceremonies and public spaces, the enslaved secured acknowledgment of their property from both their masters and other enslaved people. And, in cases of theft, some of the enslaved resorted to special committees to ferret out the culprit, while others resorted to verbal accusations and arguments over alleged thievery. In July 1805, for instance, Arch, an enslaved member of the Bryan's Station Baptist Church, "complained against yellow Daniel for the nonpayment of a just debt." It is unclear whether "yellow Daniel" was a free person or the property of a church member, but the church ruled that he owed Arch $2.25. Daniel agreed to pay it, and the "business [was] dismissed." What is remarkable is that members seemed to have few qualms about the fact that an enslaved member had freely made a contract with another person.[91]

Theft cases between enslaved people not only legitimized their property holdings but could implicate multiple owners and ultimately lead the church to extend its authority beyond the bounds of the immediate neighborhood. In November 1824 a Tennessee church heard charges against Brother Luke, the property of Jethro Fork, for acting "disorderly in detaining an old bed." Luke had been given the bed by Violet, the slave of David Smith, and had agreed to deliver it to Violet's daughter, who belonged to another man. Luke "converted [the bed] to his own use instead of delivering it agreeable to bargain," however, and had since left the neighborhood. Although Luke had "obtained a letter of dismission, and moved away," the church sought to rectify the situation. Members directed the clerk to "get his letter back." Luke was subsequently excluded in March 1825. The clerk did not record who brought the complaint to the church body, but the charges against Brother Luke most likely emanated from the wronged Violet, who had trusted him to deliver the bed. Having moved, of course, Luke may not have had the opportunity to deliver the bed and took it with him. In any case, the theft charge leveled at him highlights how enslaved people used their churches as venues to police the slave quarters and how churches at times extended their authoritative reach to former members who had departed from the immediate watchcare of the congregation. Moreover, the church's hearing of the case demonstrates white members' acknowledgment that Violet possessed a proper claim to the property and that Luke had a responsibility to fulfill his agreement to deliver that property. Local churches, then, served as sites for enslaved people not only to claim rights to property but also to punish those who ignored such claims.[92]

Church tribunals heard a disproportionate number of theft accusations aimed at their Black and enslaved brethren for several reasons. As a form of property themselves, claims to property on the part of the enslaved were always tenuous and contested. The need to publicly display their property to claim rights over it may also have opened them to charges of theft, either from their fellow bondsmen or their owners. In some cases, too, pilfering by enslaved people derived from sheer necessity. One enslaved man in Kentucky noted that he and his fellow bondsmen believed it was "a kind of first principle" that those who labored had "had a right to eat." Another claimed it was his "moral right" to take small amounts from the "abundance" he had helped to produce.[93] Such assertions echoed throughout the slaveholding region. The formerly enslaved Henry Bibb, who had worked in the cotton fields of the Deep South, insisted that "I had a just right to what I took, because it was the labor of my own hands."[94] Historian Walter Johnson has noted that food rations for some enslaved people in the Mississippi Valley proved so meager that stealing provisions became a requirement. After emancipation, formerly enslaved people asserted that white ministers focused almost exclusively on the issue of theft, reminding them they should not steal their "master's turkey" or their "master's chickens" or their "master's hawgs."[95]

These conditions may have been the reason that, although accusations of theft against enslaved Baptists revolved around a variety of forms of property, provender items routinely appeared in such cases. In 1811 the Red River Baptist Church charged Hannah, the property of a Mr. Langston, with "taking sugar that was not her own, [and] boiling the same away to a small quantity & secreting it." The Big Cedar Lick Church charged Kate "for concealing stolen goods and money" in 1814. Mr. S. Smith's Peter was charged by the Bryan's Station Church for "theft in taking his Masters Bacon."[96] Interestingly, the appellation of "Mr." rather than "Brother" signifies that Peter's owner was not a member of the church but that he, or someone directed by him, brought the complaint to the church—perhaps knowing or hoping that Peter's exclusion from the church body would be punishment enough for his transgression. The church clerk, unfortunately, did not specify who brought the initial complaint against Peter, so we do not know whether this was a case in which the master sought to punish an enslaved man directly, or just a prying church member—maybe even a fellow enslaved person—who witnessed or heard of Peter's theft and who sought out the authority of the church in order to purify its membership ranks.

By the second decade of the nineteenth century, Lexington was home to a large African American community made up of both enslaved and free individuals and rooted in church institutions. Free Blacks could be found peddling foodstuffs in the town square outside the market house, while enslaved Blacks roamed the city on tasks from their owners. Of Fayette County's 1,484 slaves, nearly half worked in ropewalks, inns, mercantile shops, and brick manufactories. Many lived in cramped urban quarters in Lexington, socializing, worshipping, and trading with other Blacks in the city. Nearby farmers also hired out enslaved persons to labor in the city's cotton and hemp industries. These and those of the city proper gravitated to Lexington's churches during the first decades of the nineteenth century, spurring the growth of the African American community. Many of the enslaved flocked to the preaching of Peter Durrett, a formerly enslaved man known as Old Captain. By 1810, on the heels of religious revival, Durrett served a congregation of about 500 members. Many whites welcomed the spiritual uplift of the Black population, but their large numbers and general autonomy under Durrett posed a significant threat to the wider region's social and religious order. Town trustees, who had long allowed Durrett's preaching in the city, fretted over the Lexington's growing Black population and Durrett's influence over it. The trustees and local white religious leaders first sought to bring Durrett under the control of the Elkhorn Association of Baptists, before sanctioning another local free Black, London Ferrell—whom the whites believed they could more readily manipulate—to preach in the city. Ferrell established the African First Baptist Church, which fell under the control of the city's white First Baptist Church. Membership numbers in the former body remained small until the late 1820s and Durrett's death, when the church reached more than 300 members.[97]

African Americans had traveled, not always voluntarily, alongside the first pioneers to Kentucky in the 1770s. Often white masters sent enslaved men to survey or clear land ahead of their families' relocation west of the Appalachians. They lived in the same stations and forts as white settlers, and some were even able to obtain their freedom by demonstrating their courage during Native attacks. Those who remained in bondage often "assumed leadership roles in the field" despite the racial barriers to their acquiring equal status with pioneer society.[98] The frontier conditions of the late 1770s and 1780s—the pioneers' stress on individual liberty, the necessity for all men (and at times women) to work or fight alongside one another—had provided opportunities for Black men, even if enslaved, that would have been out of the question in the more settled regions of the East. But the gentry who increasingly arrived in Kentucky during the 1790s pushed forward a less fluid racial hierarchy.

Slowly, after Kentucky's first state constitution of 1792 had sanctioned slavery, the gentry eroded Blacks' economic and political autonomy. Early measures sought to curtail enslaved people's participation in the economic marketplace. An expansive 1798 slave code forbade free Blacks and mulattos to testify against whites at court, mandated that enslaved people carry written passes from their owners when away from home, and severely restricted nonwhites' access to weapons. The revised state constitution of the following year went even further, disenfranchising all nonwhites—including free Blacks who owned property.[99] City leaders and state legislators continued to restrict Black autonomy over the next decade. In the late 1790s, Lexington's trustees ordered those on patrol to arrest all "suspicious blacks who may be found on the streets in doubtful situations."[100] Subsequent measures focused on the autonomy of free Blacks, further constructing a racial hierarchy in Kentucky that by the War of 1812, historian Craig Thompson Friend has argued, cemented Kentucky as an Old South state that uplifted the privileges of white men to the detriment of Blacks, women, and Natives.[101]

This process occurred largely through the state's legal system—which constructed watch houses and coordinated slave patrols, for instance—but also through informal networks such as church disciplinary practices. The Fox Run Baptist Church of Shelby County went as far as organizing special Sunday morning sessions so that "Black members" could hold disciplinary sessions. So, while at times enslaved members could benefit from church tribunals—using them to secure property claims and punish thieves among their own—as white Baptists across the Upper South set aside their emancipationist impulses during the first decade of the nineteenth century, and as Kentucky's Bluegrass region cracked down on Black autonomy in general, churches followed suit, singling out Black brethren for crimes seldom alleged against white members. For white Baptists, discipline became less about regulating sexual offenses and more about policing transgressions related to church affairs. This category includes an array of charges: interacting with another religious group, criticizing the church or minister, breaking the Sabbath, failing to attend meetings, leaving the church without a dismission letter, and refusing to submit to a church decision. Between 1801 and 1815, 29.8% of charges fell under the umbrella of failure of church duty. More than 90% of those charges were against white members, and they accounted for 40.2% of all charges directed at white members during the period. From 1831 to 1845, while the overall number of charges dropped, the share related to failure of church duty increased, accounting for 35% of all charges and 50% of charges against white members.[102]

We have seen how Baptists at times, in insisting on the spiritual equality of all members, challenged prevailing gender and racial norms in Kentucky and across the slaveholding states. Churches in Kentucky clearly did not shy away from regulating household relations. They disciplined errant patriarchs and disobedient spouses. Abusive masters and stubborn enslaved persons also faced the authority of the congregation during the late eighteenth and early nineteenth centuries. Yet the rigor and focus of church discipline also subtly changed as Kentucky became an Old South state, firmly committed to white patriarchy and the institution of slavery. This fell in line with developments throughout the South as once-marginal religious groups, such as the Baptists, moved from the fringes to the mainstream of Southern society. As Christine

Heyrman notes, church discipline faded after 1830, with evangelicals less willing to involve themselves in familial matters.[103] At the same, however, discipline's focus, while on decline, seems to have shifted to Black members, with meetinghouses emerging as central sites through which white Kentuckians policed free and enslaved Blacks.

The clerk of the Pleasant Grove Baptist Church in Shelby County may have best summed up white Baptists' feelings in 1845. That year the church heard charges against Brother and Sister Netherton for separating. The case wore on for nearly four months. Brother Netherton, after being censured by the church, eventually gave satisfaction to the charge and immediately thereafter requested a letter of dismission—perhaps because he did not appreciate his fellow church members' prying into his private affairs. Sister Netherton, making clear her thoughts on the church's role in the case, "refus[ed] to hear the church" on the matter and was excluded in March 1846. The church clerk, Williamson, in a rare candid moment, scribbled in the margins, "Oh that the church could be freed from such perplexing difficulties." In the following years, the church did free itself of such difficulties involving its white members. Of the five cases centering on adultery, seduction, or marital separation that the Pleasant Grove Church heard from 1846 through 1860, all charges were directed toward Black members.[104]

CHAPTER THREE

A "Habitation of Justice?"

The Market Revolution and the Search for Dispassionate Arbitration

> Is it lawful, to swap, or exchange horses? Answer: It is in cases of necessity, but not for [the] filthy lure of gain, which case the Church may be a judge of.
>
> —Mount Pleasant Baptist Church, August 1795

In November 1831 Jacob Creath Jr. became guardian to the infant son of the recently deceased Sydney Bedford. He also agreed to manage Bedford's estate, which included four enslaved people. Henry Foster and two other men agreed to serve as securities on Creath's behalf until the ward Bedford came of age in 1848. Creath and Foster were both members of the David's Fork Reformed Church located outside of Lexington. After hearing that Creath planned to relocate with his wife, ward, and enslaved people to Missouri, however, Foster made clear in October 1839 that he would withdraw from the contract if Creath left Kentucky. Creath refused to release Foster from the bond and claimed that the original agreement made no stipulations about remaining in Kentucky. Seeking release from his security—and a return of the money he put forth in the original agreement—Foster sued Creath at the Fayette County Circuit Court. The David's Fork Church took up the dispute as well, deciding that Foster had committed no wrong by initiating the lawsuit. Having already moved to Missouri, Creath exclaimed, "If I was [still] in the neighborhood, I would live and die out of religious society, before I would trust my character and property with [the church] again."[1]

Creath published a sixteen-page pamphlet describing his version of the dispute. He charged Foster with gambling, speculating, and slander, insisting that the whole affair stemmed from Foster's covetousness. In the end, Foster's turn to civil authority, and the subsequent failure of the David's Fork Reformed Church to resolve the dispute (at least to his liking), upset Creath just as greatly as Foster's covetousness or his slander. "Foster put legality above morality," Creath lamented. "I put the divine laws above human laws. I complied with the spirit of the laws of man—he trampled the divine laws under his feet." Creath "complied with the spirit" of worldly law, and indeed churches called upon their members to respect state authority when it did not conflict with scripture. But Foster had committed the sin of suing "his brother before infidels."[2]

Creath's accusations against Foster and the David's Fork Church reflect a broader reconceptualization of churches' roles as legal venues during the post-Revolutionary period. From their expansion in the late eighteenth century through the early republican era, Baptist churches and their counterparts across the West and South sought to contain property-related disputes within church walls, a practice that persisted in these regions much longer than in the North. Churches insisted members refrain from "going to law" and assumed jurisdiction over a range of disputes typically considered matters for common law, equity, and criminal courts. Church record books are peppered with disputes over trespassing, land, probate, slave sales, and theft. Religious historians have noted that after 1830 church discipline shifted focus and declined.[3] This chapter is concerned with why Baptists turned away from regulating members' monetary, business, and property-related disputes.

Concurrent transformations in the economy and legal culture diminished churches' authority over their members' business and financial matters. Trying to pinpoint the moment when churches stopped disciplining members for indebtedness, usury, or any property-related dispute is like trying to locate when the United States became "capitalist." When Creath responded to Foster, however, more Americans than ever before engaged directly or indirectly with national and international markets, their economic fates entwined in a complex web of transactions made with or by unknown actors. Whereas individual debt had once been derided as a moral failing, it now emerged as a near prerequisite for participation in the marketplace.[4] This emerging conception of debt, along with liberal market relations that stressed white men's ability to contract freely, strained the communitarian ethos upon which church fellowships had been constituted.[5] The ascendant economic order depended upon a uniform legal system for continued expansion. Antebellum legal reformers exclaimed that law should be formalized, providing for dispassionate and predictable outcomes. For many, state law assumed precedence over legalities rooted at the local level, where decisions were often idiosyncratic and based on local knowledge—not on precedent.[6] These transformations—

compounded by the Bluegrass region's growing gentry class, which propagated middle-class values and family privacy—led many of the faithful, such as Creath, to question their churches' role as local legal venues. Although church discipline dwindled, it continued sporadically in Kentucky and elsewhere throughout the nineteenth century. The panics of 1819 and 1837, though, made apparent to Baptists that their churches' ability to police members' engagement with the "world" was difficult indeed, and perhaps even dangerous to the fellowship.

With the expansion of the market revolution in the early nineteenth century, church charges appeared regularly until 1820 and declined precipitously thereafter. In the late 1830s, when economic panic mired much of the country, Kentucky Baptists seemed uninterested or unwilling to arbitrate members' business activities. Tensions between traditional Christian teachings and prevailing economic norms are part of this story. Such tensions might lead a member to question church members' ability to judge whether he acted morally in a business deal with someone they did not know in a business in which they had no part. They could encourage whole congregations to second-guess their prerogative to meddle in disputes that might endanger church harmony. Another component of this story, however, concerns how and why Baptists designated some activities as "secular" and others as "religious."[7] That line was always blurry at best. But within that gray area, churchgoers' myriad decisions with their neighbors, kin, brethren, and business partners highlight how church authority, as seen through the ritual of discipline, changed alongside that of the state.

Some churches, rather than insisting upon their jurisdiction, sanctioned members' recourse to state-based venues to avoid implicating the fellowship in messy economic disputes. When churches litigated members' property disputes, their actions at times became entangled with local courts' operations. Other churches directed their proceedings toward restoring member relations instead of decreeing an award. Like Jacob Creath, many churchgoers expressed dissatisfaction with church rulings. They pointed to factionalism, jealousy, and covetousness as the prime movers in church-based arbitration, a far cry from the churches' central purpose of maintaining a harmonious fellowship in their disciplinary activities. In contrasting their churches' legal activities with those of the state, these same individuals implicitly highlighted the objective of the civil courts: predictable jurisprudence over the particular, prejudiced rulings of local churches.[8] Religious treatise writers lamented the passions that drove churches' disciplinary actions and, similar to antebellum legal reformers, sought to formalize churches' legal operations by publishing tracts devoted to their authoritative scope, proper procedures, and punishments. Despite religious leaders' attempts to reinforce "Baptist jurisprudence," many church bodies had already ceded authority over economic matters to local and state courts. Churchgoers may not have "trampled the divine laws" under their feet, as Creath accused Foster, but in subtle ways they had placed the authority of the state above traditional church practices.

". . . leave the matter to Brethren chosen."

Samuel Harris, an evangelical Baptist preacher, spent much of his life trying to convert souls in Virginia. Observers reported that when preaching to large groups, Harris seemed to pour "forth streams of celestial lightning from his eye," and wherever he turned, his gaze "would strike down hundreds at once." Exaggerated perhaps, but on numerous occasions before the Revolutionary War, his preaching ran afoul of both magistrates and mobs. Harris was so devoted to proselytizing that he refused to sue a debtor in court fearing it would distract him from the cause, leaving "the souls of men to perish." Harris instead decided to sue his debtor "at the court of heaven," which ruled to forgive the debt. This weighed heavy on the debtor's conscience, and he soon after sent Harris "wheat enough" to make payment. Though Harris did not seek arbitration at his local meetinghouse, the Baptist historian Robert Semple used Harris's actions to criticize a growing failure to trust God among "christian worldlings" of the early nineteenth century. They would rather, Semple declared, "not only go to law with the wicked, but with their own brethren!" Writing in 1810, Semple quickly added that such instances "have seldom (we wish we could say never) occurred among the Baptists."[9]

Semple's addendum insisting that church authority take precedence over that of the state demonstrates the importance that post-Revolutionary Baptists placed on the ritual of discipline. It was a reminder to his readers that they should strive to be not completely of the "world" and that they could easily fall from their sacred pedestal if they chose to embrace state authority over trust in God. Baptists did not eschew civil authority completely. The Baptist preacher George Waller noted in 1818 that professing Christians must "strive to fulfil the law of Christ, through which we shall not dishonor the laws of our Government."[10] Nevertheless, churches expected members not to seek justice with one another at the courthouse. Baptists' insistence that members refrain from suing one another in local courts paved the way for churches to assume jurisdiction over a variety of economic and property-related matters. In January 1806, for instance, the Mount Pleasant Baptist Church excluded Brother Davies for "killing a hog supposed to be Br. Masey's property." That same year the Long Run Baptist Church heard complaints from Brother Collins against Brother Chimmith for "detaining his property from him illegally" by "attempting to keep one of his negro girls." The Stamping Ground Baptist Church ordered a member's debt "paid immediately" and assigned "guardians" to "attest to the [Brother's] conduct." Members extended their authority over their brethren's real estate activities as well. The Cane Run Baptist Church, for example, excluded William Harris for "failing to comply with promises with respect to some land" in 1815.[11]

In the first decades after settlement, land disputes overwhelmed Kentucky's local and state courts, their dockets bogged down in suits arising from the region's chaotic settlement. Overlapping claims and fraudulent surveying practices, combined with a lingering animosity between settlers and a speculating, often absentee, elite, engendered litigation ensnaring nearly every parcel in central Kentucky. To sum up the land situation in 1797, Kentucky's surveyor general reported that grants for nearly 24 million acres had been approved, yet the state contained only around 12 million acres. Litigation abounded well after statehood and into the early nineteenth century.[12] The tremendous number of land cases in early Kentucky highlighted uncertainty over legal authority among Kentuckians, as politicians, jurists, lawyers, and observers argued over the proper way to resolve these disputes. The eventual triumph of a privatized property regime backed by the rule of state law during the early republican period did not rule out other forums for litigation. While in the more settled Eastern states an increasingly formal and professional legal system replaced extrajudicial arbitration, the latter persisted much longer in Kentucky.[13] Residents across the social spectrum questioned their ability to find justice in the formal legal system. To many, the rule of law "was synonymous with the misrule of lawyers."[14] This suspicion drove some to seek land-dispute arbitration outside formal courts. Responsive state legislators, in turn, enacted measures that strengthened extrajudicial arbitration, serving as a foundation for subsequent laws through the antebellum period.[15]

Kentucky churches arbitrated a variety of land disputes, including those revolving around land sales, tenancy, and trespassing. Churches, of course, did not solve all land disputes and did not possess the state's authority to enforce decrees.[16] Rather, churches relied upon the fear of eternal damnation and the social repercussions arising from excommunication. In 1799 Brother Ashurd asked the Mount Pleasant Church to investigate a land dispute between himself and Brother Chilton, a member of a nearby church. The church appointed two members to go to Ashurd's land and determine whether "he did get half of the Land in Value or not." The committee reported that Br. Chilton "had the Advantage in Quantity 196 Acres, and the quality entirely superior to that of Brother Ashurd." The church took these facts under consideration but were unsure what to do next, since Br. Chilton "had not agreed to choose his Men" to arbitrate and further "seemed to [be] astonished at it, (or rather at our proceedings) and the Minds of the members were severely divided." At their next meeting, members of Mount Pleasant admitted that "the Matter had not been rightly managed" and wished "to say no more about it at present, except one should take the other under *legal* dealings before either of the Churches they belong to."[17] Although the dispute had already divided the brethren, the church body still thought it best that any "legal" actions be taken within church walls.

Resolution through churches often proved less expensive and much quicker than litigation at local courts. Whereas civil suits could drag on for years and rack up considerable legal fees, churches generally dispensed with cases within weeks and charged no fees. They did, however, assign monetary penalties. In 1805 the Stamping Ground Baptist Church ordered Brother John Cook to pay a fellow member "forty shillings for 20 gallons of whiskey."[18] At the Harrod's Creek Baptist Church, Brother Jacob Booker and his wife, Cathy, were charged with trespassing on another member's land and cutting "down a large poplar" tree. The Bookers made acknowledgment to the church at a Friday meeting the following week—held specifically to adjudicate this dispute—but may not have been content with the church's role in the matter as they immediately requested and were granted letters of dismission. The offended member must have been satisfied with the church's proceedings; if not, that member could have objected to the Bookers' request to exit the fellowship.[19]

Other cases dragged on much longer, implicated numerous church members, and required assistance from outside the immediate church body. The Tick Creek Baptist Church spent nearly a year trying to resolve a complicated land dispute in the mid-1810s. In August 1815 Brother Roulet Rice complained against Brother Robert Tyler for his actions in a land purchase from a nonmember. Two members of the church, Brother and Sister Neal, occupied the land bought by Tyler. According to Rice, Tyler intimated that he would let the Neals have the land outright if they paid him the purchase money and "a reasonable compensation for his trouble." Rice said, "I think [Tyler] stated that 40 or 50 dollars" would be sufficient. When they met, Tyler rejected the idea that any agreement had been previously reached. The controversy continued through the rest of that year and into the next, leading the Tick Creek church to request assistance from six nearby churches. The committee representing the visiting churches confirmed that Tyler had been wrong and called for an admonishment but not his suspension or exclusion. Rice did not let the matter rest, and in July 1816, eleven months after it heard the initial charges, the church formed a committee of seven to reconcile Rice and Tyler and reported satisfaction between the two at their next meeting.[20] Tyler's quest to profit off the land, to the detriment of Brother and Sister Neal who occupied it, contradicted the communitarian ethos propagated by the church. Tyler, it seemed, placed speculation and profit above the good of the church community.

Baptist churches in Kentucky and throughout the Upper South also brought up members on charges of indebtedness. These served not only to punish transgressors but also to resolve matters and maintain peaceful member relations. In 1811 Brother Rucker complained against Brother J. Shepherd at the Buffalo Lick Baptist Church "for refusing to pay a just debt." The church formed a committee that investigated the matter, ruling that Shepherd owed Rucker three barrels "& half a bushel of Corn." At the next church meeting, Shepherd expressed dissatisfaction with the committee's decision. Yet he did not push for the church to dispense with the case. Rather, he wished "to leave the matter to Brethren chosen" by himself and Rucker. The church encouraged both members "to bring forward what testimony" applied "to their case" in order "to settle the matter to satisfaction."[21] As the church clerk made no additional mention of the dispute between Shepherd and Rucker, the self-chosen arbitrators must have successfully resolved the dispute.

Churches at times simply suspended indebted members until they paid their debts. The Garrison Fork Church of Tennessee did just so in 1816, ordering member Ransom Pruit suspended from church privileges until he could produce payment receipts for all his creditors, including at least one who was not a church member.[22] A Kentucky church ordered that Bro. Poindexter, having detained "money after several promises of payment," would be acquitted if he made "payment on or before our next meeting."[23] Other churches, too, ordered debtors to pay their creditors. In the spring of 1823, the Red River Baptist Church resolved that Brother Matt Williams owed $9.12 to Bro. Betts for some bacon he had purchased but not paid for. At the church's meeting in June, the clerk recorded that Williams came forward and paid his debt.[24] In these instances, both reconciling the disputing brethren and resolving the point of contention—decreeing a financial liability—proved equally important. Rather than pursue debts owed in local courts, risking the admonishment of their fellow brethren, potential delay, and legal costs, individuals such as Williams's and Pruit's creditors relied on church authority and successfully obtained monetary recompense.

Even while arbitrating disputes involving land and debt, some Baptists were unsure about their churches' authority amid the changing economic landscape. This lack of certainty becomes apparent when state laws clashed with religious injunctions involving money dealing. In 1805 Mayslick Baptist Church members considered whether it was consistent "with the gospel for Brethren to go to law with their Brother and collect their just debts by the laws of the country." Members heard the query, referred it to their next meeting, then dismissed it.[25] Likewise, the Red River Baptist Church in Tennessee debated in 1808 whether it was right "for a Baptist to take from any man, for money lent, more than four times as much Interest as the law allows." Members agreed "it is not right," claiming that churches should not "hold such members."[26] In 1800 the Bullittsburg Baptist Church in Boone County had ordered Brother Chichester Matthews to pay Brother John Hall $12 owed for acting as security in a Virginia land deal.[27] Yet three years later, members of the same church grappled with its authority in worldly matters. When Brother Forest Webb proposed that the church form a special committee to handle all "temporal" disputes arising among members, his brethren declined.[28] Churches may declare they would not "hold such members" who engaged in usury or failed to pay a just debt, but cracks in their ability to effectively arbitrate these matters had begun to appear. Robert Semple claimed he was happy to know that most Baptists had not turned into "christian worldings" and continued to adhere to church authority when settling member disputes. Yet by the time he published his history in 1810, the United States was ensconced in rapid economic change that reformulated Americans' vision and pursuit of authority. This led Baptists to embrace aspects of the "world" and to rethink their churches' oversight over how members did business or conducted their financial affairs.

"Did we not drink deeply of that (speculative) spirit of infatuation[?]"

At their November 1819 business meeting, Mount Pleasant Baptist Church members learned that Brother Thomas Haydon had initiated a civil suit against Brother Simeon Frost. To provide satisfaction, Haydon agreed to withdraw the suit and pay the court costs. Haydon also made it known that a member of the nearby South Elkhorn Baptist Church, William Stephens, had sued Haydon successfully for $300, and that was about how much Frost owed him. Hoping to resolve the initial dispute between Haydon and Frost, the Mount Pleasant Church ordered that Frost "meet the payment of sd. debt" to Stephens. If Frost could not pay the debt, then he should attend the next "open Court" and "confess judgement for the amount he may owe Haydon and pay the cost" of the suit that Haydon had agreed to withdraw. Members then turned their attention to a lingering matter of debt between two other brethren, extending Brother Lockett's payment deadline for a $20 debt by a month. Over the next year, the church heard accusations of gambling, dancing, intoxication, breaking of the Sabbath, slander, and adultery. Members certainly took their duty to provide watchcare over one another seriously. In the shadow of the church's operations, however, loomed the authority of the civil courts, as clearly shown by the members' recommendation that Frost admit in open court his inability to pay Haydon and take over the costs. In April 1820, when the church heard that Haydon had reinstated the suit, they dismissed their case but charged Haydon with "disorderly withdrawing at [its] last meeting."[29] Haydon satisfied the church on the latter charge, but his actions within the church meeting and at the county courthouse hint that Baptists were grappling with church authority amid an economic foundation in flux. Historians label this economic transformation the "market revolution." Also hanging over the Haydon-Frost dispute was the onset of the Panic of 1819.

No matter when one posits the emergence of capitalism in the Western world, one cannot escape the fact that between the 1783 Paris Peace Treaty and the Civil War Americans experienced a revolution in how they conducted business and provided for their households. Through much of the colonial period, ordinary Americans pursued their subsistence largely removed from international trade markets. While the fortunes of a small, coastal merchant elite were entwined with the rise and fall of an increasingly global market, most people's economic lives were shaped by local markets and neighborly agreements.[30] This reality changed gradually over the course of the eighteenth century, especially after the American Revolution, when transportation improvements allowed more Americans to take advantage of opportunities to consume from, and produce for, distant markets. Small-scale manufacturers and artisans embraced technological advances. Farmers took on debt to make capital improvements, and households became sites of consumption (of necessities and luxuries) rather than simply production. Faceless transactions facilitated by instruments of credit, bills of sale, and bank notes eclipsed informal agreements made between neighbors and kin. Community-based standards of fairness receded in an impersonal marketplace governed by legal contracts. These transformations quickened after the turn of the century.

Like much of the republic, Kentucky's Bluegrass witnessed complex economic and social transformations in the half-century after the Revolutionary War. During the 1770s and 1780s, Euro-Americans had settled the greater Lexington area in hopes of taking advantage of the "best poor man's country." Their expectations for finding agrarian independence through landownership were curtailed considerably by the arrival of the gentry in the 1790s. Although many of the wealthier newcomers added to their substantial fortunes by taking advantage of the chaos arising from disputed land titles, they also established churches and courthouses and helped integrate the state's transportation and local markets with sites in the East and abroad. These changes in turn transformed Lexington into an economic hub for the surrounding region.[31] By the second decade of the nineteenth century, the greater Lexington area had transitioned from an agriculturally oriented society to one in which entrepreneurs, manufacturers, lawyers, and merchants dominated the political and social landscape. Textile manufacturers were replacing household production of many goods, while other budding industries and technologies pushed aside independent artisans.

By 1810, historian Craig Thompson Friend notes, Lexington had developed into "the most urban of western towns."[32] A population influx of lawyers, merchants, artisans, and free Blacks helped make up the city's 4,279 residents. A vibrant manufacturing sector, revolving mainly around hemp production, strengthened the city's blossoming economy. Over the course of the first two decades of the nineteenth century, a new-monied gentry emerged from the ranks of manufacturers and other entrepreneurs. "As the nineteenth century proceeded," Friend writes, "refinement, capitalistic investment, and lines of distinction spread from Lexington outward." Along the way, individuals' relationships to the wider community were transformed. Participation in the expanding market economy was not inimical to communal bonds. As Friend demonstrates, when cloth production expanded in central Kentucky during the 1790s, so too did the demand for private investment, which expanded communal networks of cooperation. Farmers supplied the card machines with dye to women who spun the textiles for market. "From field to carding machine to loom to bluedyer to local store to exporter," Friend continues, "the domestic production of cloth illustrates an interconnectedness of farm to community to commercial economy." This cooperative action, though capitalistic in nature, did not harm the stability of Kentucky's rural, farming society in the Bluegrass region. It instead fostered continued communal cooperation, interconnecting the producers of various products and allowing them to come to a "premarket price through neighborly agreement," This process produced a synergy between the market economy and the moral obligations that underlay community relations.[33]

Kentucky Baptists did their part to uphold the moral obligations at the base of local communities. In 1810 Brother Lewis Dimney of the Stamping Ground church complained against Brother Toliver Craig "for the nonpayment of money." A committee reported subsequently that Craig satisfied the debt and the brethren by signing over a $75 note to Dimney. Five years later, members of the Pleasant Grove Baptist Church in Shelby County settled a dispute over inheritance between a member and his mother. Members of Fox Run in Shelby County, meanwhile, granted a letter of dismission to Sister Brown but denied one to her husband, Francis, "on account of an objection against him, for not having settled some of his contracts." One church even picked up the tab when a member fled the neighborhood, leaving behind disgruntled creditors.[34] In their disputes over debt, land, probate and other property, Baptists clung to the notion that communal authority funneled through the church fellowship could authoritatively shape members' public activities.

The country's first widespread economic collapse, the Panic of 1819, strained the moral obligations constituting community relations. The conclusion of the War of 1812 ushered in an economic boom. As exports and productivity increased, so did state and local banks' reckless printing of paper money. In the summer of 1818, the Second Bank of the United States stopped transferring specie to irresponsible institutions throughout the country, demanding as well that these banks pay outstanding balances totaling millions of dollars. Cash-strapped banks responded by calling in specie payments from their debtors. Urban areas saw a marked rise in unemployment. Prices of cotton and land in the West plummeted while business came to a near halt. Farmers unable to repay loans were at risk of losing their property. Country merchants, stocked with valuable merchandise bought on credit, shuttered their doors as customers cut their spending and retreated at least temporarily to semi-subsistence living. Americans watched with horror and puzzlement as their assets' value dwindled.[35]

The distress did not spare Kentucky. A slight economic downturn following the war had passed by 1819, yet the gains had been largely due to speculation, a weak currency, and the shortsighted loan policies of the nearly four dozen banks established in Kentucky during the previous two decades. "Rag money" flowed through the state's economy. When the speculative bubble burst and banks demanded hard currency for outstanding debts, hard times proliferated as quickly as had baseless paper money. Businesses failed and banks foreclosed on farms and homes. Lexington's artisans, already strained by increased imports from places such as Philadelphia, left the city en masse looking for new opportunities. Those who remained found it difficult to sell their specialized, pricey wares to pinched farmers. Though in 1821 the state authorized the construction of poorhouses, other residents demanded that the legislature do more. A relief bill for indebted farmers was later declared unconstitutional by Kentucky's Court of Appeals, which itself was abolished and replaced by a "New Court" composed of pro-relief justices. The Old Court–New Court controversy continued until 1827 (when the legislature reinstalled the Old Court), and it, alongside the economic downturn, had far-reaching effects. It was clear that the communitarian ethos heralded by the first generation of Kentuckians had succumbed to the self-interest of an increasingly atomized society.[36] It is no wonder then that in late 1819 Brother Haydon so needed the $300 from Frost to pay off his own debt he sued his brother twice at the courthouse. Fellow members, perhaps themselves distressed by the deepening economic crisis, did little to stop him.

The economic fallout lasted two full years. Not until 1822 did Kentuckians and Americans in general find themselves on a stable economic footing. But times had changed. The 1819 Panic demonstrated to acute observers that a new economic order had arrived. Faceless exchanges through national and international markets, governed by the depersonalized "sanctity of contract," had eclipsed neighborly exchanges based on good faith, character, and moral economy.[37] Kentucky's middle class weathered the storm, emerging from the panic years "thoroughly in control of economic and political life" in the Bluegrass region. The "refinement, capitalistic investment, and lines of distinction" that had begun appearing in the early 1800s rebounded quickly during the late 1820s and 1830s. The division between public and private hardened, weakening sources of communal regulation over familial matters and freeing the "self-made" men of Kentucky to pursue economic advancement with less moral responsibility. Indeed, by the mid-1830s, as Friend argues, the "extramoral workings of capitalism seemed more rewarding" for central Kentuckians "than traditional patterns of familial and communal obligation."[38]

Kentucky church leaders fretted over the emerging economic order's ramifications for their flock. The Presbyterian minister David Rice surveyed the landscape and lamented that a spirit of avarice, "cherished and strengthened by the opportunity for speculation . . . was extremely inimical to the spirit of the gospel. A sense of moral obligation," he concluded, "unless it was sanctioned by some legal form, which could not be evaded, was almost destroyed."[39] In its 1820 circular letter to member churches, the Long Run Association warned Baptists of the danger of succumbing to such worldly temptations. "Did we not drink deeply of that (speculative) spirit of infatuation which has well-nigh ruined our country, in common with other people[?]" The letter continued:

> Have we not participated in those schemes of speculation, which have been invented, and in consequence of which the country is now groaning; (viz:) the banking institutions, which have been founded in unrighteousness, and that detestable practice of usury, which is so prevalent in this our day . . . [All Baptists, but the ministry especially needs to] be vigilant. Be instant in season, out of season, reprove, rebuke, exhort with all longsuffering & doctrine.[40]

The author of the circular letter, John Wells, seemed astonished that Baptists had become the very "christian worldlings" whom Robert Semple had decried just a decade before. They had participated in the profane, unrighteous financial schemes alongside the "common people," the unconverted bankers and usurers. His guidance to "reprove, rebuke [and] exhort" served as a plea to watch over oneself and one's brethren as they meddled with the "world."

Overall, the years preceding the 1819 Panic and those of the subsequent financial fallout saw churches reproving and rebuking members for business or property-related matters. Churches in the data set leveled seventy charges related to business transactions, theft, and members' legal doings from 1810 through 1822. Forty-five of these charges, about 64%, were accusations of criminal actions involving stolen property or covering up a crime. Four of these charges went against white members: one larceny allegation against Loid James in 1820, one theft charge for Sally Jones in 1821, and one charge against each Abigail and John Shotwell for covering up a crime (it seems the Shotwells were privy to a family member's giving birth to a child out of wedlock and her abandonment of the newborn across state lines).[41] The remaining forty-one charges were directed toward Black members, the bulk of which (85%) were for theft or concealment of stolen property.

The other twenty-five charges ran the spectrum from brethren "going to law" and hassles over probate and other property, to breach of contract and failure to pay a debt. Of these, 23% involved members' indebtedness to one another and to those outside the fellowship. In September 1818, for example, the David's Fork Baptist Church discovered Brother Poindexter failed to turn over "money after several promises of payment." Members ordered him acquitted if he paid the debts "on or before" the next meeting.[42] At times, an apparent unease with churches' handling of these disputes appeared, as in 1816, when the Old Mill Creek Baptist Church heard allegations against Brother Bennett "for refusing to settle & pay Mrs. Sarah Hall" money he owed her. Bennett denied the charges, but his brethren determined that Hall had "not paid." Bennett finally agreed to make payment, which satisfied the church. At the next meeting, in January 1817, however, two members came forward "casting reflections" on the church for its decision in the Bennett case. The two aggrieved members later apologized and made satisfaction, but that did not end the ordeal. A year and a half later, the church received reports that Bennett had never repaid Hall, and a "large majority" of the members voted to exclude him. When Bennett asked for a rehearing the following year, the church upheld his exclusion.[43] The church's censure did not convince Bennett to repay Hall. Perhaps the "legal form" that the minister Rice noted had eclipsed the "moral obligation" of the original contract.

". . . business very difficult to settle."

At their December 1826 business meeting, Mount Pleasant Baptist Church members learned of a difficulty between Brethren Robert True and Thomas Lyne. Members of Mount Pleasant had not heard any charges related to members' business activities, financial quarrels, or legal affairs in nearly three years. Charges of theft, fighting, adultery, and drunkenness against enslaved members, mixed with a handful of allegations against white members for adulterous behavior and failure of church duty, kept members busy with discipline. The church formed a committee to investigate and resolve the True-Lyne affair. In February the committee reported that it could not reconcile the disgruntled brethren. Claiming that the dispute between Lyne and True was "business very difficult to settle," the church dissolved the committee and "advised the two brethren to settle the matter between themselves." Earlier that year, too, Mount Pleasant's sister church at Bryan's Station, upon hearing a case of breach of contract, claimed that it was "a matter over which we have no control" and authorized the disputants "to act at [their] discretion."[44] Churches did not often suggest that disputing members settle affairs themselves. Doing so suggested negligence in discipline, a failure of ritual, and perhaps a crack in church authority over members' activities.

Historian Robert Elder argues that in the Deep South during the early nineteenth century, church discipline's goal transformed from upholding Christian standards in members' economic relations—precepts set apart from worldly rules—to ensuring that members' actions conformed to "the prevailing economic standards" of the day. Rooted in a culture of Southern honor that stressed communal authority, Elder concludes that churches served as "traditional venue[s] to address the emerging concerns over authenticity and trustworthiness that accompanied the modern era."[45] Arbitration of usury and extortion became less common, and rather than providing a financial remedy for breach of contract or debt, churches punished those who had acted dishonorably: failing to pay a just debt, absconding from creditors, or acting clandestinely in financial transactions. Without a doubt discipline across the board, not just in economic matters, waned after 1830 and, as Elder notes, at times took on a new direction more aligned with worldly prescriptions. This transformation not only redirected the focus of church discipline but held far-reaching consequences for churches as local law-producing sites. In many parts of the country, communal authority over these matters was already declining, in part owing to the sheer difficulty of pinpointing transgressions. Christians often discussed debt's moral underpinning, but they had a harder time identifying usurious acts or extortion amid the ascending economic milieu. What did debt signify about one's moral righteousness? Was it usurious if one charged interest equal to that of the local bank or as legally mandated by state law? Others simply disregarded church procedures and practices, turning to the civil authorities to arbitrate their economic affairs. Authoritative judgment became less likely to be found in the church, where godliness and individual character reigned. Parties had to look beyond church walls for effective arbitration within an economy shaped by impersonal market forces.

Debt proved a source of tension for churches as its necessity and prevalence increased in the early nineteenth century. Through much of the colonial era, a "moral economy of debt" governed debtor-creditor relations. A debtors' inability to pay was akin to a moral failure. Slowly during the Revolutionary Era, as debt became more essential in an integrated market economy, indebtedness transformed from a moral to an economic failure.[46] The "moral economy of debt" was never practiced in total, of course, but as it disintegrated amid ascending economic liberalism, ministers reminded Americans of debt's moral components. Noting that simple instances of debt or speculation were not necessarily illegal, many Baptists wished churches would still pay them mind. As early as 1792, the Bryan's Station Baptist Church resolved that it was "not agreeable" for a church member "to suffer themselves to be sued or warranted for a plain just debt while they have property enough in their hand to discharge" it.[47] This sentiment continued well into the nineteenth century. The editor of the *Christian Baptist* in 1828 prayed that churches would take greater interest in the financial dealings of their members. If a member was sued for debt or breach of covenant, whether it was by another professing Baptist or not, the case fell within his church's jurisdiction. "No man can be sued [in courts] justly unless he has violated some law of Christ, or departed from the spirit and design of christianity." This proved true "under the code of laws which govern our commercial intercourse in this country," he continued, and churches possessed the responsibility to investigate all instances of speculation, indebtedness, or covenant breaking among their membership.[48]

Baptists were not the only churchgoers critiquing new understandings of debt. The Episcopalian Rev. John T. Brooke of Cincinnati explained in 1841 that debt, though "a temporal concern," involved "moral obligation." In a "trading community" like the one that had arisen since the turn of the century, debt occurred frequently, with "many adverse influences" combining "to loosen the morality of pecuniary obligation." But debt was not all bad in Brooke's view, it was crucial to civil society. To interpret the biblical injunction "owe no man anything" as forbidding debt outright "would be unreasonable and unscriptural." Brooke specified four types of debt forbidden by the scripture: those of "Willful Dishonesty," "Avaricious Speculation," "Vanity," and "Imprudence." Categorizing these as "blamable debts," Brooke argued that each violated the law of love, that dishonesty was the same as stealing, and that speculation equated to gambling—the opposite of "virtuous commerce" or "judicious" investments." In contracting imprudent debts, a man endangered others and "even the welfare of his own family." As far as vanity went, Brooke claimed he was in no position to judge "how far opulent Christians may indulge themselves in such things as splendid mansions, elegant furniture and costly apparel," but the acquisition of such "luxuries" by "persons of limited resources, is clearly indiscreet." Throughout his sermon, while seeking to not offend his wealthier congregants and benefactors, Brooke legitimized debts as "the vehicles of commerce," key to the expanding marketplace, and not automatically subject to Christian censure.[49]

If debt's righteousness was in flux for Christians, fraud, extortion, and usury, perhaps even covetousness, simply became harder to nail down during the first half of the nineteenth century. Even before the turn of the century, some Baptists grappled with morality and the marketplace. In 1797, for instance, a member asked the Stamping Ground Baptist Church, "What is Considered to Constitute the Sin of Extortion?" The church referred the question before the member withdrew it two months later.[50] Religious commentators agreed that commerce in and of itself was not sinful. The faithful, however, needed to transact business in a way that did not violate the conscience. When buying and selling or entering a contract, one was required to deal fairly. But as the Unitarian minister Orville Dewey admitted in 1838, the difficulty lay in determining a just price. In primitive states of society, that endeavor proved much easier than in a complex and dynamic society like the United States, where liberty had given rise to "universal and unprecedented activity among all the classes of society, in all the departments of human industry."

> The wants, fancies and fashions of society; the state of crops and markets, and of trade all over the world; the variations of the seasons; the success or failure of fisheries; improvements in machinery; discoveries in art; and the regulations of governments—all these things and many more, conspire alternately to fix and disturb from day to day, that ever fluctuating thing called price.

Thus, Dewey concluded, conscience did not govern honesty in price setting. "All that conscience has to do with price . . . is, not to go beyond the usage of the market."[51] Dewey did not divorce individual acts from market actions completely; one should, for example, still avoid false representation of goods. But his comments shed light on an inherent difficulty of church tribunals: determining sinful actions in an economic system in which transactions—the parties, price, and terms—were often bound up in conditions beyond local control.

Both Dewey's and Brooke's sermons appeared within the context of another economic collapse that began with the Panic of 1837, deepened in 1839, and persisted into the early 1840s.[52] By the 1830s the previous panic appeared to have been a blip in the fading horizon. Americans had certainly regained their economic confidence. In ever-greater numbers, farms and households took advantage of easy access to credit, chancing that capital improvements would give them their portion of rising prices on land, cotton, and other agricultural exports. The march of prosperity, real and potential, came to an abrupt halt, however, during the first half of 1837, when failures in European broker houses rippled through markets on both sides of the Atlantic. Banks in cities such as New York, Philadelphia, Baltimore, and New Orleans once again stopped specie payments and called in outstanding loans. With easy credit gone, payments ceased and business slowed to a crawl. Urban wage earners lost their jobs in droves while indebted farmers went belly-up, losing the land on which they subsisted. Merchants and manufacturers failed, and as historian John Larson notes, "Men of property whose conduct had been impeccable nevertheless were ruined" by their creditors' demand for quick payment.[53] Too many Baptists may have drunk deeply of the speculative spirit of the age, as John Wells had claimed during the previous panic, but this bursting bubble touched even those who were conducting business morally.

That may be why the economic bust of the late 1830s did not generate a rash of business and property-related disputes in Kentucky churches: how could brethren decide which activities were honorable and which violated the laws of conscience? Either way, churches' actions diverged between the two panics. During the ten years preceding the 1819 Panic, church members regularly pursued discipline for a variety of property or business matters. Not so by the time of the next panic. From 1830 through 1843, the seven churches in the data set heard thirty-five charges dealing with property, business transactions, or members' legal troubles. Twenty-eight (80%) of the thirty-five were accusations of theft, concealment of stolen property, or covering up of a crime—twenty-seven of which were directed at Black members. From the onset of the panic in 1837 through 1843—when historians generally agree the economic distress subsided—churches leveled seventeen charges against Black members (all related to stolen property) and one charge of forgery, also against a Black member. Church clerks left no records of white members haggling over monies owed or services not rendered.[54]

"I have lost little in being excluded from their fellowship . . ."

Church tribunals served as effective sites for dispute resolution only when members acted dispassionately in their decrees. Members, when "called upon to testify, judge, and advise," had to be objective or risk their prejudices tainting the proceedings. Even a slight "defect, in their temper, testimony, judgment or advice, may turn the scales against success."[55] As Jacob Creath Jr. would certainly agree, individuals possessed a right to procedural fairness in both church-based and state-based courts. Proper church discipline required impartiality. By the 1830s and early 1840s many disputants, however, decried the unfair, factionalist-produced decrees coming from their local meetinghouses. Witnessing a decline in disciplinary activity, church leaders throughout the country set out to strengthen churches' law-making functions by formalizing their procedures, stressing the importance of predictable and dispassionate arbitration. The very stability and continued progress of their respective organizations was at stake. Their efforts fell in line with leading legal thinkers of the antebellum period, who "sought to depoliticize the law" by insisting "upon its objective, neutral, and facilitative character."[56]

As early as the 1820s, trans-Appalachian Baptists began calling for a more uniform system of discipline, though not until the 1840s did church leaders take serious steps to formalize their procedures. The First Baptist Church of Frankfort composed a letter in 1823 to the Franklin Baptist Association asserting "that every society should have a compendium of discipline under which offenders of every grade might be easily arraigned, reclaimed, or censured."[57] Two decades later members would get their wish. In the 1840s numerous ministers devoted tracts to church government and church discipline. Eleazer Savage gave two reasons for publishing his *Manual of Church Discipline* in 1844. "Disciplinary measures, as they exist," he contended, "are more frequently the offspring of *passion*, than principle." Moreover, church members possessed no guide "to scripturally instruct church members, as to the *different kinds* of offences" and "the *proper methods* of treating them."[58]

The Reverend Warham Walker concluded his own treatise, *Church Discipline*—also published in 1844—by claiming that an adherence to the principles elucidated within his text "by any church, would be found highly conducive to its true prosperity." He continued: "The discipline of a church, if it be conducted according to the law of Christ, will be characterized by harmony, simplicity, and regularity. The law leaves nothing doubtful, in respect either to the mode of disciplinary actions, or the spirit in which it should be performed." Walker further warned churches that governed discipline "by no rule, save their own discretion" that their path could be "fraught with peril." Those churches risked "introducing corruption, disorder, and dissension" into their ranks, maladies that eventually would render them "incapable of united, vigorous, and well directed action" toward their secular or regular enemies.[59] William Crowell's *The Church Member's Manual*, appearing in 1847, proved so popular that three years later he published a condensed version as a handbook. In 1873 a new revised version was issued.[60] Like Savage and Walker, Crowell stressed the importance of discipline. "The course of the church should always be uniform and consistent in its treatment of offences," he wrote, lamenting that some churches "notice some offences and pass by others." He then elaborated a number of procedural requisites for proper administration of church-based justice, including sections devoted to ruling according evidence, the various punishments available for churches, and the treatment of excluded persons.[61] In sum, Crowell devoted more than sixty pages to the various procedures, attributes, causes, and types of church discipline. Tracts such as Walker's and Crowell's echoed Baptist concerns throughout the United States. A Virginia minister, Thomas Hume, insisted in June 1844 that "a more efficient discipline" was essential for churches' "spirituality, and a necessary remedy for much of the evil" that afflicted them. He put aside concerns that rigorous discipline led to short member rolls, arguing instead that while the practice was often "painful" in "application," its benefits when "faithfully and judiciously" used were "promotive of the spirituality and healthfulness of those that remain[ed] in the church."[62]

Religious leaders' calls for a formalized church disciplinary system aligned with contemporary legal thinkers, who called for law to be objective and formal in nature. By the 1830s the American legal profession had developed a treatise tradition that sought to present law as scientific, emanating "not from will but from reason." Law, prominent legal intellectuals insisted, was "an objective, neutral, and apolitical system."[63] As the jurist James Kent stressed in his *Commentaries on American Law*, it would be "extremely inconvenient to the public if precedents were not duly regarded, and pretty implicitly followed. It is by the notoriety and stability of such rules, that professional men can give safe advice to those who consult them; and people in general can venture with confidence to buy, and to trust, and to deal with each other." If judicial decisions were ignored, he continued, "we should disturb and unsettle the great landmarks of property."[64] Indeed, by the late antebellum period, state legal reformers in the South increasingly infringed upon local authority over property matters, claiming the state's protection of property was in the public interest.[65] Local legal venues persisted throughout the period, with legal reformers deriding localized law's inherent flexibility and unpredictable nature. Parties in property disputes at church meetinghouses made similar arguments, and their indictments of churches' juridical proceedings and decrees hint at a larger reconceptualization of law, its location, and sources of governing authority during the first half of the nineteenth century.

In his quarrel with Henry Foster, Jacob Creath Jr. insisted that the David's Fork Reformed Church had failed in is scriptural duty to settle member disputes. The church's decision, in his view, was compromised well before its official decree. Creath charged that from the beginning of its proceedings the church had erred in handling the case. At one point during the trial, Foster reportedly "flew into a violent rage." For that action alone, Creath exclaimed, Foster should have been "*marked* and turned out of the society of good men."[66] The church instead pronounced Foster innocent "on his own bare word," without evidence, and "contrary to all the laws of all civilized countries . . .

contrary to all Protestant Christendom." Only after declaring Foster innocent, for example, did the church encourage Creath to send any evidence he possessed. The timing of this request unnerved Creath. "Can such a church be called a habitation of justice?" he asked. What if a state court "should give a verdict first, on the accuser's word and then seven months afterwards call for evidence? What would the community say of such a court?" Furthermore, "whose character or property would be safe in such hands?" The church, rather than upholding scripture and fairly resolving her members' disputes, had failed to properly pursue justice. "I have begged this church to settle this matter," Creath exclaimed, but "she would not."[67]

The church's decree reflected larger problems within the church at David's Fork, complications that hindered its ability to dispense discipline and resolve disputes. Covetousness and speculation were the central charges that Creath had leveled against Foster, but he extended the charges to include the entire church, exclaiming that it had become "a *nest* of traders and Southern speculators."[68] Creath alleged that with its character in question, the church could no longer judge objectively. By contrasting its operations with the workings of secular courts—asking what if "the courts of the country" operated by issuing a verdict before receiving all the evidence—and declaring that he could no longer trust the church with his character and property, Creath hinted that the David's Fork Reformed Church had lost credibility as an effective law-producing site. Insisting it had departed from all "Protestant Christendom," he implicitly raised the "civilized" operations of the commonwealth's courts above those of the church body. Given that his former brethren at David's Fork seemed reluctant to sufficiently investigate the matter, the feeling may have been widespread in the church and beyond.[69]

Witnesses, observers, and participants across the trans-Appalachian West echoed Creath in accusations against their local churches. William Collins expressed as much not long after Creath's dispute with Henry Foster. In the spring of 1841, Collins, a member of the Elizabeth Church of Particular Baptists in Bourbon County, Kentucky, held in hand thirteen tons of hemp. William Anderson, a lifelong acquaintance of Collins and fellow member of the Elizabeth Church, expressed interest in buying the crop but needed to do so on credit. Following a church meeting in April, Anderson and a handful of other members assembled at Collins's home to broker the deal. There, according to Collins, the two drew up contract terms, eventually agreeing to those stipulations two days later. Upon receiving payment of up to $300 on May 1, Collins contracted to deliver a corresponding quantity of hemp to Anderson, with the rest to follow at his discretion over the summer and fall of 1841. Anderson further agreed to make payment in whole with 10% interest by June 1842. In late April, amid a wet spring, Collins called upon Anderson to ensure that he still wanted the first part of the hemp delivered. Not having completed his hemp house, Anderson declined delivery at that time. Collins ultimately delivered more than two tons in June but received no money from Anderson. "After waiting several days and receiving no money," Collins later wrote, "I concluded that he had violated the contract, and that therefore I was absolved or released from any further obligation according to law." Collins did not trust his personal judgment, however, and called in help from "some eight to ten persons, all of whom coincided with [his] own opinion."[70]

Collins's appeal for confirming opinions proved simply the first step in a long process that went from informal arbitration with church members serving as referees, to a church vote, and eventually to the Bourbon County Court. After hearing testimony from a female church member who had been present when Collins and Anderson had agreed to the contract, the two arbitrators ruled that Anderson had indeed violated the contract and owed Collins for the two tons already delivered. Both Collins and Anderson agreed with the ruling, but Anderson did not immediately hand over the note. At the August church meeting, two members agreed to enter as security for Anderson's debt to Collins. "I then felt that I was perfectly safe," Collins insisted, "having three Particular Baptists bound by honor," and Anderson agreed to draw up a note for Collins. A few days later, however, he demanded that Collins "make confession to him or [they] could not live together in [the] Elizabeth Church." Collins refused, and Anderson "lodged a complaint" against him at the July church meeting, claiming injury done "in purse and feelings."[71]

The dispute continued for months, with Collins, Anderson, and numerous other church members leveling accusations at one another. Part of the problem, according to Collins, was Anderson's refusal to turn over a promissory note for the hemp. At one point, Collins told Anderson that he "had proved the contract by testimony sufficient to indict any man in Bourbon county for murder," and further that his actions justified an exclusion from the church.[72] Anderson responded by accusing Collins of usurious practices, fraud, and disorderly conduct and charged Collins's son with false swearing. After numerous failed attempts, the Elizabeth Church eventually called a special meeting to settle the issue. By this time Collins had grown tired of Anderson's stalling and believed the church was hardly in a position to settle the matter effectively, as "all the members had taken sides," making it unlikely that they could reach an objective decision in the case. Instead of tackling the facts of the dispute, however, the church members voted that they were distressed with both Anderson and Collins. Collins stood, expressed his confusion about the vote, and left the meetinghouse. The church eventually resolved that Collins had erred in so quickly discarding the contract and that Anderson was at fault for not adhering to the decision of the previous arbitration committees. As Collins tried to explain himself to the church, the moderator cut him off, claiming his words reflected badly upon the church body. "It then seemed to me," Collins later wrote, "that I could say nothing but what was deemed out of order or unnecessary." He relented. Upon request from the moderator, Anderson again refused to turn over the note. A motion for both men's exclusion from the church passed.[73]

Collins believed the church had made a mockery of the whole affair and, like Creath, implied that the local court would have handled such a contract dispute more effectively. The moderator had even reportedly "remarked that it had been the worst managed case he ever knew." Following his exclusion, Collins asked one member why the church did not allow him and Anderson to settle the matter at law. The brother replied that a lawsuit would engender "cross swearing among the members of the church, and a jury might decide differently from a committee, which would place the church in an awkward position." Another member admitted that the exclusions of the two men were handled as one vote—a rather rare occurrence—because "otherwise, there would have been a split in the church." The church's actions may have protected the coherence of the membership body, but its failure to protect its members' individual rights upset Collins, convincing him of the necessity of state law. "I conclude from it that if professors of the religion of Christ can act as here stated," he exclaimed, "I have lost little in being excluded from their fellowship and communion." After their exclusions, Collins initiated a suit against Anderson, "and there was cross-swearing, sure enough." Collins prevailed, though the court awarded him only a little over $100, some $300 less than he claimed Anderson owed.[74]

Collins insisted on multiple occasions "that is was not the money [he] was contending for," when he sought the church's assistance. Soon after the dispute began, one neighbor told Collins that word had circulated about his backing out of the contract. Surely the awareness of rumors spreading throughout the neighborhood and the surrounding area of his alleged failure to live up to his contract with Anderson drove Collins's actions during the church proceedings. Once that legal venue legitimated the rumors by excluding Collins—labeling him as both a less-than-straightforward businessman and an unrepentant moral transgressor—he first found solace at the local court before making "public in pamphlet form the causes that led" to the degradation of his civil and religious identities. He claimed to be perfectly satisfied "that all who heard the trial"—and, he noted, "they were a good many"—were "satisfied" that he deported himself throughout the endeavor "above board," taking "no ungentlemanly advantages" of Anderson.[75] His account—which primarily describes the church's handling of the case—ends with his triumph in a court of law whose ruling eclipsed the church's actions, restoring his rightful property and reputation.

Not far from the Elizabeth Church, members of the Washington Baptist Church were embroiled in their own disagreements over church discipline and the "exercise of arbitrary and lawless power" during the mid-1840s.[76] The consternation aroused within the Washington church centered upon actions taken by their sister churches and governing association. In 1845 the printed minutes of the Bracken Association noted rumors about the alleged actions of Elder Gilbert Mason (minister for the Washington and Lewisburg churches) while serving as preacher at the nearby Mayslick Baptist Church during the early 1840s. Along with five other charges, Mason was accused of "serious impropriety as to the disposition" of monies collected for Georgetown College.[77] The Washington Church took up four of the six charges against their pastor immediately after the conclusion of the association meeting in September 1845, and "[Mason] was unanimously acquitted." The church members decided they had no jurisdiction over the two other charges.[78]

Three months after the association's meeting, the Mayslick Church held a council—attended by members of churches in both the Bracken and Elkhorn Associations—that touched upon the charges against Elder Mason. Given that Mason had already been dismissed from the Mayslick Church on good terms in 1843 and accepted as the pastor of the Washington Church soon after, members of the latter charged that the Mayslick proceedings were illegal, "altogether unauthorized, and unprecedented in Baptist jurisprudence."[79] Any effort "to arraign, try, or even prefer charges against any individual member, out of his own immediate church," Washington church members asserted, "is an act of usurpation; and is wholly *unauthorized* by Baptist Law, or scripture teachings." Not only did the Mayslick Council overstep its authority by hearing charges against a member of another church—who was not present and had already made satisfaction for the offenses in 1842—but the council ignored overwhelming witness testimony in favor of Mason.[80]

The Washington Church disregarded the decision of the Mayslick Council, and the controversy continued throughout 1846. In January the Washington and Lewisburg churches published a reply to the Mayslick Council, which further stoked the controversy and led to another gathering of an advisory council in July. After hearing testimony and examining evidence, the Lewisburg Council—as the July meeting came to be known—ruled that Elder Mason deserved "expulsion from [his] church."[81] The Washington Church retorted that the council's proceedings against Mason were tainted by prejudice and illegality and refused to follow its recommendations. As in the cases of Creath and Collins, Washington Church members believed their pastor's reputation was being trampled by extralegal procedures propelled by passion and faction.

In defending their position to the Bracken Association, the church called upon Judge Adam Beatty, a circuit court judge in Mason County who had participated in the Lewisburg proceedings. Beatty submitted a long letter in Mason's defense, claiming that after Mason defended his actions to the council, the delegates changed the charge—in relation to the Georgetown donation—from embezzlement to breach of trust. Thus, he continued, the council made "it a crime in Elder Mason to have defended himself against" the embezzlement accusation "by the production of evidence showing that he was not guilty of the charge!!" Its procedural tactics shocked the judge. "Was such an anomaly ever before witnessed in a judicial tribunal?" he asked. "Could anything else but a judgment of condemnation be expected from a tribunal, which was of opinion that *an endeavor*, on the part of the accused, to defend himself, served only to aggravate his offences." Moreover, the council had found Mason guilty of slander based upon evidence of confession. This evidence, the judge continued—pointing to a ruling made by the Kentucky Court of Appeals—holds "very little weight" in state-based courts. As twenty-seven individuals corroborated the preacher, in contrast to the confessions of a few, "this species of testimony ought not to have the weight of a feather in deciding the facts of [Mason's] case." On another charge related to a debt owed a Mr. Kirk, Beatty claimed there was ample evidence to disprove the accusation, yet the council voted the charge sustained. Despite Beatty's defense of both Mason and the Washington Church, delegates to the Bracken Association cut ties with the Washington Church in 1846 for its refusal "'to abide by and perform the decision of the [Lewisburg] Council in Elder Mason's case.'"[82]

The Bracken Association's actions incensed members of the Washington Church. Not only had the association severed ties with the Washington

Church, but it had adopted a resolution calling for Mason's retirement. In turn, Washington Church members invoked several Baptist authorities—including John Taylor and Warham Walker—who highlighted the danger of power-usurping associations. For Mason's congregants, in dissolving ties with their church and casting aspersions against their pastor, delegates to the Bracken Association had acted from passionate malice, wielding "lawless power" against the church's scriptural rights:

> We are greatly deceived if what we have set forth does not convince all candid and *dispassionate* men, whose minds have not been warped by preconceived opinions, that the action of the Association at its present meeting . . . has been a violation of the first principles of justice, and inconsistent with Baptist law and usage, in cutting off the Washington Church from its association with its sister churches, and thus attempting to degrade and dishonor the said church for doing what it had a clear legal right to do.[83]

Such outcomes were exactly what writers like Savage, Walker, and Crowell hoped to avoid when they published their treatises devoted to church discipline in the 1840s. In each case the deciding tribunal strayed from procedural corrections and fell into the pit of passionate resolution. This is not to say that passion or faction was absent from churches before the late-antebellum period. But amid the expanding, integrated marketplace of the early nineteenth century, as debt transformed from a moral to an economic failing and refinement spread outward from urban centers such as Lexington, individuals, church members and not, sought more formal, seemingly unprejudiced, and relatively predictable arbitration for their property disputes. This led to a weakening of church authority over white members' property-related matters and a disproportionate focus on Black members' transgressions.

Although Creath, Collins, and the members of the Washington Church disagreed on doctrinal principles—Creath was a Reformer, Collins was a Particular Baptist, and the Washington Church was in the Regular Baptist Order—each could agree they had been wronged by the workings of prejudiced tribunals. And, as Judge Beatty pointed out, Mason's reputation had been attacked by a council that paid no heed to the rigors of law. For them, and surely other churchgoers throughout the region, their churches lacked the attributes of state law's professional, formal, and objective procedures and outcomes. The fact that each of the above disputes centered upon white men's property and reputations compounded the matter and impelled the respective parties to detail their disputes' particulars in published form. Yet a central theme in each account was the contrast between church-based and state-based legal venues. For Creath, no "civilized" tribunal of a secular nature would proceed as had the David's Fork Church. The Washington Church, too, denounced the "arbitrary" rulings of the association's councils. Not only did it lack authority, but it had acted contrary to both state and Baptist law. Collins also relished finding recourse at the local court, noting that he had become "perfectly satisfied lawing such men as Anderson." He concluded his pamphlet noting the subsequent disciplinary paralysis that plagued the Elizabeth Church following his exclusion. Pointing to one case under consideration, he exclaimed, "having been, I think, for five months before the church," without movement, "I really fear the church is almost afraid to make an attempt to regulate her own business."[84]

CHAPTER FOUR

"The Putrid Carnage of Contention"

Religious Insurgency and Church Authority

> Beware of false prophets, who come to you in sheep's clothing, but inwardly they are raving wolves: Ye shall know them by their fruit.
>
> —Matthew 7:15

> It is [Alexander Campbell's] interest to scatter the Baptists awhile, [so] that he may rake up all he can.
>
> —John Taylor, in *History of Clear Creek Church; and Campbellism Exposed* (1830)

When in April 1831 members of the Fox Run Baptist Church gathered for their monthly business meeting, Brother John Ford charged Brother James Drane with breach of contract. The church clerk recorded little detail initially but noted that a committee would "examine into the merits of the case, and their Decision [was] to be final." After its investigation, the committee ordered Drane to pay Ford "a reasonable rent for the use of [Ford's] 35 acres of land." At the church's next meeting in May, members admonished Brother Jeptha Brite "for opening his doors to disorderly preaching." The two cases appear to have little in common. But a closer look reveals that Drane and Brite were in-laws; the latter's wife, Elizabeth, was a Drane by birth. The "disorderly preaching" that allegedly took place at the Brite home, moreover, was the handiwork of Jacob Creath Jr. or his uncle of the same name—two men whose allegiance to the reformed views of Alexander Campbell was well known throughout the region. By 1831 Baptists in Kentucky and throughout the trans-Appalachian West viewed Campbell and the two Jacobs as false prophets in sheep's clothing, and many churches excluded any member who associated with such "reformers."[1]

The cases against Drane and Brite encapsulate Baptists' expansive vision for church discipline, as well as that practice's prevailing weakness in the face of economic and religious transformation. John Ford's charge against Drane for breach of contract was not unusual in the post-Revolutionary period. It aligned with the Baptists' insistence that members refrain from "going to law" with one another. And the church's action against the Brites for hosting dissenting preachers in their home appears to be an effort to police the fellowship's doctrinal purity, a matter certainly under the purview of church discipline. Indeed, the practice of watchcare imbued churches with broad authority over members' public actions and private lives. Pushing back against their brethren, however, Drane and Brite, along with their wives, submitted a remonstrance against the church's decision in both cases. Their arguments mirror those grievances put forth by disgruntled church members in many business- or property-related disputes and hint at individuals' reconceptualization of church authority. The Dranes and Brites agreed that, instead of serving as a rational, dispassionate tribunal, the church had been pervaded by a factionalist spirit that hindered its ability to dispense discipline fairly. Religious controversy also hovered in the background and certainly animated Fox Run's handling of the Drane-Brite affair.

The two couples' contumacy before church authority came at a transformative moment for Kentucky Baptists and people of faith across the nation. Between the turn-of-the-century Great Revival and 1831, Kentucky Baptists experienced three decades of institutional growth alongside recurrent controversy from within and without. The revivals had not only helped push Protestant evangelicalism into the American mainstream, it also planted the seeds of later dissension and schism. Throughout the young republic, democratization of religious belief and sectarian competition characterized the religious landscape, with the legal separation of church and state providing for twice the number of denominations competing for adherents. Once-marginal groups such as the Methodists and the Baptists grew by leaps and bounds—the latter's membership multiplied tenfold, with more than 2,000 new churches organized in the three decades following the Revolution. Never a unified bloc—doctrinal quibbles led to the formation of "Freewill" Baptists and "Primitive" Baptists, for instance—Baptists nevertheless found themselves at the forefront of a religious culture in which organizational authority was in flux.[2]

Following their General Union in 1801, many Kentucky Baptists shifted slowly from strict Calvinism and incorporated a more Arminian approach to salvation, one that over time gave birth to various reform efforts. This decline of a certain Puritanism—a rigorous Calvinism exemplified by the "Particular" or Regular Baptists—in some ways signaled the end of congregational control over the disciplinary process. Protestants across the United States, and in ever greater numbers, began turning outward, embracing an evangelist spirit that required they carry the Gospel directly to sinners. "They shared," historian Sam Haselby writes, "a conviction that American missionary and moral improvement associations, acting as instruments of spiritual regeneration, would remake the world."[3] Everyone could be saved. And by the antebellum period the Protestant majority, though divided on various religious and political issues, had seized the levers of state power. Evangelicals began using law and government to police all of society, buttressing their "moral establishment" and punishing transgressors of the religious and civil peace.[4]

Religious controversy was a vital stream in the confluence of factors hindering church authority over neighborhood affairs. Kentucky Baptists' hesitant adoption of missions was fraught with tension from the time the first missionaries trekked through the state seeking support and funds. Baptists' initial missionary efforts during the 1810s provoked controversy and fizzled early in the next decade. Their attention then turned to the insurgent movement led by Alexander Campbell and Barton Stone, often referred to at the time as either the Restoration or Reformation.[5] Well before Campbell and Stone united their followers as one movement in 1832, their critiques of sectarian designations and various Baptist practices split churches and neighborhoods. Notions of fellowship and community did not disappear, but for many churchgoers the religious controversy reformulated how they understood and approached local law. Bogged down in abstruse theological debates, with neighborhood relations marked by distrust and schism, churches no longer appeared the authoritative venues they had once been. Disciplinary practices did not cease completely during the schisms of the 1820s and 1830s, but afflicted churches recorded fewer or no charges amid the dissension. The success of the Stone-Campbell movement, moreover, propelled many Kentucky Baptists to turn to more centralized religious institutions in the 1830s, just as the most vociferous controversy with the "Campbellites" subsided. They revisited the "mission question," eventually supporting a series of innovations, from a statewide general association to local temperance, Bible, and education societies. Thus, as they turned away from congregational discipline, churchgoers developed a more far-reaching form of discipline, one carried out through centralized organizations that in some cases sought to funnel their directives through the authority of local, state, and federal governments.

". . . the odious names of heretic, infidel . . ."

In 1814 Barton W. Stone, leader of the "Christian Church," published an address to churches in the trans-Appalachian West. He aimed the 110-page tract at the sect's detractors, articulating his views on various aspects of theology, from Christ's divinity to proper church government. Stone also reminded readers of his chief goal: to rid society of sectarian distinctions and form a Christian union based solely on the Bible. "The doctrines of the Bible," he declared, "have never divided christians; but human opinions of those doctrines without charity, have always done the mischief." Stone did not advocate banishing diversity in religious opinion among Christians—he pointed to the presence of Calvinists and Arminians within his ranks—but he believed that "christians living together in love and union, who differ in opinions," would best promote the Redeemer's kingdom and most effectively combat infidelity's advance. As long as a man professed the "divinity of the Bible, and walk[ed] humbly in all the commandments and ordinances of the Lord Jesus Christ," then he should have no problem worshiping alongside those who viewed Scripture differently. In a society free of religious establishments, men should not "dictate to the consciences" of their neighbors, branding them "with the odious names of *heretic*, *infidel*, &c.," simply because their beliefs diverged. Stone's 1814 plea for Christian unity was not his first, and the epithets of "heretic" and "infidel" had already been hurled at him and his followers for some time.[6]

Stone was born on Christmas Eve in 1772 in Charles County, Maryland. His parents baptized him into the Church of England, but as a young man in the 1790s, Stone converted to Presbyterianism. After North Carolina's Orange Presbytery ordained him a minister in 1796, Stone itinerated briefly through western Virginia, Tennessee, and Kentucky before settling with Presbyterians at Cane Ridge and Concord, located in Bourbon County, in the heart of Kentucky's Bluegrass. From his first years as a minister, however, he harbored uncertainties over various aspects of orthodox Calvinism, including ideas about the total depravity of man, predestination, and reprobation. Despite his qualms, after examining him extensively on the Westminster Confession of Faith, Kentucky's Transylvania Presbytery ordained Stone.

Like so many others in Kentucky, Stone was excited by the news of the outdoor revivals occurring throughout the southern part of the state in 1799 and

1800. The man responsible for many of those assemblies was the Reverend James McGready, Stone's one-time teacher, and in early 1801 Stone traveled to Logan County to witness a meeting for himself. Convinced the revival was God's doing, he returned to his congregation with news of the ecstatic gathering: of men and women falling to the ground, singing hosanna, and proclaiming their love of Christ. A revival followed at his Concord Church, and Stone began planning for an extended meeting at Cane Ridge. Advertised for a month in advance, the Cane Ridge revival was the best-known of its time, drawing an estimated 10,000–25,000 individuals to hear preaching from Presbyterian, Methodist, and a few Baptist ministers. Camp meeting revivals continued in Kentucky the following year, and as historian John B. Boles notes, "Religion came to monopolize the attention and talk of a substantial portion of the population."[7]

For Stone, the revivals confirmed his lingering unease with the doctrines of predestination and reprobation. He began insisting that all sinners could be saved simply by coming to and believing in Christ. While some of his brethren accepted this more expansive view of salvation, others derided the minister's unorthodox musings. In September 1803, after the Kentucky Synod convicted one of Stone's cohorts, Richard McNemar, for preaching false doctrine, Stone, McNemar, and three fellow ministers denied the synod's authority over them. When efforts to reclaim the five recusants failed, the synod suspended them from their pulpits. The five ministers responded by withdrawing from the church; shunning sectarian designations, they insisted that the only appellation a true believer needed was "Christian." Over the next seven years, internal divisions and continued doctrinal controversy with Presbyterians beset the Christians, and by 1811 Stone found himself the sect's sole leader. His movement, a product of the Great Revival, continued to gain adherents across the trans-Appalachian West over the subsequent two decades.

Stone and other emerging religious leaders of the post-Revolutionary period took advantage of a fluid religious-legal landscape, one in which state-established churches were virtually absent, to build grassroots movements that appealed to common people. Though historians may have overstated these movements' democratic character, the religious insurgency did encourage ordinary Americans to question their inherited beliefs and take their religious future into their own hands. Organized, dedicated, and eager to take advantage of new communication tools, such upstart "reformers" further stressed the already withering power of established denominations. Episcopalians in the southern colonies found themselves in disarray in the wake of evangelical attacks and loss of state support in the years after the War for Independence. The Congregationalists in New England, while tenuously hanging on to their state support, were ill equipped to deal with a mobile population rapidly expanding into the Western frontier. Even the Presbyterians, institutionally better prepared to missionize and convert frontier settlers, found themselves under siege from revivalist fervor and doctrinal disagreements that drew away both clergy and members. Methodists, Baptists, and later the sects associated with the Stone-Campbell movement found themselves at the center of a competitive marketplace for people's souls. And though ministers like Stone sought to mitigate them, divisions over doctrine festered in this fertile ground.[8]

Doctrinal quibbles had existed in Kentucky well before statehood. Disagreements between Regular and Separate Baptists within Lewis Craig's convoy demonstrated just a small segment of theological variety. The early trans-Appalachian experience helped break down barriers between the two groups, as a shortage of preachers led to pulpit sharing. Still, in the founding of the Elkhorn Association in 1785, the Regular Baptists (Calvinists subscribing to the Philadelphia Confession of Faith) proved victorious, voting that the new organization would adhere to that confession's stipulations. Separate Baptists, more evangelical and less devoted to human instruments of faith than their "Particular" or Regular counterparts, responded by forming the South Kentucky Association and binding themselves to no such confession of faith. In 1801, fourteen years after their Virginia counterparts had united, and in the midst of an ecumenical revival, the two Baptist strands in Kentucky finally formed a general union. These United Baptists agreed to an eleven-point plan in which a moderate Calvinism prevailed, but it also left room for dissenting opinions on predestination and atonement and thus space for those with more expansive views on salvation. Such doctrinal wiggle room led to sectarian battles within Kentucky's General Union of Baptists over the next three decades. As early as 1803 Baptist preacher and Kentucky governor James Garrard became implicated in an "Arian" heresy—denying the Trinity—and his church at Cooper's Run was expelled from the Elkhorn Association.[9]

Concerns over heterodoxy and infidelity combined with a broader fear of religious declension. A subtle give and take between anxiety and optimism, between spiritual drought and religious fervor, proved a constant theme for faithful Kentuckians in the three decades following the Great Revival. Initial church growth surely comforted many observers. The Methodist Western Conference (Kentucky and Tennessee) more than doubled its number of ministers between 1800 and 1805, from 14 to 30. During those same years, the conference grew from just over 3,000 members to 10,158.[10] Kentucky Baptists added more than 10,000 members to their ranks between 1800 and 1803.[11] Nonetheless, within only a few years following the revival, deism and infidelity, which had been "almost silenced" during the revival period, "began to vaunt [themselves] again." According to the nineteenth-century Baptist historian John Spencer, lawyers, doctors, and even mechanics joined newly formed infidel clubs in droves. Moreover, the three major denominations—not buying Stone's message of Christian union—continued to argue over various doctrinal and personal differences and received few new members. All the churches of the Elkhorn Association, for instance, reported only nine new baptisms in 1808, making it "the gloomiest year" of the young century. By 1810, however, Spencer insisted, "some light showers began to relieve the thirsty land, and more fruitful seasons followed."[12] Fruitful at times, but future seasons also witnessed much turbulent weather that produced uncertain harvests.

". . . the new theories of the day . . ."

In the summer of 1812, Presbyterian missionaries John Schermerhorn and Samuel Mills, "under the patronage" of missionary societies in Massachusetts and Connecticut, embarked on a tour of the West. The two missionaries reported back to their benefactors in a series of dispatches they later designated as *A Correct View* of the region. Steeped in condescension and pandering to their readers in order to raise funds, Schermerhorn's statement had few positive things to say about Kentucky, other than that the Bluegrass's "abundance of . . . crops is not exceeded, if equaled, by any portion of upland in our country." Unfortunately for Schermerhorn, Kentuckians' behavior did not rise to meet their soil's "excellency." Infidelity ran rampant, he reported, and the "loose" morals of the area's inhabitants, many of whom were "extremely ignorant, as well as very vicious," promoted vices such as drunkenness, fighting, gambling, and breaking of the Sabbath. He insisted, however, that Kentuckians "generally treat missionaries with respect." Schermerhorn and Mills performed some actual missionary work while in Kentucky as well, assisting the Lexington Bible Society in reorganizing its constitution. They left behind 100 Bibles for the group to distribute.[13]

The missionaries' motives aroused the suspicions of many Kentucky Baptists—which was not surprising after publication of *A Correct View*. Though Schermerhorn noted the presence of revivals for Baptists and Methodists throughout the state, he derided both groups. Their mode of selecting preachers (presumably their lack of hierarchical control over the choice) and the manners of those selected (often uneducated and of the people) engendered disrespect for the "clerical order." And, Schermerhorn continued, "wherever you find men well informed," they spoke of their "decided preference" for a Presbyterian minister "rather than hear the Baptists and Methodists." He claimed that doctrinal disagreements among the latter two groups made it nearly impossible to spread the Gospel in certain parts of the state.[14]

Spreading the Gospel served as the missionaries' primary goal, and in the American West they saw great opportunity. Since the 1790s many Protestants had embraced their duty to evangelize—to spread Christ's teachings and baptize converts—but it was not until the second decade of the nineteenth century that the movement succeeded in building centralized institutions. New England Congregationalists formed the first American missionary organization, the American Board of Commissioners for Foreign Missions (ABCFM), in 1810. Missionaries were soon commissioned to bring the Gospel to remote overseas locations, while others eyed inhabitants just west of the Appalachian Mountains. As Schermerhorn, Mills, and other pro-mission religious leaders noted, the West was primed for mission work and its salvation was crucial to that of the nation. For there, the Episcopalian cleric George Washington Doane insisted, the future marched on, "in arts, in wealth, in power, a progress such as earth has never seen, outrunning even fancy's wildest dreams." Why not proselytize there? So, with hopes of establishing a Christian commonwealth that included the trans-Appalachian region and beyond, Eastern evangelicals organized a variety of benevolent and missionary societies during the 1810s and 1820s—including the American Sunday School Union (1814), the American Bible Society (1816), the American Tract Society (1826), and the American Home Missionary Society (1826). Some of these endeavors were ecumenical, and others were denomination specific, such as the Baptists' Triennial Convention, founded in 1814, and the American Baptist Home Missionary Society, formed in 1832 and focused on spreading the Gospel in North America.[15]

The missionary cause reached Western Baptists in force with Luther Rice's travels through Kentucky and parts of Tennessee in 1815 and 1816. One-time leaders of the Congregationalists' ABCFM, both Rice and fellow traveler Adoniram Judson had embraced Baptist doctrine while missionizing in India in 1812. The following year, Rice completed a tour through Virginia, the Carolinas, and other Eastern states, raising $1,012 (after expenses) and acquiring support for a denominational apparatus to further the mission cause. By 1814

Rice had helped found the General Missionary Convention of the Baptist Denomination in the United States for Foreign Missions, better known as the Triennial Convention. The convention immediately asked Rice "to continue his itinerate services . . . with a view to excite the public mind," to complete missionary work, "and to assist in originating societies or Institutions" that could further its missionary goals.[16] Rice complied and soon brought numerous Western churches and associations into the fold, succeeding where local organizations had previously faltered. Years earlier, the well-known Kentucky preacher and lawyer Silas Noel had tried in vain to organize local missionary societies.[17] The gains he *had* made dissipated after Rice and Judson funneled the resources of local organizations into the coffers of national institutions. Upon his first visit to the Elkhorn Association's meeting in 1815, Rice collected a "liberal contribution of 150 to 200 dollars . . . for missionary purposes." Member churches followed suit: the Mayslick Baptist Church, for instance, called for donations to the missionary movement in June 1816, with funds to be sent to the next association meeting in August.[18] Over the next few years, the Lexington-based Kentucky Baptist Society for Propagating the Gospel appeared alongside five branches in Bardstown, Washington, Shelbyville, and elsewhere. The Long Run Association even sponsored a missionary's trip to the "frontier" of Missouri in 1815.[19]

A growing yet nebulous coalition of trans-Appalachian Baptists distrusted the flurry of missionary behavior, spying in it Eastern designs on Western church autonomy. During their tour of Kentucky, Mills and Schermerhorn veered off course to visit John Taylor. They had hoped to find out more information on the state of the Baptist cause in the region, as well as promote Rice's upcoming tour through the state. But during their visit to Taylor's home, they also inquired into Baptists' fund-raising techniques in general, asking the minister "what amount of supplies [he] generally received from [congregants] for preaching." Taylor recalled that the two men scoffed upon hearing his "very puny" remuneration and "blamed the badness of [his] policy." With such a large number of Baptists in the state, they urged Taylor to "stir up the people to Missions and Bible Society matters." If you "get the people in the habit of giving their money for any religious use," the two missionaries insisted, then "they will continue to appropriate for all sacred purposes." "[T]hese respectable young men being strangers" in his home and in Kentucky, Taylor bit his tongue. Yet he later asserted it was at that moment he began "strongly to smell the *New-England Rat*."[20]

Anti-mission Baptists (often labeled "anti-effort" or "Primitive") distrusted expansive denominational apparatuses that stretched beyond the local level and appeared to place value in the wrong principles. For many anti-missionists, governing associations themselves inspired distrust, so they could not stomach providing funds, and presumably relinquishing control over church affairs, to centralized and distant benevolent institutions—perhaps ecumenical ones at that. The president of the Baptist's Triennial Convention, Richard Furman, could insist, as he did in 1814, that churches' autonomy would "be steadfastly maintained" if they participated in missionary efforts, yet the convention's stated goal of "eliciting, combining, and directing the Energies of the whole Denomination in one sacred effort" probably proved a greater concern for anti-missionists. Fragmented by doctrinal disagreements, anti-missionists never coalesced as a unified group. They *were* successful—in the short run at least—in curbing the missionary spirit during the late 1810s.[21]

Although missionaries had found support after Rice's 1815–1816 travels through Kentucky and other parts of the West, by 1820 the opposition had organized around the ideas of two prominent preachers: Daniel Parker and the ever-present John Taylor. For both Parker and Taylor, the missionary effort was really an aristocratic plot bent on swindling decent churchgoers while sapping control from the Baptists' highest earthly authority, the local congregation. Parker, who the Baptist U. B. Chambers claimed held "wild and peculiar notions in theology," emerged as one of the missionary system's most strident critics. Parker lived in Tennessee, not far from the Kentucky line, when the mission question reached the West. He soon moved to southeastern Illinois, where he propagated his anti-mission views more actively. In 1820 Parker published *A Public Address to the Baptist Society* in which he charged missionary societies—specifically the Baptist Board of Foreign Missions—with being unscriptural and dangerous to the Baptists' democratic form of church governance. Later that decade Parker advanced his theological basis for anti-missionism, known as the two-seed doctrine. God, Parker claimed, had created Adam and Eve in his likeness (the good seed), but after the fall of man, he planted in Eve, and all the daughters of Eve, the "seed of the serpent." Those sprouting from the former were the children of God; the latter, the devil's offspring. Thus, in bringing the Gospel to foreign lands, to the descendants of the devil's seed, missionaries embarked on a worthless endeavor.[22]

Parker's anti-missionary views echoed Taylor's more well-known and certainly more influential views (at least among Kentucky Baptists). Later, in 1830,

Taylor would deride Parker, claiming that both he and Alexander Campbell were "distracting the Baptists in the Western country." He also questioned whether Campbell and Parker were religious at all.[23] In 1819 Taylor wrote *Thoughts on Missions*, a brief screed in which he relayed his impressions of Mills, Schermerhorn, Rice, Judson, and the missionary cause in general. He compared the missionary system with the Catholic Church's selling of indulgences during the pre-Reformation period. He denounced theological schools devoted to educating ministers and decried the "artful measures of those great men [missionary agents]" that were used to pilfer money from common church members. "How is it," Taylor exclaimed, that "these white-handed gentry [are] always stretched out for money, and like the horse-leech, ever crying *give, give!!*" Taylor submitted his "thoughts" to the Elkhorn Association in 1820, and although delegates did not refer the pamphlet to the association's member churches, three churches immediately queried about the mission cause. The next year Elkhorn's delegates, "for the sake of the peace," ceased correspondence with the Baptist Board of Foreign Missions. Kentucky Baptists' enthusiasm for missions subsided.[24]

For Taylor and other anti-missionists, the appearance of benevolent organizations coincided with increasing suspicion of other overbearing governing organizations. One of Taylor's chief objectives in publishing *Thoughts on Missions* was "to drive [missionaries] out of Baptist associations."[25] Taylor was not anti-association. He had been crucial to the founding of the Elkhorn Association in 1785, and during his nearly five decades of preaching, Taylor visited various associations throughout the state, sometimes attending numerous meetings each year. He believed associations' power should be limited, especially over church disciplinary matters. Taylor and others did not want associations to assume power similar to that held by Presbyterians' regional presbytery courts or state synods. As he noted in 1823, "a number of poor Baptists" were in the habit of using associations "as a kind of appellate court," which only hurt congregational authority.[26] Pastor Peter Gayle of Tennessee agreed, lamenting that there appeared to be certain groups "anxious to introduce the system of making Associations Ecclesiastical Courts to regulate and bind the consciences" of churchgoers.[27] The question over associations' authority even led to church schisms. The South Elkhorn Baptist Church, founded by Lewis Craig in 1783, divided in the early 1820s. The majority faction withdrew from the Elkhorn Association, and, after a brief account of the division, the clerk reiterated the majority's stance: that the church "is a worshipping congregation & is the highest Court Christ has fixed on earth." The association's only purpose was as an advisory council, the clerk continued, "not as some would have it, a legislative one."[28]

Tensions within the Baptists ranks would not soon diminish. The 1801 union of Separate and Regular Baptists had eased tensions between the two groups and set Kentucky Baptists on a road to institutional growth. By the 1820s, however, churches throughout the state had found themselves engulfed in new challenges from nearby proselytizers such as Stone, Protestant nationalists from the Northeast bent on building a missionary movement, and questions over the utility of governing associations—each pitting the faithful against one another and threatening the very unity for which the architects of the 1801 General Union had hoped. Into this atmosphere charged a Scots-Irish preacher, a sometime Baptist based in western Virginia. Alexander Campbell first traveled to Kentucky in 1823, and within only a few years, his views on missions, governing associations, and other human-made instruments of the church splintered families, congregations, and neighborhoods along doctrinal lines. By 1830—after he had lured nearly a quarter of all Kentucky Baptists to his Reformation movement—many Baptists equated Campbell with the wolf in sheep's clothing of whom Matthew had warned.

". . . the disorganizing sentiments of Alexander Campbell."

In August 1823 Alexander Campbell published the first edition of his monthly periodical, the *Christian Baptist*. He dedicated it to those who, among other things, felt "duty bound, to search the Scriptures for themselves" and "reject all doctrine and commandments of men." Campbell desired a return to the apostolic age, to the condition of the primitive church when members united solely through faith in, and submission to, Jesus Christ. "No subscription to abstract propositions, framed by synods; no decrees of councils, sanctioned by kings; no rules of practice commanded by ecclesiastical courts," Campbell wrote, "were imposed on [the first professors of Christianity] as terms of admission into, or continuance in this *holy brotherhood*." Sounding much like Barton Stone in his 1814 address, Campbell pointed to the lack of divisions among the first Christians. "Their churches were not fractured into missionary societies, Bible societies, education societies; nor did they dream of organizing such a world." They would never give any of these organizations "*a cent or a prayer*, lest in so doing they should rob the church of its glory, and exalt the inventions of men above the wisdom of God." Campbell wanted nothing less than a return to an "ancient order of things," to a primitive church of like-minded members attuned to the scriptures.[29]

Campbell was born in the Broughshane parish of Ireland on September 12, 1788. The son of a Seceder Presbyterian minister, he grew up in a devout family and as a teenager joined the church led by his father, Thomas. Thomas Campbell left for the United States soon after, and at the age of twenty his son set out to join him. A shipwreck derailed his first attempt (while confirming his life's calling as a minister) and redirected him to Glasgow for a year of study. There, Campbell imbibed Lockean and Scottish common-sense philosophy, strands of thought that shaped his scriptural interpretations for the rest of his life. Though he became disgusted with the sectarian bickering permeating his church and the Scottish reform movement as a whole, church leaders in Glasgow influenced his thinking on everything from congregational autonomy, weekly communion, creeds, and the restoration of primitive Christianity. In 1809 he joined his father in Pennsylvania. The two Campbells, with hopes of promoting Christian unity, soon formed the Christian Association of Washington, which later became the Brush Run Church. Alexander married in 1811 and took up a farm in what is now Bethany, West Virginia.[30] The following year, the Campbells repudiated infant baptism and aligned with the Baptists' doctrine on full-body immersion for converted believers. So began the nearly two-decade, tumultuous relationship between the Campbells and the Baptists. Though he itinerated under the Baptist banner and though two of his early churches belonged to Baptist associations, the younger Campbell's connection to the group remained tenuous. By 1816 his solitary investigations of scripture led him to uplift the New Testament over the Old, a stance he made public that year in his "Sermon on the Law." The sermon instigated a slight controversy among Baptists, and some historians have pointed to 1816 as the beginning of his reform movement. Not until the 1820s and his publication of the *Christian Baptist*, however, did true dissension emerge within Western Baptist churches.[31]

Campbell's Reformation reached Kentucky in the early 1820s. Campbell's first visit to Kentucky in 1823 included his well-attended debate with a Presbyterian minister in the town of Washington in Mason County, about sixty miles northeast of Lexington. Many Baptists attended and praised his handling of the debate. The prominent Baptist preachers Jeremiah Vardeman and James Fishback invited Campbell to their Lexington pulpits, providing greater credence to his views. But even then, in 1823, Campbell understood that his positions on church government strayed from mainline Baptists, and he reportedly told some Baptist admirers soon after that he had "almost as much against you . . . as . . . against the Presbyterians. They err in one thing and you in another." Both groups, he concluded, were "each nearly equidistant from original apostolic Christianity."[32] Those who in the next decade came to agree with Campbell and who sought to re-instill "the ancient order of things" came be known as "reformers" or, pejoratively, "Campbellites." Critics responded to Campbell's critiques with their own periodicals, including the *Baptist Chronicle and Literary Register,* which declared Campbell and his *Christian Baptist* (and his later publication, *The Millennial Harbinger*) "decidedly hostile to evangelical truth and piety."[33]

His doctrine nevertheless found a receptive audience among many Kentuckians, as well as among Americans across the South and West. In addition to denouncing creeds, confessions of faith, and other human instruments of church governance, Campbell denied the agency of the Holy Spirit in conversion and downplayed the importance of moral law. Grace could be obtained simply through belief. Soon, dissension and schism marked Kentucky's religious landscape. Just a year after Campbell's visit to the state, churches began questioning regional associations about whether confessions of faith or scripture were the basis for faith and practice. Many churches soon found themselves excluding dissenting "reformers" or paralyzed by schism. The controversy continued through the rest of the decade, its intensity alleviated only briefly by revival as the 1820s came to a close. "[F]rom what you say about the principles and Doctrine of A. Campbell," one observer wrote his brother in 1830, "I inferred that you thought all Kentucky was in a distressing state." The writer insisted on optimism, however, reminding his sibling that though "in some parts the Baptists have been wickedly mangled," the day was coming when the Lord would uplift his "true followers."[34]

To an outsider, the doctrinal disagreements between Campbell and orthodox Baptists may appear slight. But many lay members distinguished the two groups. Jasper Morris, remembering the schism that took place in Mason County's Mayslick Baptist Church in 1830, insisted that the two churches had since "been two distinct and separate sects having . . . different rules of church government." Another observer, James Ingels, agreed, noting that Baptists and Reformers "entertain different principles of religious faith both in theory and practice." Ingels himself had departed the Bethlehem Baptist Church soon "after the Campbellites commenced preaching there" because, he claimed, "their doctrines didn't suite me." Others did not bother with the theological niceties. As Nancy Pierce exclaimed, "I don't know [the Reformers'] rules, but I do know they do not hold the same faith and doctrine that we [Baptists] do."[35]

Although the laity did not always wade deep into the technical theological points, church leaders took those points seriously. From the late 1820s through the next decade, Baptist leaders obsessed over Campbell's influence in the West. The *Baptist Banner* devoted column after column to anecdotes of Campbellite hypocrisy or blasphemy, usually alongside details of the Reformation's continued advancement among trans-Appalachian Baptists. At times, the editors veered toward an anxious obsession in their quest to root out dissenters. "Some of our readers may suppose that we devote too much of our paper in noticing the Campbellites," the *Banner* proclaimed in 1835, "but we think the state of things in Kentucky imperiously demands it." Kentucky was "doomed to be a battle ground," as the reformers "are organizing and have already commenced a systematic attack upon" Baptists throughout the state. "The Campbellites traveled in all directions to dispense their false doctrine," the editor concluded, "it therefore becomes us to be on the alert and to repel the various slanders and misrepresentations that are afloat."[36]

John L. Waller, the editor of the *Banner* from 1835 to 1841, may have genuinely feared Campbell's insurgency. He came from a family of prominent Baptists, and this history also framed his reaction to the changing religious landscape. In the early 1760s Waller's great uncle, also named John, had been known in Virginia as an "exceedingly wicked man" before finding Christ later in that decade. He carried out a long preaching career and was one of the three arrested with Lewis Craig at the Spotsylvania meetinghouse in 1768. Six years later authorities again arrested Waller for preaching without a license. The preacher refused bail and remained in jail for two weeks. The younger John Waller and a whole generation of Kentucky Baptists had been reared on such stories of preachers persecuted by their neighbors and the state. Five decades later, with no official state repression and evangelicalism positioned at the center of the United States' social and cultural mainstream, Waller and his cohorts may have employed a bit of hyperbole when describing the advancing Campbellite phalanx, seeing the controversy as a way to remind Baptists of the constant need to stay vigilant.[37]

Hyperbole or not, Baptists throughout the West equated their encounter with the Stone-Campbell movement with war. The Franklin Association of Baptists urged its member churches to "make no compromise with error; mark them who cause divisions; [and] divest yourselves of the last vestige of Campbellism." A church in Washington, Kentucky, charged that the "tenants, doctrines, & views preached" by the Reformation Church "are at war with the principals & doctrines" of the Baptists. Likewise, to the south, R. B. C. Howell, editor of the *Tennessee Baptist* and pastor of Nashville's First Baptist Church, lamented that the city served as "Headquarters of the Reformation." The insurgency's "ablest exponents" resided in the vicinity, "and the influence they exerted, both in the city, and throughout the country, was of immense magnitude." On the positive side, Howell beamed, the continued religious strife had turned Baptists into "theological combatants . . . ever ready to meet the enemy, and strike him down."[38]

The combatants even sparred over control of a new Baptist college in Georgetown, Kentucky, founded in 1830 with the purpose of educating Baptist ministers. The trustees of the Kentucky Baptist Education Society, who oversaw Georgetown College, were split between anti-mission Baptists, pro-mission Baptists, and Campbellites. Such divisions chased away the college's first president, a frustrated Joel S. Bacon of New York. Thornton F. Johnson, a professor of mathematics and a Campbell sympathizer, took the helm in 1832, only to be followed in 1836 by "a staunch Baptist" from Massachusetts, B. F. Farnsworth. Farnsworth's appointment led the Campbellite faction to leave and organize Bacon College, just a few miles from Georgetown. Owing to this "act of treachery," Farnsworth resigned, and Georgetown College foundered until 1840, when a former Baptist pastor from Massachusetts assumed control.[39]

The most divisive conflict, however, took place in churches and associations. John Taylor insisted that the Clear Creek Baptist Church in Woodford County "had been so overwhelmed with sorrow and confusion" because of Campbell's influence during the late 1820s that "a number of [the church's] best members had taken [dismission] letters and gone elsewhere." Those who left were unlikely to find peace in nearby churches. Taylor warned that Campbell's followers had a special knack for taking advantage of a squabbling congregation with the goal of snatching away members. After faction and "bitter conflict" began spreading through the South Benson Baptist Church, for instance, he claimed "those buzzard-men [Campbellite leaders] smelled the putrid carnage of contention, and flew with speed, perhaps 20 miles," to effectuate a division. It was not just church leaders, or even church members, who decried the religious controversy as strife coursed through local communities. Roadham Rout, a resident of Mount Vernon, Kentucky, testified that the neighborhood church had "been torn asunder by internal dissension." His neighbor, Spencer Anderson, unaffiliated with any church, agreed that "the peace of the neighborhood is broken and as I consider on account of the division in the Church."[40]

Owing primarily to the growing influence of the Stone-Campbell movement, Kentucky Baptists experienced a period of prolonged dissension and schism during the 1820s and 1830s. The religious controversy held lasting consequences for church discipline, and thus the broader practice of local law in Kentucky. The Elkhorn, Long Run, and Franklin Associations, composed mainly of churches from north-central Kentucky, serve as useful case studies through which to uncover how religious strife affected the operation of Baptists' disciplinary procedures. Although churches had sought to promote neighborhood peace, the "democratization" of American Christianity had given birth to a religious insurgency that unwittingly weakened churches' authority in matters of local governance.

". . . them people who call themselves Reformers."

Lewis Craig, John Taylor, and other Kentucky Baptists constituted the Elkhorn Association in 1785, the first such body organized west of the Appalachians. Within a decade the association had united thirty churches that collectively claimed just under 2,000 members.[41] By the turn of the century, membership in Elkhorn's affiliated churches more than doubled to 4,853. Even before the Stone-Campbell movement, Elkhorn's churches had experienced some years of schism. Nonetheless, between 1826 and 1840, from the first rumblings of Campbellism through the 1830s, the Elkhorn Association averaged 3,742 members and remained a leading association for Kentucky Baptists.[42] Its counterpart, the Long Run Association, sprang from the turn-of-the-century revival. Responding to a rise in membership, twenty-six churches from seven different counties came together in 1803. By 1810 an additional thirteen churches had joined Long Run, bringing its total membership to 2,851, making it at that time the largest association in the state. For the next thirty years, the association averaged nearly 3,200 members.[43] Churches from Elkhorn, Long Run, and the North District Associations formed the Franklin Association in 1815. Fifteen years later it boasted nineteen affiliated churches and claimed a membership of 1,728. Though never as large as Long Run or Elkhorn, Franklin did average nearly 1,700 members during the 1820s and was made up of churches from in and around the state capital, Frankfort.[44]

Delegates to the Long Run Association were the first to encounter strife. In 1823 Campbell preached at a Baptist church in Louisville, and two years later that church queried the Long Run Association over the scriptural justifications for various Baptist practices. "Is there any authority in the New Testament for a Religious body to make human Onsets, and confessions of faith[?]" Furthermore, does the New Testament provide justification for governing associations, the church asked; "If so what is it?" The nearby church at Shelbyville followed suit, wondering whether "our associations as annually attended [are] of general utility?" Long Run delegates did not immediately answer the questions. Instead, they referred them to the association's member churches, requesting that each send a reply the following year. These questions stirred up some consternation, as the exclusion-per-member rate for all of Long Run's reporting churches jumped from just 1.04% in 1825 to 4.56% the following year, its highest level in more than two decades.[45]

The year 1827 was tumultuous for the Elkhorn Association, and, as with Long Run, Campbell's critiques of Baptist church governance lurked behind the contention. At its August meeting, held at the David's Fork meetinghouse, two sets of delegates arrived claiming to be the true representatives of Lexington's First Baptist Church. Apparently, a minority faction led by James Fishback had sought to change the church's appellation from "Baptist" to "Church of Christ" and subsequently excluded seven "of the most prominent members opposed to them." In response, their opponents (the church majority) excluded forty-two members associated with the Fishback's faction. At the association meeting, each group desired recognition as the true church. Elkhorn's delegates, admitting their hesitance to interfere "in the internal government of the Churches composing her body," claimed that the majority formed the true First Baptist Church of Lexington. The minutes from 1827 do not mention Campbell or Stone, but the title "Church of Christ" was rooted in the Reformation movement. Fishback was also a prominent Baptist turned reformer who figured in several church schisms. Behind their silence, however, delegates understood the divisive forces at play and warned Fishback's faction "of the awful danger and alarming tendency of causing divisions in [religious] society by [the] introduction of a system of things by which the name and character of the Baptist denomination would be essentially changed." Elkhorn's delegates then retreated, denying the association's authority to settle intra-congregational disputes. Their newfound reluctance stemmed at least in part from a request by the church at Versailles, represented by Jacob Creath Sr. and others, which asked the association to cease accepting queries from its member churches, as the practice was a "great evil" and "the cause of disquiet among the members." The Versailles church claimed that, rather than "an advising council," the association "would be more profitably employed as a worshipping assembly." The other delegates agreed and resolved that "Churches themselves are the highest ecclesiastical authority known in the word of God, and we earnestly advise them never to bring their difficulties to the Association for adjustment."[46]

At about the same time that Long Run delegates heard questions about their churches' creeds and confessions of faith, the Franklin Association warned its member churches of prevalent "*heresy* and *unsound doctrine*." The new doctrine had reportedly become "a very frequent subject of conversation" and advocated a "Christian union" (a goal of the Stone-Campbell movement). Two years later, the association, in an unusual move, opened its minutes with a letter denouncing Campbell, Stone, and another prominent reformer, Thomas Smith. The three had apparently attacked the Franklin Association's 1826 circular letter, which had stressed the importance of creeds and questioned the ability of anti-creedists to maintain the "unity, purity, and harmony" of their churches. To the orthodox Baptists of Franklin, Campbell and his coterie were "puissant pugilists" and dangerous to Christianity, for without a creed protecting its doctrinal borders, a church had to harbor "under her wings, the vilest heresies that now disgrace the Christian name."[47]

Despite proclaiming to be under attack by heretics and false doctrine, Kentucky Baptists witnessed a revival that lasted from 1827 to 1830. Coinciding with some of the harshest anti-Campbell rhetoric, churches across the state reported a combined increase of more than 15,000 members. In one year (1827–1828), Elkhorn's churches received 1,500 members. While strengthening membership rolls initially, the revival probably owed a great deal to Campbell's teachings and may have silenced dissension only temporarily. The early 1830s witnessed some of the most vociferous fighting between Baptists and reformers, with the former losing many of the membership gains of the late 1820s. Even the nineteenth-century Baptist historian John Spencer admitted the revival "greatly favored [Campbell's] reformation" and left Baptist churches in Kentucky "proportionately weakened in moral power."[48]

Associations throughout the state continued to deal with dissension provoked by Campbell's movement during the last years of the 1820s. The Elkhorn Association dropped communication with the Versailles Church in 1830 for "receiving into her membership" Jacob Creath Jr., who had "in faith and practice, departed from [Elkhorn's] constitution" and had been active in "constituting minorities." Elkhorn delegates then resolved to cease "further correspondence with churches and Associations that hold to certain doctrines of Mr. Alexander Campbell." As it terminated correspondence with the Mahoning Baptist Association for its Campbellite ties in 1829, the Franklin Association reminded its brethren that "before Alexander Campbell visited Kentucky, you were in harmony and peace." Now discord reigned in "families, neighborhoods, and churches." Delegates to the Long Run Association sought to shore up their stance on creeds, clarifying in 1830 that it was "constituted on a Baptist Philadelphia Confession of faith." They further urged transgressors to cease their "rebellion against the principles of our associational existence." Campbellite doctrine stood "in direct opposition to the existence and general dictates of our constitution."[49]

In the following years, much of the Baptists' membership gains from the late 1820s revival dwindled away. The Long Run Association reported a loss of just over 1,100 members between 1829 and 1831. Elkhorn's churches noted a concurrent decline of 892. In just one year, 1829 to 1830, Kentucky's Baptist churches lost more than 5,500 members.[50] "All the intelligent of the denomination saw [by 1830] that the cause of Christ was languishing," the historian Spencer wrote some fifty years later, "that the churches were diminishing in numbers, and still more in piety, intelligence and the enforcement of discipline."[51] To be sure, Spencer was no fan of Campbell, or anti-missionists for that matter, but a closer look at disciplinary activity within churches bears out his charge of lax regulation. The influx of members during the revival, followed by the exodus of so many "Campbellites," appears to have affected member relations enough to paralyze churches' disciplinary mechanisms in many cases.

The dissension wreaked havoc in many churches. At times, whole church bodies departed from the Baptist faith and adopted Campbell's views. As reports from churches flooded into associations, and associational minutes then reached editors of Baptist periodicals, word of church schism spread throughout Kentucky and other parts of the West. U. B. Chambers, editor of the *Baptist Chronicle & Literary Register*, published in Georgetown, reported that in "Fayette, Woodford, Franklin, and Jessamine [counties], the afflictions of the churches have been severe." In Montgomery County, too, he lamented, "almost whole churches have gone with the [Campbellite] current."[52] To the south, the pastor Andrew Nuckols worried in 1830 about the "great divisions in the Green River Association" and feared that "a small minority only [would] be saved" at his Glasgow church.[53] The North District Association sounded a familiar chord that same year, reporting that ten churches had "in faith and practice, departed from [the Association's] original constitution."[54] Perhaps hoping to calm anxious congregants, Elkhorn's 1829 circular letter noted the "great agitation" that plagued the state but reminded brethren "that in all cases of difficulty and grievance, there are proper tribunals to which we may resort for satisfaction."[55] From the records of many afflicted churches, however, it appears that churchgoers became less likely to resort to those "proper tribunals."

The Flat Rock Baptist Church of northwest Shelby County divided as a result of Campbell's teachings in August 1831, and the schism slowed church discipline to a halt. At that month's business meeting, twenty-one church members, a minority, composed a letter to the Long Run Association requesting recognition as the true church of Flat Rock. "[A] majority of the church," they claimed, had departed from "not only the Faith but also the Rules and Regulations of the Baptists." In the decade before the split, the church clerk recorded charges ranging from "going with vain company" to intoxication, fighting, adultery, mistreatment of children, "joining the Methodist Society, and "going to law" with a fellow member. From 1815 to 1825 (when the Long Run Association referred queries about Campbellite doctrine to its churches) the church averaged one charge per 5.5% of the church membership.[56] For the last six years of the period (1820–25) that average reached 7.34%. In contrast, in the decade following the association's first grappling with Campbell's budding insurgency (1826–1836), that rate collapsed to a mere 0.85%, including no recorded charges for nearly seven years, from October 1829 to July 1836.[57] From the first signs of doctrinal controversy within the Long Run Association in 1825, then, the Flat Rock Church witnessed a decade of declining discipline. This decline included a complete lack of disciplinary activity in the years immediately before and after the 1831 schism. For many members, their church apparently no longer seemed an authoritative, neutral site amid the backdrop of doctrinal contestation.

Deeper in the Bluegrass, the David's Fork Baptist Church of Fayette County, a member of the Elkhorn Association, experienced similar controversy and schism during the early 1830s. From 1824 through 1829, the church recorded one charge for every 3.49% of its membership. In 1830 a Campbellite minority seceded from the church, and that same average—enlarged with excommunications related to the schism—more than doubled to 8.71%, the highest such yearly rate between 1824 and 1840, and nearly three points higher than the next closest year, 1824, which had averaged one charge for every 5.88% of the membership. After the schism, however, the church documented only one charge for every 1.52% of the church membership. The drop in discipline is even more significant if the charges are broken down by race. By the late 1820s churches emerged as crucial sites for the maintenance of the region's race relations. The church at David's Fork was no exception. After 1825 it aimed its discipline almost exclusively at Black members. From 1831, the year after the schism, through 1860, moreover, the church recorded 186 charges, only 49 of which were leveled against white members (and more than one-third of those charges were for non-attendance at meetings or interaction with another religious body).[58] It is clear that soon after the 1830 schism, white members had reimagined the ritual of discipline. Showing an increased reticence to regulate brethren of their own race, whites at David's Fork transformed their church tribunal into a venue through which to police Black members, free and enslaved.

The Franklin Association's member churches witnessed a similar decline in discipline as the Campbellite insurgency battered its membership ranks. The Mount Pleasant Baptist Church—considered "one of the most prosperous churches in the Franklin Association"—divided when a visiting preacher, who had been granted the use of Mount Pleasant's meetinghouse, began siphoning members from the Baptist congregation. In July 1825, only seven months after the Baptist church had opened its doors to Thomas Smith and his followers, the church rescinded the order. The records contain no hint of what specific doctrine Smith preached in 1825, but in 1827 the Franklin Association coupled him with Campbell and Stone as an opponent of the creed system of church governance. And at the time of the 1825 resolution, Mount Pleasant Baptists were engaged in debates over their church constitution. During the ten months following their barring of Smith and his followers from their meetinghouse, the Baptists excluded seven members for joining Smith's church. From about the time that Smith initially requested use of the church, in late 1824, through at least 1828, the church did not record any disciplinary activity other than the excommunications of those joining Smith's congregation. Prior to Smith's appearance and the subsequent excommunications, members had consistently turned to church discipline to regulate their community (the charge-per-member rate from 1820 to 1824 was 5.9%), citing members for, among other offenses, failure to attend business meetings, disorderly conduct, and joining the Free Masons. From 1825 to 1828, when the church record book abruptly ends, that rate fell to 3.66%. If the charges that arose directly from the religious controversy are removed, the rate is zero.[59]

Churches witnessed a decline in discipline that correlated with the dissension arising from the Stone-Campbell movement. Some Baptists even implied that the dissension had rendered their tribunals less effective. Elder George C. Sedgwick published a short article, "How to Deal with Campbellites when they First Appear in an Orthodox Church," in an Ohio newspaper, and the *Baptist Chronicle* reprinted it in 1830. Baptists who crossed over to Campbell, Sedgwick claimed, were often quick to denounce those who held opposite views, but "as soon as the [Baptist] church attempts to deal with them for their peculiar Campbellite views . . . [they] immediately deny being Campbellites, and cry out persecution!" Other church members then sympathized with their cries and grew lax in discipline. Instead of being cut off from the fellowship, he continued, the transgressors remained to further circulate "Mr. Campbell's writings, and vindicate his views." Once they obtained enough converts, "they proclaim themselves the church."[60] Of course, church discipline did not cease completely, and churches continued to expel many members who strayed from Baptist principles. But Sedgwick's charge highlights the challenges churches faced in the post-establishment era. As historian Nathan Hatch argued, increased competition for allegiance from civic associations and other religious groups, meant that "many denominations maintained their authority only by seldom exercising it."[61]

Indeed, churchgoers throughout the country fretted over their churches' role in the new world of association. In late 1835 members of Philadelphia's Bank Street Church—affiliated with Campbell's Reformation—battled over its members' overlapping allegiances. Elder Henry Grew and several others opposed a new member's reception into the church because of his affiliation with the local Masonic lodge. "Some of its principles, contained in [its] oaths," Grew insisted, were "gross violations of the laws of God and man." Those who supported the new member countered that "the subject of masonry or anti-masonry" were simply "matters of opinion" with which "the church had nothing to do." Grew disagreed that the church should treat her members' involvement with civic associations "of a vicious character" with indifference. The authority of the church, the maintenance of its "purity and honor" necessitated rigorous discipline and allegiance to the laws laid down in Scripture. The church refused to hear Grew and his supporters, while another church leader, Elder William Ballantine, instructed members to think not of the various "agitations" coursing through society: "Speculation with which this age abounds, besets you all around. Masonic questions—anti-masonic questions—slavery and anti-slavery agitations—the dogmas of the sects, Catholic, Episcopalian, Presbyterian, &c." all worked against "the holy commandment." For Elder Ballantine, those issues constituted a sideshow. All one had to do was love God and love one's neighbor.[62]

This flummoxed Grew, who immediately asked what Ballantine's comments meant for church authority in a profane world:

> What is the position assumed in these letters? Is it not that Polygamy, Slavery, Free Masonry, and other "evils," are no matters of church discipline, because they are *political*? But may not a matter be political and immoral? And if it is immoral, is it no subject of discipline in that holy kingdom in which the workers of iniquity have no inheritance? Are the political principles, practices and associations of the men of this world "undefiled and separate from sinners"?[63]

Grew was grappling with the dividing point between the secular and the religious in people's lives and the role of the church in combating "the evils of the present age." Continuing stubbornly, Grew visited the home of the Free Mason church member. The new member refused to leave his Masonic lodge. Just days later "a small majority" excluded Grew from the church. Some of his followers withdrew their membership in support and drew up a list of their grievances. The church, they claimed, had failed its scriptural duties by refusing to consider proper "subjects of church discipline, because they are *political*." Grew proceeded to list numerous scriptural passages, from Corinthians to Matthew and Revelations, which bound the church to combat societal evils through discipline. For Grew and his followers, the church's tribunal had become one governed by partiality and particularity, with little adherence to God's law.[64] Beset by challenges to their authority from within and without, churches could not muster the procedural rigor and neutrality that a proper court needed.

There is evidence that the sectarian squabbles affected other aspects of Baptist ritual beyond discipline. For some people, Campbell's elevation of individuals' interpretation of the scriptures on salvation undercut Baptists' attempts at maintaining a communal order. Continued dissension would have instilled distrust or disillusionment among the brethren. Kentucky Baptists had their fair share of religious controversy during the 1820s and 1830s. Churches across the state witnessed a period of membership expansion and retraction as the Campbellite revivals developed into schisms. Congregants certainly took notice of both neighbors and strangers moving through their ranks, and this may have altered their sense of community, making them less willing to air grievances or envision their churches as the proper sites for keeping the peace. John Taylor noted that amid its dissension in 1829, the Clear Creek Baptist Church "had no communion at the Lord's table during the whole year; indeed they were not in circumstances so to do, and scarcely any [had] been baptized."[65] The consternation also fatigued many. M. A. Crute wrote her aunt that there had been "considerable excitement" and "much controversy" about the "Campbellites" who "appear[ed] to be carrying the day" in her Kentucky neighborhood. "I have less faith than ever in religious controversies," she admitted, for "nothing is better calculated to make infidels than angry religious disputes."[66]

Changes in religious doctrine also played a part in declining discipline numbers. The period from 1800 to 1830 witnessed many Baptists embrace a more spacious, Arminian vision of salvation, departing from the strict Calvinist focus on the elect and predestination. The exponential growth of missionary societies alone attests to the fact that many religious men and women sought to convert sinners the world over. Pro-mission Baptists uplifted these efforts above all else in promoting morality and God's kingdom. Delegates to the General Meeting of Western Baptists in 1833 were reminded that "preaching the gospel" to sinners was "the leading instrumentality which christians are to use for extending the knowledge of the truth and promoting the glory of God." While in certain instances other methods may be relied on to promote "christian morals," missionary work derived from "the express command of Christ."[67] Discipline as a means to promote Christian morality is nowhere to be found in the meeting's minutes. It seems as if the "good old disciplinarians" of the previous generation had been replaced by missionaries whose work "God [had] stamped [with] a peculiar honor." One delegate went so far as to exclaim that missionary work, and supporting it, was such "an important duty" that it "should engross most of the time, of the feelings, and of the efforts of all christians, throwing into the background all the driveling policies and little businesses" that generally occupied "the hearts and energies of men." Another attendee seconded this notion, exclaiming that preaching the Gospel was "the commander-in-chief of all the gospel's instruments, being in subjection only to the gospel itself."[68] Not all Baptists shared this approach, but local church discipline, it seemed, had been eclipsed by the broader agenda of converting the sinful masses.

The appearance of other benevolent and reform associations—covering everything from temperance and abolition to prison reform and Bible distribution—alongside the Stone-Campbell insurgency and shrinking discipline rates, shows a greater concern with reforming the world than with simply purifying the congregation. Such endeavors necessitated some degree of institutional centralization. They required church members to at times go beyond the bounds of their immediate fellowship and place trust or money in the hands of an organization based a town over or in a city on the East coast. Campbell denounced any institution not found in scripture, and many Baptists agreed—whether they joined his Reformation movement or not. But ultimately some Baptists sought to maintain their denomination's strength by forming those very organizations. As historian Richard Traylor notes, the Campbellite exodus left Baptist pews filled with individuals often less suspicious of governing associations or other human-made religious instruments. This situation paved the way for missions and other benevolent organizations to advance in Kentucky.[69]

Although the "mission question" had arisen in the early 1810s, serious proposals for a Kentucky state convention devoted to missionary work did not appear until 1827 and failed to really take hold until late 1831—after the most contentious controversy over the Stone-Campbell movement had subsided. In that year Elder Spencer Clack called for a meeting to be scheduled for the spring of 1832, its object "to form a better acquaintance among distant brethren" and devise "some plan for a more general diffusion of the gospel." Campbell's insurgency had not only postponed the organization of a state convention but served as justification for many Baptists to support expansive missionary endeavors. In late 1831, in a letter to Clack, Elder John Wilson noted that his position had not changed since 1829 when he first heard of the proposed state convention. But "[j]ust after that period," Wilson wrote, "we were visited with such a tide of polemic confusion from the fountain at Bethany [Campbell]" that it was necessary to "wait for the favorable calm which has now ensued." A state association devoted to the missionary cause was necessary, he concluded, as it would "constitute a formidable phalanx in opposition to the Immorality and Heresy of the times." Without such an extended, coordinated effort the Baptists remained "scattered, and comparatively defenseless . . . exposed to the ravages of wolves in sheep's clothing."[70]

Clack and Wilson claimed that a state convention would not infringe on congregational autonomy. "The convention ought not and cannot be an ecclesiastical court possessing appellate jurisdiction," Clack reassured skeptics. It would have no "jurisdiction whatever over the churches or associations" that chose to join. Wilson advised as well that the "State Association" should be based on the terms of the "'General Union' which are so well understood and so universally received among us." Pro-mission Baptists asked, did not Christ want "the strong [to] sustain the weak" and for "churches, ministers and members, rich and poor, strong and feeble" to serve as God's instruments "in the conversion of a world lying in wickedness?" How else but through a statewide association would "these great ends be accomplished?" Replying to that very question, one anti-missionist, writing under the pseudonym "A Baptist," reminded his opponents that God had already created a system to combat wickedness and unite church members: the maintenance of "proper gospel discipline," a plan "better than man can devise."[71] Resistance continued, perhaps summed up best by members of the Buffalo Lick Baptist Church of Shelby County. In 1832 they declared that the church had no "legal authority" to participate "in the new theories of the day, such as the Bible Society, Missionary, Tract, Temperance, [and] Sunday School," which along "with the Baptist Convention Scheme" were "but man made [organizations] at best, & consequently [have] more of the love of money, and self, than the Glory of God."[72] The growth of the state's missionary organizations during the following decades, however, implies that the missionary cause had eclipsed rigorous church discipline.

The Kentucky Baptist Convention did not fulfill the hopes of its organizers, but its animating principles would shape Baptist activity in the 1830s and beyond. Only nine of Kentucky's six hundred Baptist churches sent delegates to the first convention meeting in 1832. The next few years, marked by the 1833 cholera epidemic, organizers' deaths, and continued suspicion of a statewide anti-mission organization, marginalized the convention within Baptist life. But the missionary impulse did not cease. Over the 1830s Baptists began organizing protracted camp meetings—long a Methodist technique for gathering converts—and marveled at their churches' membership gains, especially, as one observer noted, additions of those from "the substantial and respectable class." While the Kentucky convention handled state-level missionary efforts, some associations set their sights on regional missions beyond Kentucky's borders. Still congregational in nature, organized missionary organizations gave Baptists a common cause and by late in the 1840s contributed to their evolution from a sectarian to denominational identity.[73]

Amid the sectarian strife and the appearance of statewide and national reform movements (which historian Samuel Haselby has termed "American religious nationalism"), some church leaders continued to insist on the broad authority held by their local churches. Preachers, ministers, and certainly many of the laity held out hope for a more rigorous discipline. Rev. Thomas Hume of Virginia connected religious declension with a failure of churches to practice "uncompromising discipline." Proper discipline could revive a spiritually impoverished church. Hume wanted to broaden his listeners' view of discipline:

> We do not alone contemplate . . . those more heinous acts and immoralities of which expulsion is the consequence; we include that necessity which exists in times of declension, for enforcing anew the obligations of church members, and urging on all, a more faithful attendance upon the means of grace, a more particular interest for their individual welfare, and a more direct regard to the spiritual concerns of the whole body. A process like this would diffuse reviving influences throughout the church and there would recur a prevailing spirituality which would draw down an enlarged blessing upon such a people.[74]

Even in more centralized denominations like the Presbyterians, ministers extended the power of churches' discipline beyond the strictures laid out in the scriptures. Rev. David Elliot of rural western Pennsylvania rebutted those critics who "utterly deny the right of the church to extend her authority to any other cases than those which are specifically, and expressly detailed" in the Bible. Acknowledging the argument that expanding "church authority" beyond "express statute" would be "highly dangerous to the liberties of the people," Elliot reassured his flock they could adjudicate cases beyond those that Paul noted in his letter to the Corinthians. To assume God, the supreme lawgiver, would demand the exclusion of fornicators, railers, and the covetous but "suffer thieves, and liars, and slanderers," those who perjure and even "knaves," was ridiculous. Indeed, the church could judge "all whose crimes" proved "destructive of the purity, peace, and edification of the church." Elliot's assertion was an attempt to buttress church authority. He provided a guide for churches in dealing with cases that otherwise could be considered outside their jurisdiction. In short, he spelled out churches' implied powers and reassured his readers that submission to church discipline did not entail trampling of one's liberties, religious or otherwise.[75]

It is unlikely that any member of the Drane or Brite households read the Presbyterian Elliot's *Letters on the General Structure, Government, Laws and Discipline of the Church*, but in the summer of 1831, they would have disagreed with his contention that submission to discipline did not endanger individuals' liberties. Perhaps Drane and Brite did see that at least one Kentucky Baptist association resolved in 1830 to bar churches and members from inviting "any Teacher or preacher to preach in their private houses, or meeting houses, who is known to be hostile to the principles of [the Baptist] Union."[76] In either case, their relationship with their brethren at the Fox Run Baptist Church would be forever altered by what they saw as an intolerant anxiety in the church, one brought on by years of religious controversy.

". . . we do not wish to have any more cases in the Court."

For Shelby County Baptists in 1831, the Stone-Campbell movement was simply one of the scourges that had swept through the area. During the previous year, the county had experienced a smallpox epidemic, a scarcity of drinking water, and an increase in "mad dogs" roaming its towns.[77] Many Baptists may have seen the rabid dogs as an apt metaphor for the Campbellites—or, as John Taylor described them, those "hairbrained [*sic*] reformers" who "in all their extravagant folly, and wicked disorder" were "tearing churches to pieces."[78] Harebrained or not, Campbell's movement divided churches, associations, and neighborhoods along doctrinal lines. Within the Long Run Association, at least four churches fractured, including Flat Rock, Harrod's Creek, and Floyd's Fork. The Elkhorn Association witnessed similar schisms in Lexington's First Baptist Church, in the David's Fork Church, and in the congregation at Clear Creek (John Taylor claimed that twenty-five of the forty schismatics were "negroes, chiefly, I think, belonging" to the fifteen whites who seceded). Elkhorn delegates also ceased correspondence with other churches, including those at South Elkhorn, Versailles, and Providence, for departing "from the faith and constitution of the Association." Likewise, in 1830 many churches of the nearby Bracken Association suffered a "thorough and Radical" division, and "that association cut off or excluded" any person or group associated with Campbell's movement.[79]

This religious dissension of the 1820s did not leave the Fox Run Baptist Church untouched. The controversy led to a period of disciplinary decline at Fox Run, similar to what had occurred at its sister congregations. From 1820 to 1824, the church recorded the likeness of one charge for each 2.59% of its membership. In 1825 the church witnessed a rash of disciplinary cases, leveling one charge for each 12.94% of members, up from only 2.22% the previous year. This drastic increase can be attributed partly to the church's starting a Sunday morning business session that allowed for its enslaved members to take part in discipline (more than half of that year's charges were against enslaved people for disorderly conduct). Yet it seems that Campbell's influence had also crept into members' doctrinal leanings. In August 1825 the church excluded Brother Thomas for making "a public declaration" against "some doctrines held and believed by this Church (and the Baptists, generally)," which happened to fall in line with the then-strengthening Campbellite movement. Over the next five years (1826–1830), the disciplinary rate dropped to one charge for 1.18% of members, with the bulk of these charges directed at Black members. In the five years leading up to its accusations against the Dranes and Brites, the Fox Run Church had heard only one case involving a white member: in 1829 against Brother William Hursk for intoxication and "whipping his two sisters."[80]

It was in this context that the Fox Run Church heard the respective cases against Drane and Brite. In neither case did the church seek the usual "satisfaction" from the transgressor. Instead, the church only disavowed Brother Brite for allowing the "disorderly preaching" (by Jacob Creath Jr. or his uncle) in his home. And Drane, it seemed, was ordered to simply pay rent on land that he was using but that belonged to John Ford. After the decrees, the Dranes and Brites submitted a joint letter of grievance to the clerk and demanded that it be recorded in the minute book. Their remonstrance makes clear that tensions had been simmering within the Fox Run congregation for at least a year. They accused Brother William Ford, a delegate to the 1830 meeting of the Long Run Association, of making "unwarranted insinuations and reflections"—perhaps related to their Campbellite leanings[81]—about the two couples in the church letter. Ford's ensuing apology did "not prove satisfactory." Ford also allegedly misrepresented church doings. He and others "held a Council," the two couples declared—"we do not mean a Church Council"—just prior to the 1830 association meeting with the purpose of examining the doctrinal leanings of the Dranes and Brites. This was too much for the two couples, who, after being examined by an unsanctioned church council and spoken ill of at the association meeting, insisted that "a spirit of intolerance and persecution" had risen within the Fox Run Church.[82]

That was not all. That hostile spirit was combined with what the Dranes and Brites insisted were the proceedings' procedural peculiarities and the church's authoritative overreach. In the case against James Drane, the church clerk had refused "to Record the Accusation" as "it was acted upon." The investigative committee concluded that the whole occurrence was simply a misunderstanding, not a willful breach of contract by either party, yet they ordered Drane to "pay fifty dollars for misunderstanding Bro. Ford." The money seemed to be a secondary concern, as Drane appears to have been more upset with the church's procedural miscues. Jeptha Brite admitted that he had allowed Creath and others into his home but simply "so that they could be accommodated with seats." He insisted that the church had no authority in the matter. There was no church resolution prohibiting a member "from inviting who he pleases [into] his private house." With their grievances heard, the accused concluded, "Now Brethren, if this is the way you dispose of business in your courts of Conscience; we do not wish to have any more cases in the Court."[83] In one swift line, the Dranes and Brites struck down the workings of the church's tribunal and the authority of the congregation over their public and private lives. Not all Baptists who were swayed by Campbell's influence attacked church disciplinary procedures directly. But few who withdrew from churches submitted a letter of remonstrance like the Dranes and Brites. Their accusations of unfair treatment and their contention that the Fox Run Church had been overwhelmed by a "spirit of intolerance and persecution" found a receptive audience. In 1834, three years after the Dranes and Brites declared their exit from the fellowship, they joined other Baptist dissenters and constituted a nearby church affiliated with the Stone-Campbell movement.[84]

Stalwart Baptists such as U. B. Chambers, the editor of the *Baptist Chronicle & Literary Register*, published predictions of Campbellism's "downward march" the very same month the Dranes and Brites protested their church's decision (so much so that Chambers devoted less and less space to the insurgency and more space to the proposed state convention and other benevolent and reform associations). But animosity between the two groups persisted through the antebellum period. Rev. Eleazer Savage claimed in 1844 that both Campbellites and Mormons were "heretics," deserving swift punishment if found within orthodox Baptist churches. As late as 1855, rumors swirled through Louisville that the city's Baptists might reunite with area Campbellites, much to the chagrin of some local Baptist preachers.[85] Stone's and particularly Campbell's theology, which highlighted individual belief, downplayed the role of the Holy Spirt in conversion, and uplifted the Bible over all man-made schemes, certainly struck a nerve. Nearly a quarter of all Kentucky Baptists left under the influence of the Reformation, and the exodus and distrust it created hindered church discipline while propelling many Baptists to embrace more centralized religious institutions. The Stone-Campbell movement overall was immensely successful during the antebellum period. By the eve of the Civil War, the Disciples of Christ were no longer an insurgent sect. Rather, with a membership of more than 200,000, they were the fifth-largest Protestant denomination in the United States.

By the 1840s Kentucky's religious landscape was even more diverse than it had been just a few decades before. The controversy over missions, governing associations, Calvinism, and the Stone-Campbell movement ripped through

Kentucky alongside the Methodist Church's exploding growth, fears of Mormonism, and the steady advance of the Shakers. At the physical center, if the not the spiritual center, of this religious pluralism rested church meetinghouses. John Taylor claimed at the high point of Baptist-Campbellite dissension that the best way to stop the advance upon Baptist society was to "give [Campbellites] no place in our meeting houses; and should they complain, let them use the common rules of society for redress." His comments point to the material concerns on which doctrinal dissension turned. And many participants on both sides sought out society's "common rules" when negotiating for control of local meetinghouses, instigating contentious lawsuits between church factions and transferring heated doctrinal disputes from houses of worship to courtrooms. Internal discipline could no longer make the grade. As Pastor James Fishback asserted in 1836, dissenters often violated others' "religious rights in seizing upon their meetinghouses" and threatened the "peace, concord and happiness" of the entire state. This, he concluded, required churches "to resort to the laws of the land for her protection and defense."[86]

CHAPTER FIVE

"A Great Curse to the Neighborhood"

Church Property Disputes and State Authority

> I do not undertake to say which party is in the wrong, but there is considerable hostility in the neighborhood between the parties.
>
> —Testimony of Roadham Rout in the Mount Vernon case, 1834

In May 1834 the members of the Mount Vernon Church of Christ in Woodford County, Kentucky, drafted a resolution detailing their property claim to the local meetinghouse. They asserted that the church considered "herself as occupying [the] house agreeab[le] to the design of the original builders" and donors of the land. According to the deed, church members had no authority to use the property "in any other way or manner than as a constituted part of the Baptist Society of Kentucky." If they allowed a preacher of "another sect or denomination" to use the building, then they might "forfeit" their own rights to the house. Members approved the resolution unanimously. Immediately thereafter, Brother John Curd produced a remonstrance signed by twenty-one church members criticizing past actions taken by their pastor, James Fishback.[1] Curd and his followers "must withdraw" from the church body, Curd insisted, and since the twenty-one dissenters possessed "equal rights" to the meetinghouse, they intended to continue using the building for worship.[2] Fishback retorted that Curd had ignored church rules and sought to organize a new church "consisting of the disciples" of Alexander Campbell and Barton Stone. Twelve of the dissenters accepted dismissal on good terms from the church, but Curd and several others refused, and the church excluded them for, among other things, breach of covenant and fomenting division within the church. Days later, Curd, his fellow dissenters, and a new pastor "forcibly entered" the meetinghouse and declared that they had formed a new church.[3] The two factions fought for control of the meetinghouse during the summer of 1834 and eventually engaged in a lengthy legal contest. Rather than rejecting the authority of secular legal institutions, the Mount Vernon Church members, along with their brethren throughout the region, resorted to local and state courts to mediate messy doctrinal disputes that implicated rights to church property.

Legal scholars and historians have examined church property disputes and their effect on church-state relations in the United States. For the most part these studies focus on United States Supreme Court decisions. In particular, they have looked to the court's application of the deference principle in *Watson v. Jones* (1871)[4] and its clarification of the neutral-principles approach a century later in *Jones v. Wolf* (1979).[5] These examinations focus overwhelmingly on schisms in hierarchically organized denominations, such as the Presbyterian, Methodist, and Episcopalian churches, from the immediate post–Civil War period through the early twenty-first century. They do not fully consider disputes within congregationally based religious groups such as the Baptists or church-property conflicts in the antebellum era.[6] Until very recently, scholars who study prewar property disputes focused on schisms emanating from the sectional split of the major Protestant denominations between 1837 and 1845.[7] Before and during these divisions over racial ideology, however, Baptists across the trans-Appalachian region found themselves entrenched in a competitive religious marketplace characterized by doctrinal dissension, church schism, and litigation.

The experience of the Mount Vernon Church is a clear example of how the pluralistic post-Revolutionary religious landscape propelled religious groups to interact with the state. In Kentucky the fierce sectarian battles altered how individuals viewed their churches' governing authority, and the Stone-Campbell insurgency, especially, split churches along doctrinal lines. A number of these schisms engendered property disputes between opposing factions. The Mount Vernon members' inability to contain the dissension led to a nearly four-year struggle for control over the local meetinghouse. The contest navigated its way through extrajudicial arbitration and the local chancery court to culminate with an 1838 decree by the Kentucky Court of Appeals, the state's highest judicatory at that time. Like similar cases in antebellum Kentucky, the ruling in *Curd v. Wallace*, as that case came to be known, demonstrated the tangled relationship of religious and secular authority in the post-establishment era. Kentucky did not possess a legacy of church establishment. Yet the state government still influenced religious groups through legislative enactments and court rulings. Amid a presumably "free" religious marketplace, one increasingly characterized by dissension and church schism, actions taken by both religious and state actors opened the door for the latter to shape ecclesiastical affairs.

This was not a top-down imposition of state authority. Lawmakers, and especially state judges, strived to avoid meddling with ecclesiastical discipline, polity, or doctrine, claiming that to do so would violate "the spirit and policy of the constitution."[8] Instead, reacting to the changing religious culture, individuals and churches *sought out* state authority to secure their temporal holdings. Local and state courts emerged as venues through which individuals debated religious doctrine, claimed religious identities, and secured property. By looking at doctrinally driven church property disputes among antebellum Baptists—disputes often overshadowed by similar contests arising from the sectional controversy—we can uncover how the democratization of America's religious culture not only begot "a jurisprudence of disestablishment" fashioned through the legal system but also allowed local and state courts to review matters of church discipline and doctrine, and thus how religious controversy shaped the contours of religious and civil authority.[9]

Doctrinal schisms and contests over church property reveal the state's role in defining sacred space and determining religious identity. Religious experience, scholar Belden Lane writes, "is invariably [a] 'placed' experience," occurring in familiar or ordinary places and legitimated as sacred through ritual practice.[10] Lane is concerned primarily with how humans come to interpret certain landscapes as sacred, not necessarily with the importance of property—meetinghouses, land, and so forth—to religious groups. Antebellum church property disputes in secular courts, however, highlight not only the continued importance of set-aside religious space (that is, many congregations' identification with specific structures) but also the state's part in legitimizing, circumscribing, or defining that space. Sacred space is often more than a site imbued with meaning. It is a nexus of politics, power, and property. The "sacred character of a place," scholars note, "can be asserted and maintained through claims and counter-claims on its ownership."[11] For many, a space assumes sacred attributes through appropriation and possession. To secure ownership, to legitimize their claim to real property, or, in many cases, to protect their meetinghouses from insurgent religious groups, churches had to turn to state authority. State law operated in often subtle ways to determine the boundaries of religious space by identifying which religious doctrine or denomination could legitimately occupy a space or which group vying for a particular place constituted the "true" church. The state was able to exert authority over religious groups precisely because individuals made spatial claims to tracts of land, meetinghouses, and other church buildings for professors of specific creeds.

Local meetinghouses also served as physical manifestations of the contested religious marketplace. Antebellum disputes over these spaces highlight how access to public meetinghouses demarcated the spatial contours of religious tolerance. The very act of excluding a sect or denomination from public meetinghouses assisted others in defining that space as sacred.[12] To claim a meetinghouse, however, groups had to use tools backed by state authority. Through church incorporation, land-deed reversionary clauses, and specifications in subscription bonds, church members, land grantors, and entire communities inscribed religious orthodoxy with rights to church property. In so doing, they assured the state a place in religious life despite the professed separation of church and state, despite the supposed inability of civil authority to "penetrate the veil of the Church."[13]

". . . there was a strong feeling in favor of Republican Meetinghouses."

The landscape of religious community extended beyond meetinghouse walls to a range of settings. Many gathered in private homes to pray, discuss doctrine, and worship with local preachers. The well-known camp meeting revivals of the period also shifted the experience of religious community from permanent structures to riversides and clearings in the woods. The 1801 revival at Cane Ridge, about twenty miles from Lexington—simply the most notable instance of camp-meeting revivalism—drew some 10,000 individuals for four days of preaching.[14] In a letter to his brother about his attendance at an association meeting in Davis County, Kentucky, Frank Stone expressed awe over "the greatest concourse of people I believe I ever saw. The woods and the church was almost alive with men, women, children, horses, [and] buggies."[15] Some congregations assembled in schoolhouses, courthouses, and other civic buildings ordinarily used for a variety of purposes.[16] Soon after its organization in early 1816, for instance, the First Baptist Church of Frankfort, Kentucky, met in the statehouse and courthouse before securing worship time at the city's public house of worship.[17] In Tennessee, Nashville's First Baptist Church spent much of the early 1830s holding services in a rented yet "commodious room in the Masonic Hall."[18]

Still, meetinghouses remained central sites for religious gatherings. During the early nineteenth century, Baptists and other evangelicals defined the church not as the physical space of worship but as the covenanted group of believers. Evangelicals may have had "no qualms about using secular structures," as scholars Anne Loveland and Otis Wheeler note, but access to local meetinghouses proved important to both church officers and the laity.[19] In 1846 Nancy Pierce, noting her age to be "somewhere in Eighty," insisted she wanted a Baptist church to worship at her neighborhood meetinghouse in Bethlehem, Kentucky (as it had done prior to a church schism brought on by Campbell's Reformation). Pierce claimed she could walk to the meetinghouse, "but not there & back in the same day." Yet "whenever the weather was suitable" she wished to attend services, and there was no other nearby meetinghouse.[20] Area Baptists so intently desired access to the space that members of a church in nearby Paris left that body and joined the Bethlehem Baptists in hopes of securing rights to the building.[21] Similarly, in their dispute with Fishback and the Baptists, Curd and his followers based their "equal rights" to the Mount Vernon meetinghouse on its proximity to their residences.[22]

The post-Revolutionary religious marketplace not only witnessed competition over adherents but also engendered new understandings of religious space. For seventeenth-century Puritans, a meetinghouse was understood as "a neutral public space," often marking the center of town and used for a variety of spiritual and secular activities.[23] Over the course of the eighteenth century, however, the religious purposes of New England meetinghouses increasingly eclipsed their civil functions. By 1850 more refined church buildings devoted solely to religious community replaced the traditional public meetinghouse.[24] In the Anglican Chesapeake of the colonial era, churches were also positioned in central community locations and used for both secular and religious undertakings.[25] From the early days of settlement, trans-Appalachian inhabitants used meetinghouses as both civil and religious spaces. Political leaders in Kentucky, for instance, held a public rally at the Bryan's Station Baptist meetinghouse in 1799 to decide on a platform for the state's upcoming constitutional convention.[26]

Various denominations held services at shared public meetinghouses. At the Lancaster, Kentucky, meetinghouse, the Methodist, Baptist, Presbyterian, and Reformation churches all "had their different days" for worship.[27] In 1822 the clerk for the Frankfort Baptist Church recorded that a committee had been appointed to converse with the local Methodist and Presbyterian churches in order "to afford [the Baptist] Church an opportunity of worshiping" in the public meetinghouse an additional two Sabbaths a month.[28] Before the two churches found themselves entrenched in litigation in the 1840s, Newton Clift remembered that the meetinghouse in Washington, Kentucky, had been "for some part past used in common by [the Baptists] and the society of Reformers."[29] This spatial ecumenicalism extended to urban areas with private denomination-specific church buildings. For the 1829 meeting of the Elkhorn Association of Baptists, for example, Lexington-area Methodists and Presbyterians opened their meetinghouse doors for the association's delegates and other attendees to hear preaching.[30]

In smaller towns religious groups often shared common worship space. A recurring sentiment expressed by churchgoers and other observers in church property disputes was that they understood the buildings or grounds in question as "republican." Pastor Fishback claimed that many such structures in Kentucky—though not the house at Mount Vernon—had been "built as Republican Meeting houses free for everybody or for preachers of all the religious sects to preach in."[31] In the dispute over the Bethlehem meetinghouse, the respondent insisted that "[a]ll denominations of Christian Baptists as well as others were permitted to use the house until the exclusive use of it was claimed by members" of the complainants' church. Likewise, referring to the "old meetinghouse" in Lancaster, Jacob Robinson insisted in 1855 "that a sufficient amount [of money] could [not] have been obtained to have built any other than a republican church," for "at that time [the late 1810s] there was a strong feeling in favor of Republican Meetinghouses." Others claimed "the church was used as common property."[32] William Huffman Sr. testified that he "never heard of any special claim set up by any denomination" to the Lancaster meetinghouse until the day of his deposition.[33] The notion of a "republican church" or "republican meetinghouse" highlights how these often-shared community spaces nurtured civil and religious identity, public virtue and private morality.

Whether seeking to build a republican meetinghouse such as the one in Lancaster or a private structure for a particular congregation, churches relied upon public donations. Once churches had secured a tract of land—usually donated by one or two local residents—for the "purpose of erecting a meetinghouse upon," they turned to raising funds for construction. Member-appointed building committees circulated subscription bonds through the surrounding neighborhood, surely hailing the positive effects a new worship space would have on the community. And many were successful. A Baptist in Tennessee noted that several of his brethren, along with a number of Presbyterians, Methodists, and individuals "of no particular church, subscribed liberally" for the construction of a Nashville church.[34] Another church member who was central in raising the money to build the Lancaster meetinghouse felt "clear to say without fear of contradiction that two thirds of the money was subscribed by persons who belonged to no church."[35] After Tavner Branham and David Harris each donated a half-acre of land for the Mount Vernon house, other local residents chipped in what they could. Subscribers agreed to pay "the sum annexed to [their] respective names," one-third "in money, the other two thirds in corn, wheat, whiskey, pork, bacon, beef, cattle or materials . . . all at market price."[36] Such meetinghouses, whether claimed by a specific congregation or not, could help cultivate "[u]niversal peace, good morals, kind feelings, & happiness . . . throughout the neighborhood."[37]

When disputes arose over access to meetinghouses, church factions pointed to their members' monetary donations to claim rights to the disputed property. At Mount Vernon, Curd and his codefendants adopted this strategy after Fishback's church secured an injunction against them at the Woodford County Circuit Court. Those who contributed to the meetinghouse, they insisted, did not intend for one pastor (Fishback) and his followers to have exclusive possession of the house. With attention to female donors, they noted a handful of original subscribers to the meetinghouse who now communed with their church. The widow of Tavner Branham "gave one half acre of the ground" and fifty dollars. Mrs. Caldwell, also a widow, donated "$70 or $80," and Mrs. Price, "a widow whose husband gave $100," had all joined the new church and were now, because of the injunction against them, "prevented from worshipping their maker in the house they aided to build."[38] Similarly, a member of Nashville's Reformation Church, which had retained property deeded to the Baptist church after a schism, claimed the Baptists possessed no right to the house, for only one member of the Baptist church had donated a mere "ten dollars." It was unreasonable to assume that a large majority of members, "embracing in their number those who had given the lot, and had been most liberal and active in getting the house built," the writer insisted, should hand over the house "to a few persons" who had donated so little.[39] In other cases, residents insisted that their meetinghouse could not be sold or repurposed "without a concurrence of all the subscribers," no matter their religious affiliation or lack thereof.[40]

Though spaces were often shared by various religious groups and nominally available to all denominations, this spatial ecumenicalism had its limits. Land deeds, subscription papers, and common understanding indicated the bounds of religious tolerance in the post-Revolutionary United States. By the turn of the nineteenth century, the federal government and most states had outlawed religious establishments. The legal practice of toleration—in which colonial and then state governments removed civil penalties for some beliefs that dissented from the established church—which had developed in most of the colonies during the eighteenth century, historian Chris Beneke argues, was replaced by a common commitment to religious liberty, with diverse religious groups receiving equal treatment. Religious-based prejudice and persecution persisted throughout American society, of course, yet they were largely unaided by a legal system devoted to liberal religious beliefs. Not only was post-Revolutionary America a much more religiously tolerant society than before, Beneke continues, but the cultural process of implementing religious liberty "established important precedents for the future" of pluralism, religious and otherwise, in the United States.[41]

Yet Americans continued to use the legal system to exclude those considered dangerous or unorthodox from common meetinghouses. Many individuals claimed openness alongside exclusion with no apparent qualms. For instance, observers could assert, as J. C. Bryant did, that local meetinghouses were built as "republican church[es], free for everybody," but these spaces were usually restricted to mainstream Protestant denominations.[42] As Bee Salter remembered, the Lancaster meetinghouse "was built for all denominations except the Roman Catholics and Shakering [*sic*] Quakers." She went on: "It was built by the public and was always a republican house."[43] Others echoed her sentiments.[44] Even Judge Alvin Duvall of the Kentucky Court of Appeals allowed that the land in contention had been donated to the public "for the use of all religious denominations professing the Christian faith—Roman Catholics and Shakers excepted."[45]

This exclusion through legal instruments was common in denomination-specific deeds as well. John Davis donated an acre of land to the Particular Baptists Society in Davidson County, Tennessee, but noted that "other *orderly* gospel ministers shall have privilege to preach" in the meetinghouse when not in use by the Baptists.[46] Though not specific, "orderly gospel ministers" implied ministers who were Protestant Christians—most likely Methodists, Presbyterians, or Baptists. Later Campbell, Stone, and their Disciples of Christ would be considered more aligned with the Christian mainline, but in the 1820s and 1830s, detractors often labeled them as "disorderly" and "disturbers of the peace."[47] The subscription paper for the Mount Vernon house noted the property and meetinghouse were "for the benefit of the Baptist Society, & when not occupied by them," they were open for any "Gospel Preacher invited by a subscriber."[48] After the 1834 schism, members of Fishback's church claimed that the reference to a "Gospel preacher" was "placed in said article for the purpose of excluding Barton Stone and his followers," based on a belief that Stone and other reformers were not preachers of the gospel.[49] Daniel Williams likewise testified that "the words gospel preacher" were inserted into the paper because "all the Baptists in the neighborhood refused to subscribe" to the building of the house "unless the above exclusion was made."[50] Without legislation, then, without meddling judges or overt institutional collusion, individuals and communities encoded religious orthodoxy in legal instruments and claimed local common property for a general set of religious principles.

"If at any time a majority of the Church should depart . . ."

Beyond subscription bonds and land deeds, individuals and churches used legal mechanisms and state authority to secure their property. Church incorporation, though controversial during the late eighteenth century, provided religious groups with a variety of legal powers, not least of which was the ability to pass property in succession. Each state handled church incorporation differently. In New England, because parishes were considered public municipal corporations, individuals residing within their geographic boundaries constituted the membership. Residents were subject to parish taxes and liable for its debts. In an arrangement that persisted until disestablishment during the post-Revolutionary period, the parish minister acted as trustee, holding fee-simple title to any donated or granted lands. Other colonies and states continued to rely on the charter system developed in the mother country—which meant petitioning the legislature for corporate status—well into the nineteenth century, only ceasing the practice when states adopted general incorporation laws.[51]

Baptists had an uneasy relationship with church incorporation during and after the Revolutionary Era. In 1784 the Virginia General Assembly passed an act incorporating the Episcopalian Church. Baptists claimed this "Incorporation Act" smacked of state preference for one religious group.[52] To compound matters, the assembly awarded the Episcopalian Church all the church buildings, land, and other property located throughout the commonwealth. Led by their governing associations, Virginian Baptists flooded the legislature with petitions attacking the new law. One petition submitted by preachers Reuben Ford and John Leland—representing the thoughts of the state's four Separate Baptist associations—described church incorporation as "pregnant with evil, and dangerous to religious liberty." Memorials that had been circulated at court days and church meetings called for a repeal of the Incorporation Act and the sale of the "public property" held by the Episcopalians.[53] Virginians' taxes had paid for the glebe lands, Baptists argued, and they should be returned to the people. Episcopalians countered that ownership of the land was part and parcel with their acceptance of disestablishment and the end of state financial support. If the legislature dissolved the church's claim to the land, it would threaten the very sanctity of private property. Though the legislators repealed the Incorporation Act in 1785, they initially left the glebe lands intact, not providing for their dissolution until 1802.[54]

Religious and state actors argued over church incorporation well into the nineteenth century. Old School Presbyterians and Anti-Mission Baptists believed that incorporation for religious groups held potential dangers for both church and state. Their experience fighting Virginia's religious establishment had not soured all evangelical groups on the necessity of religious corporations, however. Into the antebellum era, church groups engaged in heated public debates in Virginia, many viewing incorporation as the best way to protect their interests. The state legislature proved more reluctant and consistently turned down churches' requests for incorporation. Such an act would be, the legislators exclaimed, "inconsistent with the principles of the constitution, and of religious freedom, and manifestly tends to the establishment of a national church."[55] Relying primarily on interpretations of the 1786 Statute of Religious Freedom and its implications for the relationship between church and state, historian Thomas Buckley noted that the General Assembly left Virginia's churches "in a legal limbo [and] without secure title to property or a recognized status in civil society."[56] Acts of incorporation were certainly important for religious societies' claims to property and the ability to pass such property in succession. Yet incorporation from the state legislature also legitimated the internal workings of the church itself: the ability to enforce group rules, bylaws, and member obligations.[57]

In Kentucky, state legislators, perhaps learning from the struggle to the east but also reacting to the local religious backdrop, sought to better define the power and place of churches in civil society. Property disputes such as the one at Mount Vernon can be traced back to the final days of 1813, when an unspecified religious congregation from Concord sent a petition to the state assembly. It claimed that some years after a tract of land was donated to the members of the Concord congregation, "several of the trustees to whom the deed was made" were removed from their position. The petitioners, unsure "as to their power to do anything relative to said land" and "the mode of appointing successors" to the removed trustees, prayed that legislators would pass a law appointing trustees and "vesting them with certain powers."[58] After investigating the matter, the state assembly's courts of justice committee reported "that other religious societies" had found themselves in similar circumstances and advised that even though the government should never seek "to control or interfere with the rights of conscience," it was "equally bound" to protect "each man" in his religious practices and enable "every [religious] society to hold a small portion of land" for erecting a meetinghouse. The state House of Representatives, therefore, should adopt a resolution to protect religious societies "from the inroads of the lawless." Moreover, the committee recommended that a law should be passed pointing "out a mode in which trustees of the property can be appointed, changed, or renewed."[59] The assembly eventually passed the measure, and the governor signed "An Act for the Benefit of Religious Societies of this Commonwealth" on February 1, 1814.[60]

The first section of the act constructed a framework for Christian groups to elect or appoint trustees according the society's internal rules, provided they gave county courts a record of who was elected. The trustees were invested "with the legal title" to the land and possessed the "power to do any legal act" that may be necessary for "the safe keeping and preservation" of the church's property. Yet, the bill continued, if a "schism or division" occurred in the church, the act should not be interpreted as an authorization for the trustees to "prevent either of the parties so divided, from using the house or houses of worship, for the purpose of devotion, a part of the time, proportioned to the numbers" of each party. Furthermore, the act was not to be understood as authorizing "the minority of any church having seceded from, or been expelled or excommunicated from the church" to interfere with the majority church's appointment of preachers or designated time of worship.[61]

Two decades later, amid congregational schisms due to the Stone-Campbell movement and dissension over the role of missionary societies, the Kentucky General Assembly provided an even simpler method for religious groups, specifically Christian organizations, to acquire and maintain a legal identity. In 1835 the assembly passed "An act to provide a remedy for religious societies and communities," granting churches the power to appoint "one or more suitable persons upon their record book" to act as a committee or trustees on behalf of the congregation to bring suit to prosecute or recover "any claim, right or title" the church had in real or personal property.[62] Kentucky's Revised Statutes, which took effect in 1852, strengthened the 1814 act by forbidding all church trustees (not simply those appointed as successors to the original trustees) from barring schismatic factions from meetinghouses. Excluded persons' rights could not be impaired unless they were excommunicated "*bona fide*, on the grounds of immorality."[63]

Even before the Baptist-Campbellite schisms of the late 1820s and early 1830s, opposing church factions understood the importance of acquiring corporate form to claim property. The Bryan's Station Baptist Church fractured in early 1811, when one faction embraced Particularistic Baptist principles. Just a year later the dissenting group appointed a committee "for adjusting and securing" their rights to the meetinghouse. Bryan's Station's sister church, South Elkhorn Baptist, experienced a similar division in 1822. After being excluded from the church by the main body, the minority group, led by none other than James Fishback, constituted a new church (also called South Elkhorn Baptist) and appointed trustees "to maintain the title of S.E. meeting house ground." Upon learning of their opposition's legal maneuverings, the majority church acted in kind, appointing two men as trustees to secure their rights to the church property. Ironically, Fishback's actions in this dispute would be turned against him a decade later when his detractors at Mount Vernon selected their own trustees to the contested meetinghouse and registered their names with the county clerk.[64]

The ability of religious groups to appoint trustees and acquire a legal identity allowed them to pursue debts, enforce member obligations, and receive or convey property. For instance, in August 1839 Thomas Berryman pledged to donate $125 to the Kentucky Baptist Education Society.[65] Berryman subsequently refused to pay his debt, claiming that the funds collected "were being used contrary" to the society's originally stated intentions. An Owen County court disagreed and ordered him to pay "the debt in the petition mentioned & one cent in damages."[66] Religious groups with civil recognition could also rely upon state authority to enforce their bylaws. Recognized Christian societies, then, could expect that, as Judge George Robertson of the Kentucky Court of Appeals declared in 1842, "civil courts" would protect churches "in the proper and undisturbed enjoyment of their religious exercises, the rightful enforcement of their ecclesiastical discipline, and the peaceful occupancy and use of their property."[67] Control of lands and meetinghouses was important for religious groups, affording congregations the ability to receive and transfer real property. In the 1840s the Methodist church in Harrodsburg, Kentucky, sold its interest in the local meetinghouse to a Baptist church. Soon after, a committee representing the Baptist church filed a bill against the Methodists arguing the latter lacked title to the property. The Baptists requested that the contract be rescinded. Writing for the court, however, Judge James Simpson ruled that since the property in question had been vested in trustees "to hold for certain purposes, their deed to the trustees of the Baptist Church certainly conveys the legal title." In receiving the property, the Baptists were "secure against any proceedings in the common law Courts to disturb their possession, or to deprive them of the use thus acquired."[68]

Religious controversy, such as that emanating from the Stone-Campbell movement, encouraged church groups to seek out state authority in hopes of ensuring subsequent doctrinal stasis. The experience of Nashville's First Baptist Church demonstrates how religious controversy led church bodies to seek out state authority. In 1821 the church received a grant of land on Spring Street. The donor deeded the property to the "United Baptist Church of Nashville," but over the course of the 1820s, the church adopted views associated with Campbell's Reformation.[69] By the end of the decade, a minority had broken away from the church and reconstituted a body based upon Baptist principles. For six years the new church battled their former brethren, now the Reformation Church, for the Spring Street meetinghouse. The Baptists' longtime pastor, R. B. C. Howell, later claimed that the "house of worship belonged justly, without a doubt, to the 'United Baptist Church,' according to the terms of the deed, and not to the church of 'the Reformation.'" Unfortunately for the breakaway minority group, Howell wrote, the original Baptist church had never incorporated and "was a body unknown to law. It was neither a person, nor a corporation, and therefore incapable of holding property." Even if a judge ruled to take the house from the Reformation Church, the property would revert to the original owner, which remained the church majority. "The legal resort to obtain [the Spring Street building] which had been talked of," Howell concluded, "was therefore abandoned."[70] In 1836, after having worshipped in the city's courthouse, a local schoolhouse, and the Masonic Hall, Nashville's First Baptist Church acquired a tract of land for a new house of worship.[71] Members had learned a harsh lesson. This time they ordered the trustees to insert the church's majority-approved confession of faith and constitution into the title papers. "If at any time a majority of the Church should depart" from the expressed doctrine, the order declared, "the property of the church shall belong to the minority, however small, who adhere to [the present] principles." And if all the members departed from the "present doctrines," the trustees were directed to hold the property for any group who "may now profess or hereafter embrace the present principles of the Church."[72]

Many land grantors took similar actions to ensure their bequests remained associated with their religious preferences. Some stipulated no particular doctrine. Jonas Bradley donated one acre to the Cedar Creek Baptist Church in Wilson County, Tennessee, for them to hold "so long as the Baptist Church shall continue a regular constituted body at said place or meeting house."[73] Others, like John Bond, who donated land to the Union Baptist Church, noted the property was for "the benefit of said Church now constituted at said meeting house & their successors in principle & practice forever."[74] Yet some donors took no chances. Charles Hays donated a half-acre in 1820 to the Antioch Baptist Church "holding and maintaining the communion of Baptized believers, the impotency of fallen man, the imputed righteousness of Jesus Christ, [and] the election of grace and eternal judgment."[75] Likewise, in 1817 Emmanuel Skinner conveyed two acres to the Spring Creek Baptist Church. He included eleven principles to be adhered to by that fellowship (which he presumably believed were the tenets of true Baptists), noting more than once that the land was for the "use and benefit of said Baptist Church and their successors of the same faith and order in religious worship." If the church deviated from its doctrinal path, the land would be returned to Skinner and his heirs.[76]

Divisions over the missionary question led churches to encode religious doctrine in subscription papers and land deeds as well. In 1838, not long after a schism over the mission question, members of the Little Cedar Lick Church agreed "to build a meeting house by subscription . . . for the use of the United Baptists and free for the Methodist and Presbyterian" churches. By deeding it to the "United Baptists," church members explicitly barred their former brethren who had denounced the Tennessee Baptist Convention (a pro-mission organization) the previous year.[77] In 1837 Thomas Bradshaw granted more than four acres of land to the Spencer's Creek Baptist Church for its "exclusive use and benefit" provided "always that [the church] shall be wholly distinct from the Baptist State Convention of Tennessee."[78] The following year Philip Smart and William Mary donated just over an acre to the Ridge Church of United Baptists, a body "disconnected from the Baptist State Convention and all other institutions contrary to the order of the *old* united Baptists."[79] For donors such as Bradshaw, Smart, and Mary, Tennessee's changing religious backdrop of the 1830s necessitated a legal bulwark to protect their property from being swept away with opposing doctrine. These actions may seem like benign, ordinary efforts to secure property, and sometimes they were. Yet by tying property to specific doctrinal principles, such stipulations hindered the ability of the church majority to direct their own theological course. If a church whose property was deeded to a body unaffiliated with the missionary movement, for example, decided to embrace the missionary cause, it could engender years of contention and negotiation between factions for rights to, or control over, the deeded property.

Land deed stipulations, then, could at times empower seceded or excluded minorities to the detriment of the Baptists' highest earthly authority: the will of the church majority. Such was the case of the Concord Baptist Church of Brentwood, Tennessee, not far south of Nashville. The church divided over the mission question in the fall of 1835. The pro-mission majority, in support of the church's long-time preacher, founder, and one of the "strongest promoters" of the missionary cause in the state, James Whitsitt, ordered the details of the split recorded in the opening pages of their new church book. In 1834 church members had voted overwhelmingly to continue Whitsitt as their pastor. Three dissenters "succeeded in agitating the church painfully on this subject," however, charging that Whitsitt, in pursuing the missionary cause, had departed from the "original principles" of the church. Members investigated the charges and acquitted Whitsitt "by a unanimous vote with the exception of his accusers." The church gave the three dissenters a month to rethink their position and fall in line with the authority of the church majority, demanding also that William Nance, one of the Whitsitt's accusers and the church clerk, turn over the record book. Nance refused, and members charged him with, among other things, "a breach of trust in illegally retaining [the church's] property." Nance and his two cohorts withdrew from the fellowship, and the majority excommunicated them for good measure. The controversy continued through that year, with the majority excluding three other members who "withdrew from the church for reasons of the same kind." Nance and his fellow dissenters claimed they were excluded simply because of their opposition to the workings of the Baptist State Convention. Though totaling only six in number, the group insisted upon recognition as the true Baptist church of Concord. The pro-mission majority, of course, also claimed to be the true Baptist church, even if—as the dissenters asserted—they had drifted from the fundamental principles on which the body was founded.[80]

Negotiations between the two parties turned on the wording of the church's land deed, which provided the minority faction with the exclusive right to the meetinghouse. Numbering near forty members, the majority had successfully retained Whitsitt as their pastor, but their embrace of the Baptist State Convention's pro-missionary principles hindered their access to the meetinghouse. During the next several years, the clerk recorded meetings that took place in members' homes and at a local school. It appears that in the early 1840s, the majority may still have had at least partial access to their original meetinghouse, for in December 1843 "the subject of repairing the old meetinghouse or building a new one was agitated." After investigating the matter, the church learned that their former brethren had claimed the meetinghouse and were "determin[ed] on hostile movements" if the majority pursued any further claims to the property. Rights to the "old meeting house and particularly the ground upon which it is built," the clerk recorded, was "connected with the old confession of faith or the fundamental doctrinal principles upon which the Concord Church was first constituted," which their body no longer ascribed to. A discussion ensued whether the church should adopt its former constitution and confession of faith, and this idea "was rejected by a very large majority." Realizing that by refusing to adopt their former principles, they relinquished their claims to the meetinghouse, the church voted to raise a subscription paper and begin looking "out for a new situation [to] build another."[81]

The Concord Church soon discovered that their lack of a written constitution or an articulation of their doctrinal principles was inhibiting their prospects of gaining a sound title to land for a new meetinghouse. In June 1844 the committee appointed to oversee fundraising and construction of the new house of worship reported they had secured a tract of land from one Lafayette Ezell yet said that "it will be very difficult for us to obtain a valid deed" to the lot unless "we have some articles or confession of faith in order to tell who we are." Nearly ten years had passed since the first rumblings of dissension had appeared over the mission question, and almost nine since the minority had seceded from the main body—claiming recognition as the true church of Concord and rights to the original meetinghouse—and the majority pro-mission body had yet to declare their theological principles in constitutional form.[82] On New Year's Day 1845, Ezell conveyed more than four acres to the "Missionary or United Baptist Church at Concord."[83] The necessity of securing legal title forced the Concord Church to make a written profession of faith, to articulate their religious identity in order to gain legal recognition. Their newly acquired property would thereafter be entwined with their pro-mission standard of faith, which would presumably protect the church from reliving the material uncertainties of the prior decade.

This is not to say that property matters wholly constructed individuals' religious beliefs. Concord Church members signified as much when they voted down the resolution to adopt their old principles—the church constitution and confession of faith associated with their former meetinghouse. But conflict over property certainly exacerbated church schisms and may have informed many individuals' denominational affiliation. In the case of Nashville's First Baptist, for instance, only five members, along with their families and a "few friends," took part in the reorganization of the Baptist church in 1830. "Not a few [individuals] were held back by social and family influences which were brought to bear upon them with great power," Howell insisted, while others "were down and utterly disgusted with the endless agitations" and ceased attending either of the churches. Yet the small number was also due to the fact that their original meetinghouse on Spring Street—the one deeded to the Baptists but retained by the Reformation Church—was "very handsome." All the members were "very proud" of it and would have been "obliged to abandon" their "spacious house of worship" and assemble instead "in an unsightly hovel." Moreover, Howell continued, "many of the most liberal and wealthy" members of the church "were satisfied to remain" with the Reformation Church. In contrast, the reorganized Baptist body was made up of only a "handful of members, comparatively poor [and] without a house of worship, or the means to build one." Thus, those who remained with the Reformation "saw no prospect for success" in leaving with the Baptist members.[84]

In Kentucky and elsewhere during the post-Revolutionary period, local meetinghouses emerged as sites of contestation over religious doctrine. Churches and land grantors entwined rights to property with specific theological principles—at times hindering the ability of the church authority to adopt new doctrines—and, through state-based law, spatially constructed the bounds of religious tolerance in the new republic. Doctrinal specification in land deeds and subscription papers were only the subtlest ways in which religious groups' used state authority to secure their temporal holdings. By the early 1830s the region's Baptists had witnessed nearly a decade of discord due to the advance of the Stone-Campbell movement. The schisms emanating from this sectarian insurgency led some churches to seek recourse for their property disputes in local and state courts. Their actions illuminate how the changing religious culture—itself engendered by constitutional enactments separating church and state—necessitated churches' interaction with state authority.

". . . if they cannot get a whole one, they will put up with a scrap."

By the time the Kentucky Court of Appeals decided *Curd v. Wallace* (1838), its first case over church property arising from doctrinal schism, courts across the United States had experienced decades of litigation between disputing religious factions. In 1790s Vermont, clashes between Congregationalists and Baptists over property erupted. Baptists demanded partial ownership in existing meetinghouses or recompense for fees paid to build and maintain them. Congregationalists also found themselves in heated, sometimes violent, conflict with Methodists and Universalists, whom they tried to bar from town meetinghouses.[85] A decade later litigation ensued when Vermont's legislature regranted all lands that had previously been allotted for religious purposes for the support of education. The battles continued for decades and resulted in two U.S. Supreme Court Cases.[86] More than eighty cases in Massachusetts alone involved Unitarian factions battling their Trinitarian Congregationalist counterparts.[87] And in Virginia, the Assembly's 1802 Glebe Act did not end controversy over churches' property.[88] Nor did it, as historian Thomas Buckley notes, "separate church and state or prevent government's involvement with religious issues or the churches."[89] Indeed, he continues, the "Virginian glebe fight demonstrated the possibilities for the entanglement of church and state, religion and politics that would follow throughout the nation's history."[90]

Although *Curd* was the first case over a disputed meetinghouse to reach the state's Court of Appeals, Kentucky courts had not been entirely free of conflict over religious groups' property. After two members withdrew from Pleasant Hill Shaker community in the 1830s, they initiated suit against the Shakers for the property they had brought into the society. In *Gass v. Wilhite* (1834), the Kentucky Court of Appeals affirmed the lower court's ruling in favor of the Shakers.[91] Writing for the court, Judge Samuel Nicholas pointed to the Shakers' articles of association, which clearly stated that new members "bring and devote to the joint interest of the church, all such property as they justly hold &c." If a court ordered the seceding members' property returned, Nicholas claimed, "it must be in direct contravention of their express agreement" made upon entering the Shaker community.[92] The material benefits of membership extended only to those who remained within the fellowship.

Local courts also witnessed disputes involving land and meetinghouses following schism. In 1832 the Fayette County Circuit Court heard a case concerning property belonging to Lexington's African Baptist Church. In the early 1820s church trustees, all free Blacks, acquired two separate tracts of land. The first lot had no meetinghouse, while the second had a "suitable house of worship." The church began worshipping at that house and never pursued construction of a house on the first lot. By the end of that decade, "several members" of the church "were expelled therefrom upon charges of immorality" and "united as a separate congregation." Acting as a new church, the excluded members erected a house of worship on the empty lot and proceeded to use that building for services. The original African Baptist Church denied the new church's claim and sued for "a reasonable compensation for the use and occupation of said property." The case dragged on until the Fayette Court dismissed it with costs in June 1837.[93]

These cases foreshadowed litigation that would appear in local and state courts over the next four decades. From the 1850s through the early 1870s, Kentucky courts arbitrated property claims in schisms over racial ideology. During the 1830s and early 1840s, however, courts heard property disputes arising from doctrinal schisms, splits resulting primarily from the Stone-Campbell insurgency. In Kentucky, with schismatic sects relying on the strictures of the 1814 act, many churches found themselves entrenched in litigation—alongside and against their friends, family, and former brethren—over local meetinghouses. In these conflicts, doctrine and religious identity often took center stage, giving the state a role in reviewing and determining each.

Thanks to the efforts of John Taylor, the 1828 schism within the Clear Creek Baptist Church of Woodford County was probably the most infamous example of Campbell's influence in Kentucky. The "intruders [had] pushed in," Taylor reported in his 1830 pamphlet, *A History of Clear Creek Church; and Campbellism Exposed*, and through their preaching "divided and distracted the church." After the division, the Baptists of Clear Creek, "like many other distressed places in Kentucky," had to share their house and "forbear to commune together at the Lord's table" with those "vulgarly called Campbellites." Campbell's adherents, Taylor remarked, "seem to be very church hungry; if they cannot get a whole one, they will put up with a scrap."[94] Taylor's comments can be read in two ways. The Campbellites, hungry for new followers and converts to their doctrine, endeavored to sway whole church bodies, or at least a minority faction, to their doctrinal position, Taylor believed. His lamentations also point to the material realities of doctrinal dissension and church schism, as church meetinghouses throughout Kentucky emerged as sites of negotiation and controversy for competing religious groups.

Not all disputes over church property arising from Campbell's Reformation revolved around legal title or even access to grounds and meetinghouses. At times, the opposing parties had to work out more mundane matters such as building maintenance. The Floyd's Fork Church in Fishersville, Kentucky, divided in the early 1830s. Both parties retained some access to the meetinghouse, though relations between the two groups continued to be strained. In December 1834 the Baptist body appointed a committee "to see the party claiming a part of this house" to inquire about "putting in a floor of plank" and installing a pulpit. The Reformation church at Floyd's Fork declined to help with the repairs, primarily because the Baptist church had not assisted them in building the church benches. Instead of voting internally to pursue construction, the Baptist church agreed to dispense with the matter for the time being. Similarly, in the early 1840s the Harrod's Creek Baptist Church appointed a committee to correspond with the Reformation church that shared its meetinghouse "to take in consideration the necessity of repairing the meeting house." Four years later, the Reformation church asked the Baptist church whether "they will give or take one hundred dollars for their interest in the meeting house." Such negotiations were certainly a more common occurrence for churches than litigation in the secular courts, but these more routine negotiations demonstrate the pervasive nature of church property concerns during and after schisms.[95]

Participants on both sides of the religious controversy understood the importance of the meetinghouse for the continued growth and success of their respective bodies. John Curd claimed that in Kentucky "the occupancy of meeting houses by opposing parties" was "a great drawback to the progress of the reformation." The actions taken by Curd and his party in their effort to retain proportional use of the Mount Vernon meetinghouse clearly shows they believed that their expulsion was unjust and that, even though they were the minority faction, they retained rights to the neighborhood's house of worship. Similarly, writing from Lexington in 1834, James Challen informed Alexander Campbell and the subscribers to the *Millennial Harbinger* newspaper—Campbell's successor to the *Christian Baptist*—that the "reformation" was suffering, and he believed the problem was due primarily to "our having an interest in so many Baptist meeting houses, which precludes the probability of meeting at the same place" and at the same time each week. "I have been almost tempted to pray," Challen continued, "that the disciples may be entirely excluded from every Baptist house in the land." Only then would they be "obliged" to construct their own dwellings. "The law of the land, I know, gives them a right to occupy . . . these houses," Challen concluded, "but though lawful, I think it is not expedient." Still, not all followers of Campbell and his Reformation agreed on the necessity of expulsion from Baptist bodies or construction of new meetinghouses.[96]

The "law of the land" to which Challen referred was Kentucky's 1814 act. Although legislators had enacted the law in hopes of avoiding the disputes that had arisen in New England and elsewhere, the statute may have propelled church factions to pursue recourse through the state legal system.[97] Before the Civil War the Kentucky Court of Appeals ruled on at least six cases in which the 1814 act became an issue.[98] In the conflict over the Mount Vernon meetinghouse, the 1814 act figured prominently, even before the case reached the Woodford County Circuit Court or the state appeals court. Fishback testified that Curd and his fellow dissenters were well aware of the 1814 act, and specifically that the dissenters believed the law provided them a right to the meetinghouse. For his part, Fishback read the statute from the pulpit in an effort to convince the dissenters that Curd had misunderstood the legislators' intent in passing the measure.[99]

No matter how disputants interpreted the law, however, the 1814 act paved the way for judges to review or revise actions taken by church majorities. In his opinion in *Curd et. al. v. Wallace et. al.* (1838), Judge George Robertson lamented that the case file exhibited "a large mass of polemical theology" that "was probably abstract and unessential" and certainly not "the province nor the inclination of this Court to consider." Civil courts had no business determining whether "the Church of Christ" under Fishback was "essentially" a Baptist Church or part of the Baptist Society as understood by Harris and Branham, the grantors of the land. Nor was it necessary or proper to determine whether the "reformers" led by Curd were part of the Baptist society or not. Instead, Robertson insisted, the court could only consider the controversy so far as it "involves the right of property or use" between the two groups.[100] Though striving to avoid meddling in church affairs, the court, relying upon the 1814 act, issued a decree that did just that. Robertson granted Curd's schismatic church proportional use based upon its seceding members, despite the fact that many of those seceding members had been excluded by a regular vote of their former church. This touches on one of the act's potential problems—specifically, its first proviso mentioning "immorality." Who defines "immorality?" The judges? The church body itself? Legislators, in both the 1814 measure and the 1852 Revised Statutes, failed to define the term. Fishback claimed the dissenters *had* acted immorally when they fomented division within the church. "By immorality is meant," he wrote, "'any act, conduct, or practice, which contravenes the divine commands or the social duties of the members of the Church.'" Fishback believed that the court's ruling, allowing individuals who had been deemed immoral by the church to continue using their meetinghouse, smacked of state interference.[101]

Indeed, during the 1830s some observers denounced the 1814 act as a threat to religious liberty. In 1835 "A Spectator" writing in the *Baptist Banner* called upon state legislators to repeal the law. During the previous five years, the writer contended, it was "believed that at least fifty adverse claims to the use of meetings houses" in Kentucky had been taken up "by a new sect that call themselves Reformers, composed of the followers of A. Campbell and B.W. Stone." These individuals may not have been pushed out of the Baptist ranks for traditional immoralities, but they had "created schisms and divisions in churches" and failed in both their religious and civil duties. Their actions constituted immorality, the writer insisted, because immorality was anything that went against the commands of God or "'*violate[d] social duties.*'" It was fine if individuals changed their religious viewpoints and left their former church in peace. But the Reformers, and especially those who sought to retain the use of Baptist meetinghouses, brought only "disorder and strife." By facilitating the Reformers, the 1814 act had brought "the destruction of the comfort, peace, and happiness of churches," as well as "neighborhoods and families," and needed to be repealed immediately. If not, then the legislature would continue to reward "disorderly and licentious men" for violating "the rights and good order of religious society" and corrupting "the good morals of the state."[102]

Some believed the act could encourage dangerous religious ideas to gain influence and adherents. On the same page of the *Baptist Banner* as Spectator's editorial, an anonymous article warned readers that the act enabled more than simply Campbellites or other reformers. "For should some two or three members of a church become Mormonites [*sic*], or followers of Matthias; or even Deists or Atheists . . . what is there [in the 1814 act] discussed by [Spectator], to debar them from using the meeting house to propagate their dangerous and demoralizing sentiments?" Already, the writer knew of meetinghouses in Kentucky where "as many as three parties" claimed the same space to worship.[103] In Nashville, Tennessee, where no law provided for proportional use by schismatic groups, observers echoed this sentiment in public arguments over access to houses of worship. One writer asked his opponents (who had retained the use of the church building after a schism) what they would do if a majority of their body suddenly became "Mormons, or Jumpers." Would they give up their meetinghouse and "walk off content with the result"?[104] This may have been a backhanded insult directed at the supporters and congregants of the Campbellite church. Yet statements such as these display the growing cultural anxiety over the prevalence of nonbelief and the rise of marginal religious movements. As communities' central social and spiritual sites, meetinghouses were too important to allow them to fall in the hands of professors of allegedly unorthodox, disorderly, or dangerous religious principles.

In their decree, Robertson and the Kentucky Court of Appeals addressed the possibility that fringe religious groups would gain access to property. Noting the "anomalous, and somewhat perplexing" provisos of the 1814 act, Robertson sought to calm Fishback and others who feared the law opened their local meetinghouses to religious outsiders. The legislature, Robertson insisted, did not intend to secure meetinghouses for those who "renounce the christian religion and become infidels or Mahometans."[105] Rather, the act was intended as a check on trustees' authority in doctrinal disputes. It sought to leave disputing parties "to ecclesiastical discipline and authority, to the protection of their own christian armor, and to the guidance of their own christian charity and prudence."[106] Yet to Fishback and his church, the act appeared to do exactly the opposite, rewarding those excluded by a regular vote of the church and submitting church authority to that of the state. Throughout his decision Robertson appeared uncomfortable applying the act. Subsequently, although several schismatic factions initiated suits based on the 1814 act, after its ruling in *Curd*, the court interpreted the statute rigidly, applying it only in cases in which the trustees had been appointed according to its directives, and dispensing with the act when the property in question remained in the hands of the original trustees.[107]

Even cases in which Kentucky courts ruled the 1814 act inapplicable, some jurists meddled with actions taken by church authorities. Frankfort's First Baptist Church divided over Campbell's doctrine in 1841. The majority excluded several dissenters, who then formed a new church and claimed a right to worship in the meetinghouse. Seeking exclusive control over the property, the Baptist majority "invoked the intervention of the civil power by filing a bill" at the Franklin County Circuit Court. That court ordered the Baptist church to hold a new election for its board of trustees and directed that members recently excluded could vote in the matter. Upon hearing the case in 1842, however, the Court of Appeals rejected the Reformation church's invocation of the 1814 act. Civil courts, "having no ecclesiastical jurisdiction," said the justices, "cannot revise or question ordinary acts of church discipline or excision." The exclusions, the court continued, meant that they are no longer members of that society and thus no longer "entitled to any rights or privileges incidental or resulting from membership therein."[108] The court deferred to actions taken by the church body, a tactic it again used soon after in *Gibson v. Armstrong* (1847) and in *Berryman v. Reese* (1850).[109] These cases and others highlight the continuing process of constructing the boundaries of civil and religious authority after disestablishment, a process that continued throughout the period at local, state, and federal levels.

The Kentucky Court of Appeals increasingly relied upon the deference principle in its decrees, yet church property cases still provided avenues for state authority to determine a group's religious identity. At the center of many church property cases was a congregation's denominational affiliation, especially when the land had been deeded to a specific group. The subscription paper for the Mount Vernon meetinghouse indicated that the house was to be "For the benefit of the Baptist Society," and both sides jockeyed for recognition as a Baptist body while insisting that their opponents were heretical in their doctrine. Curd and his codefendants denied that they or their pastor, F. Palmer, held any heretical beliefs, expressing their willingness "to submit to the most rigid scrutiny on these points." When asked if Fishback's church was "any part of the Baptist Society," member Robert Risk asserted, "I did not join it on such & joined believing it to be the Church of Christ." Risk's sentiments were echoed by former member Robert Adams, who averred that "so far as I know they are not recognized by the Regular Baptist Society as a Regular Baptist church." Adams had heard from current members, too, that Fishback's church had changed its name, established open communion, and asked to be dismissed from the Elkhorn Association of Baptists. William Poindexter testified that he had personally heard Fishback declare that "the name Baptist was a sectarian tag & the association a biding place for the devil."[110] According to another witness, Fishback claimed that "if the house was not awarded to them he would advise [his] church" to rejoin the Elkhorn Association or General Union of Baptists, "by which means [his church] would be able to get the house."[111] Fishback, of course, claimed his church was of the Regular Baptist order, yet it went by the appellation "Church of Christ" and had voluntarily departed from the Baptists' regional governing association. Indeed, before the court case an arbitration committee ruled that neither Fishback's nor Curd's church was a Baptist organization.[112] Despite the land deed strictures and testimony, however, the Court of Appeals awarded control, though not exclusive use, of the meetinghouse to Fishback's church.

In other cases, too, the appeals court strayed from the original land deed's doctrinal or denominational specifications. In 1847 it awarded a meetinghouse to the *United* Baptist church in the town of Washington despite the 1797 deed's stipulation that the property was for the use of the town's *Particular* Baptist church. Observers testified that the United Baptist church was not a Particular

Baptist church, that it adhered to a different doctrine of salvation, and that the Particular Baptist governing association in Kentucky did not recognize or correspond with that body as a Particular Baptist church.[113] The court insisted that a change in name did not entail a change in religious identity. Throughout the early nineteenth century, however, United Baptists and Particular Baptists distinguished themselves from one another, and at times the differences caused schisms in both individual churches and their regional governing associations.[114] The following year, in *Scott v. Curle*, the court again deviated from the strictures of the land deed—which had clearly directed the property to the Regular Baptists—and awarded the meetinghouse to the schismatic Reformation church, even after acknowledging that the latter had "dissolved all connection with the Baptist order."[115] More than twenty years later the United States Supreme Court insisted that civil courts could not deviate from property donors' express terms, claiming "it is not in the power of the majority of [a] congregation, however preponderant, by reason of a change of views on religious subjects to carry the property . . . to the support of a new and conflicting doctrine."[116]

The Kentucky Court of Appeal's rulings in these cases were not the last word on matters of church property in that state or throughout the nation. From the 1850s through the early 1870s, disputes over church property percolated through Kentucky's courts. In cases such as *Harper v. Straws* (1853)[117] and *Gartin v. Penick* (1868),[118] the court continued crafting its jurisprudence of disestablishment. This process came to a head in Kentucky with the dispute over the Walnut Street Presbyterian Church in Louisville, where the congregation's allegiance was divided between the denomination's Northern and Southern branches. After the Civil War, leading members of the Walnut Street Church, influenced largely by their opposition to emancipation, severed their connection with the Presbyterian Church USA, the denomination's Northern wing. They and most other Presbyterians in central Kentucky aligned themselves with the Presbyterian Church–South. The church members who remained, however, pressed for control over the church building. The Presbyterian Church USA and their allies in the Walnut Street Church argued that since Presbyterians were a hierarchical organization, the property was held in trust by the denomination. By leaving the church, the seceders had forfeited their right to use the church. The dispute made it all the way to the United States Supreme Court, which ruled in *Watson v. Jones* (1871) that the Presbyterian Church USA retained ownership of the property, holding it in an "implied trust." For nearly a century, judges used the *Watson* decision as precedent, arguing that courts had to defer to the determination of the religious authorities in matters of church polity and discipline.[119]

But rather than a beginning, the Civil War era cases arising from divergent views of slavery's righteousness served as bridge between antebellum doctrinal schisms and those of the twentieth century.[120] The prewar cases in Kentucky not only illuminate the connection of church and state—despite no legacy of establishment in the state—through the first half of the nineteenth century and beyond, but also show how the democratizing religious culture propelled churches to seek out state authority to protect their property. In his answer to the original suit at the Woodford County Court, John Curd lamented his "mortification and pain" in arguing "spiritual matters in a temporal court." Yet this discomfort did not stop him or his codefendants from attacking Fishback's doctrinal inconsistency and heralding their own orthodoxy in testimony or, when the lower court's ruling went against them, from seeking further recourse at the Court of Appeals. Like their counterparts throughout the region (and across the young republic), they appealed to state authority to settle disputes that their church tribunals could not successfully mediate.

It is a mistake, however, to center the examination solely upon cases that reached local and state courts. Neighborhood meetinghouses served as important sites for individuals' spiritual and social interaction, and from the earliest days of settlement, churches looked to the state in order to claim and maintain their property. State authority worked in subtle ways to shape religious matters. Whether through incorporation or stipulations in land deeds and subscription bonds, civil authority protected churches' temporal property and implicitly constructed the boundaries of sacred space, upholding communities' understandings of religious orthodoxy while barring others from "republican" meetinghouses. Rather than moving in "clearly defined" and "separate spheres," as Judge Robertson claimed in *Gartin*, religious and secular authority often crisscrossed, the contours of each murky and mutually constituted during the early republic and antebellum periods. Baptists especially, but other religious groups as well, often pride themselves on their autonomous natures. Yet as disputes over church property demonstrate, churches rely on the state for protection and are subject to its authority. By seeking out state assistance, Baptists, who had fought so passionately for the separation of church and state during the Revolutionary era, inadvertently opened the door for civil authority to shape ecclesiastical affairs.

> But let it not be supposed that we mean that legal thing abstractly called discipline . . .
>
> —Franklin Baptist Association, 1837

"I think it's a mistake for any country," Louisiana governor Bobby Jindal insisted in January 2015, "to allow the development of areas within their country, whether it's neighborhoods or other areas, where the same laws, the same values, the same rules, simply don't apply." Speaking at a conservative think tank in London, Jindal was referring to no-go zones purportedly set up by Muslim extremists in the United States and Britain in an effort "to colonize Western countries." Such no-go zones, the author Steven Emerson had told Fox News nine days before Jindal's comments, barred non-Muslims and relied on religious authorities to enforce faith-based laws. Fox News ran an on-air retraction just days later, noting there was "no credible information" to support Emerson's claims, and British prime minister David Cameron responded by calling Emerson a "complete idiot." This apparently did not sway Jindal. He insisted the "huge issue" was that such groups "want to come to our country but not adopt our values," that they desired "to set apart their own enclaves and hold onto their own values." Jindal's comments reflect debates over sharia law's influence in American communities that have only increased in recent years.[1]

Yet Jindal's remarks also echo fears expressed more than two hundred years ago by Virginia's colonial authorities as they faced the growth of the Baptists, a group whose first churches in the Old Dominion had been planted by outsiders. In the late 1750s Regular Baptists from Pennsylvania and Separate Baptists from New England migrated south and began proselytizing in the countryside of Virginia. Over the next two decades, these preachers set up dozens of churches, religious enclaves that challenged the existing social and religious order. While extending spiritual equality to all members regardless of their race or sex, Baptists eschewed the dancing, preoccupation with social rank, and ostentatious dress of the Virginia gentry. Moreover, Baptists' "bizarre" practices of full-body immersion and internal discipline stoked animosity among all ranks of their Anglican neighbors.[2] One historian notes that pockets of "rather thick Baptist dissent" appeared in areas where the preachers gained a foothold.[3] As Baptist ministers continued to shun civil authority by preaching without a license, and as their churches attracted a greater number of adherents, state authorities and Anglican church leaders often labeled the upstart Baptists "disturbers of the peace." An irate magistrate even charged a group of Baptist preachers with "carrying on a mutiny against the authority of the land."[4] Many dissident Baptists joined other Euro-American migrants over the course of the 1770s and 1780s in settling the region that became the state of Kentucky. By the time Jefferson's religious freedom bill became law in Virginia in 1786, trans-Appalachian Baptists had already begun constructing an expansive institutional network of churches and associations that sought to regulate morality in their budding communities through the ritual of discipline.

Baptists understood the purpose of church discipline as peace—in the fellowship and in the surrounding neighborhood. As we have seen, Kentucky Baptists did not shy away from arbitrating a variety of disputes, from intoxication and adultery to indebtedness, theft, and slave warranty. They insisted that congregational authority trumped that of the state when disgruntled members found themselves at odds. Not simply a form of social control, discipline was meant to bring about repentance and brotherly feelings within a group that strived to set themselves apart from "the world." It made little sense to an early nineteenth-century Baptist to sue his brother at the county court when he could find resolution at the meetinghouse. If neighbors or kin were disorderly, take them to the church, where other neighbors and kin could summon religious authority, the fear of potential damnation, and community pressure. In other words, keep matters in house.

But the world beyond the meetinghouse was never set apart, and it was changing—rapidly. Looking back a half century to the formation of Kentucky's General Association of Baptists, the Rev. James M. Pendleton claimed, "The line of demarcation between the churches and the world was much more distinct in 1837 than in 1887." The Baptists of the 1830s, he wrote, "dreaded anything that looked like an obliteration of the line between [the church] and the world," and a key part of maintaining this distinction was the practice of rigorous discipline.[5] By 1837, however, that rigorous discipline was already on the decline. Baptists and religious groups throughout the country were repositioning their churches within a landscape marked by transformations in household and market relations, law, and religious controversy. Indeed, that rigorous conception of discipline practiced by the "good old disciplinarians" of John Taylor's generation had receded. By the 1840s discipline seemed not only to have lessened within churches, but also to have been redefined. More than in the quantified data, this shift is evident in the pleadings and accusations of men like Jacob Creath Jr., William Collins, and James Fishback. In 1840 the Franklin Association's circular letter addressed "the exercise of christian discipline." "But let it not be supposed that we mean that legal thing abstractly called discipline," the association clarified, "by which brother is arraigned by brother at the bar of the church." Rather the new code of discipline was "love." It hoped that all members would live "in the fear of God, disciplining our own hearts and watching over another in love."[6]

Disciplining one's own heart, watching over your fellow members with love, represents a shift in how Baptists conceptualized discipline. No longer a "legal thing" of charging brethren "at the bar of the church," discipline became simply about maintaining one's morality and keeping watch over members in their Christian and church duty. Pinpointing the exact reason that Baptists in Kentucky and through much of the South and West moved away from rigorous discipline is impossible. But as they and Americans of all faiths navigated an environment of individualism set loose by the American Revolution, transformations in the economy, household, and religion itself drove Baptists to, in historian Mark Noll's words, define "a functional division of life" between the sacred and the profane. The areas in which they had previously tried to "exert self-conscious control" became matters for authorities beyond the meetinghouse walls.[7] In some ways, declining discipline set Baptists apart from the world, making it less likely that the congregation would be exposed to contentious debates over members' financial dealings or treatment of their family.

This did not stop Baptists and other Protestants from trying to shape the world around them. As churches wavered on strict discipline and localism dwindled, Baptists were just as likely to forsake the peace, abandoning their disciplinary mechanisms and turning instead to other legal strategies and drawing on power often exerted through centralized institutions. Yet churches' need for state authority was made apparent by their inability to mediate doctrinal quarrels, wrangling that propelled churchgoers into local and state courts to secure rights to their meetinghouses. Some of the faithful, like John Curd in his dispute with James Fishback, lamented the need for civil authorities. Others pressed judges to involve themselves in ecclesiastical matters, even calling on them to assign a church a denominational identity. When a judge assigned use of the meetinghouse to a dissenting faction, even when that faction had been excluded by a vote of the church, state authority eclipsed that of the congregation. Fishback and others could claim that doctrinal divergence and disruptions to the peace of the church constituted "immorality"—and thus that, according to the 1814 statute, the dissenters had been rightly barred from the meetinghouse—but disputes over church properties highlight the subtle ways that church groups were artifacts of, and ultimately subject to, state authority.

In the twenty-first century, contentious debates over the place of religion and the influence of religious authority in the United States still rage. Contemporary news cycles are dotted with disputes over religious symbolism in state buildings or civic ceremonies. Advocacy groups and politicians weigh the benefits and pitfalls of state funding of religious groups' various charitable endeavors. The politics of LGBTQ rights and abortion have led to a new installment of church-state jurisprudence, as churches and businesses point to religious beliefs in hopes of sidestepping laws geared toward marriage equality or access to birth control. Meanwhile, congregations divided over gay marriage or doctrine are seeking state recourse to secure their property claims. During the COVID-19 pandemic, churchgoers once again turned to the courts, arguing that stay-at-home orders and bans on large gatherings infringe on their free exercise of religion, despite the overwhelming risk large worship meetings pose to the health and safety of the congregation and those beyond meetinghouse walls. The roots of these issues, far from novel, go back to the republic's founding. They are entrenched in not only our nation's experiment with religious liberty, but individuals' divergent conceptions of law and authority.

ACKNOWLEDGMENTS

Like any book, this one was not a solitary effort. While its shortcomings reside with the author, *Law in American Meetinghouses* exists only because of the support I have received over the past decade. I know it would not exist without two mentors who shaped my interests and views on American history more than any others. John M. Belohlavek, at the University of South Florida, was my history professor when I was a first-year undergraduate and over the past twenty years has morphed from instructor, to mentor, to friend, and officiant at my wedding. His passion for the period led to my interest in the formative era of the early republic. He and his wife, Dr. Susan Turner, opened their home to me for months at a time while I was a graduate student, providing me invaluable time to research and write, and catch up with friends and family in the Tampa Bay area. My dissertation advisor, Yvonne Pitts, took me in as a first-year PhD student at Purdue University. She pushed me, often not subtly, to expand on my interest in legal history. And she never stopped pushing even when I thought I had done well enough. Without such prodding, this book would never even have been an idea.

I have been honored by support from several public and private institutions that have generously funded research for this book. A National Endowment for the Humanities (NEH) fellowship from the Library Company of Philadelphia gave me a much-needed semester break from teaching so I could focus on research and writing. The American Society of Legal History awarded me a William Nelson Cromwell Early Career Scholar Fellowship, which reduced financially related stress as I sought to travel to archives and conferences. The Kentucky Historical Society (KHS) supported five weeks of research at its archive and the nearby Kentucky Department of Library and Archives. Meanwhile, Stephanie Lang and the KHS staff sat through two separate research presentations on Baptist church discipline and assisted immensely in locating relevant sources. The same can be said of the Filson Historical Society, which funded my first foray into the archives for this project, at a time when I had only a nascent idea about extrajudicial arbitration on the frontier. Grants from the Tennessee Historical Society and the Alabama Historical Society, as well as an Andrew W. Mellon Research Fellowship from the Virginia Historical Society, allowed me to provide important context for the Kentucky Baptists' experience, as did the Lynn E. May Study Grant from the Southern Baptist Library and Archive in Nashville, Tennessee. Shell Dunn at the University of Kentucky's Special Collections Research Center scanned several church record books for me, for which I am grateful.

I am much indebted to the Purdue University History Department and Purdue's Graduate School, which awarded me a Frederick N. Andrews Fellowship, allowing me to pursue my doctoral studies. While I was in the department, John Larson, Yvonne Pitts, Frank Lambert, Nancy Gabin, Michael Morrison, Doug Hurt, James Farr, David Atkinson, Caroline Janney, and Darren Dochuk all contributed to this project indirectly or directly and certainly shaped me as a scholar and teacher. I am grateful to the friends I made in West Lafayette, many of them among the best I have. Trevor Burrows, Joshua Jeffers, Timothy Olin, Brandon Ward, and Andrew McGregor have all heard and read much more about Baptists than they ever wished, and often against their stated objections. Two friends and colleagues that date to my undergraduate days at the University of South Florida, Kyle Burke and Naomi Williams, deserve a special mention. Though we all went to different doctoral programs and are now spread from Tennessee to New Jersey and New York, they remain old-school confidants.

Perhaps the most enjoyable part of academic life is attending conferences and taking part in workshops. Sections of this manuscript have been presented and critiqued at the Society for Historians of the Early American Republic, the American Society of Legal History, the American Society of Church History, and the Ohio Valley History Conference. Summer workshops such as the NEH's "Problems in the Study of Religion" at the University of Virginia, Stanford Law School's "Religion and the Constitution" 2015 seminar, and the Fifth International Summer Institute on the Cultural Study of the Law in Osnabruck, Germany, were experiences I will not soon forget. I am much indebted to Barbara Welke, Kellen Funk, Karl Shoemaker, and Mitra Sharafi for my experiences as a fellow at the 2015 J. Willard Hurst Summer Institute in Legal History, hosted by the University of Wisconsin–Madison Law School. I also thank Sarah Barringer Gordon, who served on my dissertation committee and has remained a source of advice and counsel, especially regarding studies of church property. Co-panelists and commentators, including, among many others, Chris Beneke, Kevin Butterfield, Stephen Marini, and Lukas Volkman, have helped shape my views on religion and its unique place in the American republic. The number of people who have read parts of this manuscript and made it better is much too long to list, but I appreciate the suggestions and critiques of the anonymous and identified readers, including Mark McGarvie, who, without knowing me personally, read and commented on later drafts of chapters. Thank you, too, to *Church History* and Cambridge University Press. Sections of the book, especially in chapters 4 and 5, appeared in an earlier form in *Church History*'s March 2015 issue in an article entitled "'Courts of Conscience': Local Law, the Baptists, and Church Schism in Kentucky, 1780–1840." Laura Davulis, Esther Rodriguez, and Juliana McCarthy at Johns Hopkins University Press, along with copy editor Heidi Fritschel, have been helpful and patient as I completed the manuscript. They have been a pleasure to work with.

My colleagues at Tusculum University have also been encouraging. The chair of the History, Museum Studies, and Religion Department, Joel Van Amberg, always has his door open and is exactly the kind of chair any junior scholar would want. Angela Keaton welcomed me to the department and has been vital in helping me navigate teaching, scholarship, and committee work. Peter Noll has done much the same and seems always available to assist anyone on campus—whether they need advice on archives or carpentry. The dean of the College of Civic and Liberal Arts, Wayne Thomas, has been incredibly supportive of me and all faculty under him, tirelessly highlighting our work and that of the students.

My wife, Katie Perry, and I have been together since about the genesis of this book, and I know she is happy to see it in print as well. She traveled along as I visited archives and gave conference presentations, and graciously proofread chapters. She and my stepson, Hollis, welcomed me into their home, and now, many years later, we are still a unit, if at times separated by distance.

This book is dedicated to my parents, Thomas and Deborah Perry. Only as I have grown older have I truly realized the sacrifices they made so that my sister, Jill, and I could acquire an exceptional education. They have never stopped supporting us, never once questioned my desire for a history degree, never asked, "What are you going to do with it?" Thank you for that, and for so much more.

APPENDIX

CHURCHES IN THE DATA SET:

David Fork's Baptist Church, Fayette County, KY
Bryan's Station Baptist Church, Fayette County, KY
Mayslick United Baptist Church, Mason County, KY
Stamping Ground Baptist Church, Scott County, KY
Mount Pleasant Baptist Church, Jessamine County, KY
Bullittsburg Baptist Church, Boone County, KY
Old Mill Creek Baptist Church, Harrison County, KY

These churches were chosen because of their location within the Bluegrass region and the relative completeness of their records during the period of study. Qualitative evidence derives as well from more than twenty-five other record books from churches located primarily in Kentucky but also in Tennessee and Virginia.

HOUSEHOLD RELATIONS / SEXUAL OFFENSES:

1. Fornication
2. Sodomy
3. Having a bastard child
4. Adultery or adulterous behavior
5. Divorce
6. Marital separation or abandonment
7. Mistreatment of family
8. Quarreling spouses
9. "Acting the harlot"
10. Allowing a disorderly house
11. Failure in family worship

12. Improperly aiding a marriage
13. Lewd conduct
14. Going with lewd company
15. Polygamy
16. Disobedience to parents
17. Failing family or spouse
18. Taking a concubine
19. Abusing a slave
20. Not providing for an apprentice
21. Abandoning an infant child
22. Having a mulatto child
23. Seduction
24. Improper conduct with a female slave
25. Base attempt on a female child
26. Destroying offspring
27. Unchaste conduct
28. "Marrying Negroes"
29. Rape

DISORDERLY CONDUCT:

1. Fighting
2. Intoxication
3. Swearing
4. Disorderly conduct
5. Slander
6. False statement
7. Lying
8. Using contradictions
9. Dancing
10. Fiddling
11. Attending theaters or balls
12. Gambling
13. Rioting
14. Gross immorality
15. Committing a felony
16. Threatening to kill or assault
17. Assault

18. Horse racing
19. Arson
20. Threatening to shoot slave catchers
21. Taking deposition in court martial
22. Joining the Masons
23. Suicide attempt
24. Taking part in a shooting match
25. Deception
26. Hypocrisy
27. Visiting a house of ill fame
28. Going with bad company
29. Negligence
30. Posting a horse improperly
31. Distilling liquor
32. Shooting dogs

ECONOMIC, PROPERTY, AND LEGAL ISSUES:

1. Breach of contract
2. Going to law with a Baptist
3. Debt
4. Theft
5. Fraud
6. Usury
7. Swindling
8. Extortion
9. Trespassing
10. Dispute over slave sale
11. Difficulties in trading
12. Not living up to profession
13. Will dispute
14. Livestock dispute
15. Punished by magistrate
16. Refusing to give up dower
17. Refusing to pay debt
18. Passing counterfeit money
19. Concealing / trading in stolen property
20. Covering up a crime

21. Forgery
22. Keeping persons out of their property
23. Disobeying employer

FAILURE OF CHURCH / CHRISTIAN DUTY:

1. Interaction of joining other religious group
2. Breaking the Sabbath
3. Nonattendance at meetings
4. Leaving church without a dismission letter
5. Dismissed member holding a letter
6. Refusing to submit to church authority
7. Criticizing church's covenant or preacher
8. Inviting non-Baptist preachers to meetinghouse
9. Propagating false doctrine
10. Claiming others as false witnesses
11. Witchcraft
12. Objection to member receiving a letter
13. "Nonfellowship"
14. Grievance against church or sister church
15. Disorder in church proceedings
16. Neglect of Christian or church duty
17. Tampering with evidence in discipline
18. Failure to pay church subscription
19. Baptizing child with a dissenting preacher
20. Neighborhood Baptist not joining church
21. Join the emancipators

CHARGES AGAINST ENSLAVED MEMBERS:

1. Disobedience
2. Running away
3. Absconding from master's business
4. Attempting to poison
5. Rebellion
6. Abusing a white person

OTHER:

1. Unspecified difficulty between two members
2. Unspecified difficulty with nonmember

TABLE 1.
All charges, 1786–1845

Race of person charged	Sex of person charged: Men	Women	Unknown sex	Total
White	1,263 (48.5%)	375 (14.4%)	2 (0.1%)	1,640 (63.0%)
Black	557 (21.4%)	352 (13.5%)	4 (0.2%)	913 (35.1%)
Mulatto	3 (0.1%)	0	0	3 (0.1%)
Unknown race	4 (0.2%)	2 (0.2%)	40 (1.5%)	46 (1.8%)
Total	1,827 (70.1%)	729 (28.1%)	46 (1.8%)	2,602

TABLE 2.
All charges, 1786–1845, by subperiod

Subperiod & race of person charged	Sex of person charged: Men	Women	Unknown sex	Total	% of all charges, 1786–1845
1786–1800					
White	123 (60.6%)	39 (19.2%)	0	162 (79.8%)	6.2%
Black	19 (9.4%)	16 (7.9%)	0	35 (17.2%)	1.4%
Mulatto	0	0	0	0	0%
Unknown race	2 (1.0%)	0	4 (2.0%)	6 (3.0%)	0.2%
Total	144 (70.9%)	55 (27.1%)	4 (2.0%)	203 (100%)	7.8%
1801–1815					
White	565 (56.1%)	111 (11.0%)	0	676 (67.1%)	26.0%
Black	192 (19.0%)	129 (12.8%)	0	321 (31.8%)	12.3%
Mulatto	3 (0.3%)	0	0	3 (0.3%)	0.1%
Unknown race	2 (0.2%)	1 (0.1%)	5 (0.5%)	8 (0.8%)	0.3%
Total	762 (75.6%)	241 (23.9%)	5 (0.5%)	1,008 (100%)	38.7%
1816–1830					
White	388 (45.1%)	135 (15.7%)	0	523 (60.8%)	20.1%
Black	194 (22.5%)	111 (12.9%)	1 (0.1%)	306 (35.5%)	11.8%
Mulatto	0	0	0	0	0%
Unknown race	0	1 (0.1%)	31 (3.6%)	32 (3.7%)	1.2%
Total	582 (67.6%)	247 (28.7%)	32 (3.7%)	861 (100%)	33.1%
1831–1845					
White	187 (35.3%)	90 (17.0%)	2 (0.3%)	279 (52.6%)	10.7%
Black	152 (28.7%)	96 (18.1%)	3 (0.6%)	251 (47.4%)	9.7%
Mulatto	0	0	0	0	0%
Unknown race	0	0	0	0	0%
Total	339 (64.0%)	186 (35.1%)	5 (0.9%)	530 (100%)	20.4%

TABLE 3.
Adulttery charges, 1780–1845

Race of person charged	Sex of person charged: Men	Women	Unknown sex	Total
White	10 (7.0%)	20 (14.1%)	0	30 (21.1%)
Black	52 (36.6%)	58 (40.8%)	1 (0.7%)	111 (78.2%)
Unknown race	0	1 (0.7%)	0	1 (0.7%)
Total	62 (43.7%)	79 (55.6%)	1 (0.7%)	142 (100%)

TABLE 4.
Adultery charges, 1831–1845

Race of person charged	Sex of person charged: Men	Women	Unknown sex	Total	% of adultery charges, 1780–1845
White	1 (2.7%)	2 (5.7%)	0	3 (8.6%)	2.1%
Black	12 (34.3%)	19 (54.3%)	1 (2.7%)	32 (91.4%)	22.5%
Total	13 (37.1%)	21 (60.0%)	1 (2.7%)	35 (100%)	24.6%

TABLE 5.
Other sexual transgressions, 1780–1845

Race of person charged	Sex of person charged: Men	Women	Total	% of all charges, 1780–1845
White	15 (15.2%)	22 (22.2%)	37 (37.4%)	1.4%
Black	20 (20.2%)	42 (42.4%)	62 (62.6%)	2.4%
Total	35 (35.4%)	64 (64.6%)	99 (100%)	3.8%

Note: These charges include lewd conduct, fornication, unchaste conduct, rape, seduction, acting a harlot, base attempt on a female slave, having a concubine, having a mulatto child, and destroying an infant child.

TABLE 6.
Other sexual transgressions, 1831–1845

Race of person charged	Sex of person charged: Men	Women	Total	% of all charges, 1831–1845
White	1 (3.3%)	7 (23.3%)	8 (26.7%)	1.5%
Black	5 (16.7%)	17 (56.7%)	22 (73.3%)	4.2%
Total	6 (20.0%)	24 (80.0%)	30 (100%)	5.7%

TABLE 7.
Failure of church or Christian duty as a share of all charges, 1801–1845

Race of person charged	Failure of church duty as a % of all charges	
	1801–1815	1831–1845
White	272 (40.2%)	139 (49.8%)
Black	28 (8.7%)	46 (18.3%)
Mulatto	0	0
Unknown race	0	0
Total	300 (29.8%)	185 (34.9%)

TABLE 8.
Economic, property, and legal charges, 1786–1845

Race of person charged	Sex of person charged			Total	% of all charges, 1786–1845
	Men	Women	Unknown sex		
White	84 (40.0%)	5 (2.4%)	0	89 (42.4%)	3.4%
Black	85 (40.1%)	33 (15.7%)	1 (0.5%)	119 (56.6%)	4.6%
Unknown race	2 (1.0%)	0	0	2 (1.0%)	0.1%
Total	171 (81.4%)	38 (18.1%)	1 (0.5%)	210 (100%)	8.1%

TABLE 9.
Economic, property, and legal charges, 1801–1845, by subperiod

Subperiod & race of person charged	Sex of person charged			Total	% of all economic, property, and legal charges, 1786–1845
	Men	Women	Unknown sex		
1801–1815					
White	40 (54.8%)	1 (1.4%)	0	41 (56.2%)	19.5%
Black	18 (24.7%)	12 (16.4%)	0	30 (41.1%)	14.3%
Unknown race	2 (2.7%)	0	0	2 (2.7%)	1.0%
Total	60 (82.2%)	13 (17.8%)	0	73 (100%)	34.8%
1816–1830					
White	28 (32.9%)	3 (3.5%)	0	31 (36.5%)	14.8%
Black	41 (48.2%	12 (14.1%)	1 (1.2%)	54 (63.5%)	25.7%
Unknown race	0	0	0	0	0%
Total	69 (81.1%)	15 (17.6%)	1	85 (100%)	40.5%
1831–1845					
White	6 (15.0%)	1 (2.5%)	0	7 (17.5%)	3.3%
Black	25 (62.5%)	8 (20.0%)	0	33 (82.5%)	15.7%
Unknown race	0	0	0	0	0%
Total	31 (77.5%)	9 (22.5%)	0	40 (100%)	19.0%

NOTES

Introduction

1. Mount Pleasant Baptist Church, Jessamine County, Kentucky, Record Books, 1801–1867, vol. 1, November–December 1803, March 1805, University of Kentucky Special Collections Research Center, Lexington, KY. For the quote that opens this introduction, see Jacob Creath Jr., *A History of Facts* (pamphlet), in *Foster et al. v. Creath et al.*, box 91, drawer 811, case 60, Fayette County Courts of Justice (hereafter FCCJ), Kentucky Department of Library and Archives, Frankfort, KY (hereafter KDLA); quote on p. 15.

2. William Warren Sweet, "The Churches as Moral Courts of the Frontier," *Church History* 2, no. 1 (March 1933): 21.

3. Walter Brownlow Posey, *The Baptist Church in the Lower Mississippi Valley, 1776–1845* (Lexington: University Press of Kentucky, 1957); T. Scott Miyakawa, *Protestants and Pioneers: Individualism and Conformity on the American Frontier* (Chicago: University of Chicago Press, 1964), 22, 44, 58.

4. Donald G. Mathews, *Religion in the Old South* (Chicago: University of Chicago Press, 1977), 268.

5. For discipline in eighteenth-century New England, see Susan Juster, *Disorderly Women: Sexual Politics and Evangelicalism in Revolutionary New England* (Ithaca, NY: Cornell University Press, 1994). On the persistence of discipline in the South and West, see Randy Sparks, *On Jordan's Stormy Banks: Evangelicalism in Mississippi, 1773–1876* (Athens: University of Georgia Press, 1994), 146–147. Scholars disagree about whether church tribunals were sites for social control. Monica Najar, in *Evangelizing the South: A Social History of Church and State in Early America* (New York: Oxford University Press, 2008), 90, looks at church disciplinary proceedings in the Upper South—Virginia, North Carolina, Kentucky, and Tennessee—focusing on how church bodies exerted their authority within individual households (thus challenging the authority of the household head) but also how church discipline "eased the progress of the market economy" for members and provided a "version of 'citizenship'" for women and free and enslaved Blacks. Janet Moore Lindman, in *Bodies of Belief: Baptist Community in Early America* (Philadelphia: University of Pennsylvania Press, 2008), 91, examines Baptist churches in the mid-Atlantic region, noting that "as a means of social control, the church courts set standards of conduct for all members." Lindman focuses less on the opportunities church tribunals presented to subordinate groups and more on the top-down imposition of church rules, insisting that church elders decided upon and enforced church regulations. In *Religion and the Making of Nat Turner's Virginia: Baptist Community and Conflict, 1740–1840* (Charlottesville: University of Virginia Press, 2008), 169, Randolph Scully contends that among southeastern Virginia Baptists during the early

nineteenth century, "despite white male control over the institution of church discipline, the process never became a straightforward application of social control," as all members fell under the church's jurisdiction. Similarly, Sparks, in *On Jordan's Stormy Banks*, devotes a full chapter to the disciplinary practices of evangelical churches in Mississippi and argues that no member, Black or white, free or enslaved, was exempt from church disciplinary proceedings, although Blacks were "disciplined at a rate higher than their percentage of membership in some churches" (p. 164). Church discipline was not solely a matter of social control, Sparks concludes, but "an effort to foster self-control, a crucial attribute in a republican society" (p. 148). Gregory Wills, in *Democratic Religion: Freedom, Authority, and Church Discipline in the Baptist South, 1785–1900* (New York: Oxford University Press, 1997), 9–10, 117, also argues that church discipline was less about social control and more about ecclesiastical control. On reading church record books for "cultural attitudes," see Robert Elder, *Sacred Mirror: Evangelicalism, Honor, and Identity in the Deep South, 1790–1860* (Chapel Hill: University of North Carolina Press, 2016), 8; see also Jessica Madison, *In Subjection: Church Discipline in the Early American South, 1760–1830* (Macon, GA: Mercer University Press, 2014).

6. As legal scholar Marianne Constable argues, with the ascendance of "law as a modality of rule" in the early republic, "legal positivists elevated human-made law, turning non-positivist conceptions of law into nonlaw. . . . Custom, for instance, [became] part of the prehistory of law proper [and] religious law [to the sociolegal scholar] is conceived as a function of social forces and interests." There remains little room for legalities rooted outside of government. Constable, "Speaking Imperfectly: Law, Language, and History," *U.C. Irvine Law Review* 5, no. 2 (June 2015): 351–352. On New England, see, for example, Bruce H. Mann, *Neighbors and Strangers: Law and Community in Early Connecticut* (Chapel Hill: University of North Carolina Press, 1987); William E. Nelson, *Dispute and Conflict Resolution in Plymouth County, Massachusetts, 1725–1825* (Chapel Hill: University of North Carolina Press, 1981); David Thomas Konig, *Law and Society in Puritan Massachusetts, Essex County, 1629–1692* (Chapel Hill: University of North Carolina Press, 1979); Cornelia Hughes Dayton, *Women before the Bar: Gender, Law, and Society in Connecticut, 1639–1789* (Chapel Hill: University of North Carolina Press, 1995). On the repositioning of religious groups in the decades following the Revolution, see Mark D. McGarvie, *One Nation under Law: America's Early National Struggles to Separate Church and State* (DeKalb: Northern Illinois University Press, 2005); Sarah Barringer Gordon, "The First Disestablishment: Limits on Church Power and Property before the Civil War," *University of Pennsylvania Law Review* 162, no. 2 (January 2014): 307–372; Steven K. Green, *The Second Disestablishment: Church and State in Nineteenth-Century America* (New York: Oxford University Press, 2010); Thomas E. Buckley, *Establishing Religious Freedom: Jefferson's Statute in Virginia* (Charlottesville: University of Virginia Press, 2013). For a brief but valuable historiography of American church-state scholarship, see Steven K. Green, "Law and Religion," in *A Companion to American Legal History*, eds. Sally E. Hadden and Alfred L. Brophy (Oxford: Wiley-Blackwell Publishing, 2013).

7. Madison quoted in Sam Haselby, *The Origins of American Religious Nationalism* (New York: Oxford University Press, 2015), 22.

8. Creath, *A History of Facts*, 15, in *Foster et al. v. Creath et al.*, box 91, drawer 811, case 60, FCCJ, KDLA.

9. Luke E. Harlow, *Religion, Race, and the Making of Confederate Kentucky, 1830–1880* (New York: Cambridge University Press, 2014).

10. John Lauritz Larson, *The Market Revolution in America: Liberty, Ambition, and the Eclipse of the Common Good* (New York: Cambridge University Press, 2009).

11. For Kentucky's social development in this period as well as its unique importance in understanding broader trends, see Stephen Aron, *How the West Was Lost: The Transformation of Kentucky from Daniel Boone to Henry Clay* (Baltimore: Johns Hopkins University Press,

1996); Craig Thompson Friend, *Along the Maysville Road: The Early American Republic in the Trans-Appalachian West* (Knoxville: University of Tennessee Press, 2005); Craig Thompson Friend, *Kentucke's Frontiers* (Bloomington: Indiana University Press, 2010); Yvonne Pitts, *Family, Law, and Inheritance in America: A Social and Legal History of Nineteenth-Century Kentucky* (New York: Cambridge University Press, 2013); Honor Sachs, *Home Rule: Households, Manhood, and National Expansion on the Eighteenth-Century Kentucky Frontier* (New Haven: Yale University Press, 2015); Harlow, *Religion, Race, and the Making of Confederate Kentucky.*

12. As historian Richard Traylor has argued, Kentucky "serves as a window into the elements of Baptist life that transcended region. Kentucky offers an excellent, representative site for understanding who the colonial Baptists had been, who they were becoming in the early national era, and who they would be after the Civil War." See Traylor, *Born of Water and Spirit: The Baptist Impulse in Kentucky, 1776–1860* (Knoxville: University of Tennessee Press, 2015), 7–8.

13. On cultural-legal history, see Ariela J. Gross, "Beyond Black and White: Cultural Approaches to Race and Slavery," *Columbia Law Review* 101 (April 2001): 640–690; for an example of this approach that looks at local courts, see Ariela Gross, *Double Character: Slavery and Mastery in the Antebellum Southern Courtroom* (Athens: University of Georgia Press, 1998).

14. See the appendix for more information on the churches included in the dataset.

15. Laura F. Edwards, *The People and Their Peace: Legal Culture and the Transformation of Inequality in the Post-Revolutionary South* (Chapel Hill: University of North Carolina Press, 2009), 4, 8, 67. Edwards notes that church discipline did serve as a form of localized law, but she devotes only two pages of her impressive book to it and does not investigate changes in church discipline over time.

16. William Collins, *Narrative: Containing a Statement of Facts in Relation to the Exclusion of William Collins and William Anderson form the Elizabeth Church of Particular Baptists in Bourbon County* (Frankfort: Hodges, Todd & Pruett, 1843), 25, in *Baptists in Kentucky: Pamphlets from the Durrett Collection* (1843), University of Chicago Library.

17. For Tomlins, law as "modality of rule" is its expression of sovereignty and reflects its central role in creating and implementing governance. Christopher Tomlins, *Law, Labor, and Ideology in the Early American Republic* (New York: Cambridge University Press, 1993); Edwards, *The People and Their Peace*, 67.

18. Warham Walker, *Church Discipline: An Exposition of the Scripture Doctrine of Church Order and Government* (Utica, NY: Bennett, Backus and Hawley, 1844), v. Although Walker's treatise, as well as a handful of others I rely on, was published in the Northeast, there is evidence they were consulted by churches in Kentucky and elsewhere. They were reviewed in religious periodicals in Kentucky, and during one contentious dispute among Kentucky Baptists, litigants pointed to Walker's *Church Discipline* to highlight proper procedure.

19. Suggestions concerning the decline of church discipline vary in scope and detail. Najar, in *Evangelizing the South*, does not specifically address the fluctuations in church disciplinary proceedings over time. Unlike Najar, Randy Sparks, in *On Jordan's Stormy Banks*, does note a marked decline in church disciplinary procedures after the 1820s in Mississippi. He attributes this decline largely to disputes between "modernists"—who wanted disciplinary power to reside with synods, conferences, or associations—and "traditionalists," who charged their opponents with being too concerned with worldly status, prestige, and membership numbers (p. 151). Christine Leigh Heyrman, in *Southern Cross: The Beginnings of the Bible Belt* (Chapel Hill: University of North Carolina Press, 1998), 159, claims that after 1830, Baptists disciplined "a steadily shrinking number of whites." Scully, in *Religion and the Making of Nat Turner's Virginia*, especially chap. 4, addresses disciplinary patterns related to the defendants' race and sex but not to the overall decline in disciplinary activities. Wills, in *Democratic Religion*, 9–10, points to a steady decline of discipline in Georgia Baptist churches after 1850, connecting it to

a number of factors, including generational change, the growth of urban churches, and a greater concern among evangelicals with reforming all of society. In *The Democratic Dilemma: Religion, Reform, and the Social Order in the Connecticut River Valley of Vermont, 1791–1850* (New York: Cambridge University Press, 1987), 282–283, Randolph Roth claims that it is difficult to know why discipline "perished" in evangelical churches, but by 1860 these churches made almost no use of disciplinary mechanisms. Christopher Waldrep, in "The Making of a Border State Society: James McGready, the Great Revival, and the Prosecution of Profanity in Kentucky," *American Historical Review*, 99 no. 3 (June 1994): 781–782, argues that the religious fervor emanating from Alexander Campbell's movement led to an upswing in the number of prosecutions for profane swearing in the county courts but does not mention how the "revival" altered patterns of discipline within church tribunals. Likewise, in his article "'So Much Sin': The Decline of Religious Discipline and the 'Tidal Wave of Crime,'" *Journal of Social History* 23, no. 3 (Spring 1990): 535–536, Waldrep argues that "southern church discipline declined because southern communities lost their cohesiveness" on more general grounds rather than simply because of the "growth of sentimentalism and industrialism," which some historians have looked to as key to understanding the demise of localism amid cultural and economic change. Focusing on Trigg County, Kentucky, Waldrep's primary goal is to show how a decline in church discipline led to a rise in vigilantism during the decades following the Civil War. More recent works concerning discipline, which do not fully address changes in disciplinary rigor include, Lindman, *Bodies of Belief*; Madison, *In Subjection*; Elder, *Sacred Mirror*, chap. 2.

20. Najar, *Evangelizing the South*, chap. 3.

21. Najar, *Evangelizing the South*, chap. 6.

22. Collins, *Narrative*, 25–26.

23. Haselby, *The Origins of American Religious Nationalism*, 14.

24. Minute Books of Eminence, KY Baptist Church (formerly Fox Run), June 1831, Archives and Special Collections, James P. Boyce Centennial Library, Southern Baptist Theological Library, Louisville, KY.

25. See, in general, Russell T. McCutcheon, "'They Licked the Platter Clean': On the Co-Dependency of the Religious and the Secular," *Method and Theory in the Study of Religion* 19, no. 3/4 (2007): 173–199.

26. Nathan O. Hatch, *The Democratization of American Christianity* (New Haven: Yale University Press, 1989).

27. On Virginia, see Buckley, *Establishing Religious Freedom*, especially chaps. 4 and 5. For Vermont and elsewhere, see Roth, *The Democratic Dilemma*, 72–73; and Sarah Barringer Gordon, "The Landscape of Faith: Religious Property and Confiscation in the Early Republic," in *Making Legal History: Essays in Honor of William E. Nelson*, eds. Daniel J. Hulsebosch and R. B. Bernstein (New York: New York University, 2013).

28. On Civil War era schisms and property disputes, see Lucas Volkman, *Houses Divided: Evangelical Schisms and the Crisis of the Union in Missouri* (New York: Oxford University Press, 2018), especially chaps. 2 and 3. For a recent investigation of church-property issues in the antebellum era of the early republic, see Gordon, "The First Disestablishment."

Chapter 1 · "The Want of Discipline"

1. For the text of Jefferson's "A Bill for Establishing Religious Freedom," see *Thomas Jefferson: Writings*, ed. Merrill D. Peterson (New York: Library of America, 1984), 346–348. For the quotes that open this chapter, see Robert Bragge, *Church Discipline: According to its Ancient Standard, as it was practiced in Primitive Times* (London; New London, CT: Reprinted by Timothy Green, 1768), Library Company of Philadelphia, Philadelphia, PA (hereafter LCP); and Bryan's Station Baptist Church Records, August 1806, Kentucky Historical Society, Frankfort, KY (hereafter KHS).

2. Madison to Jefferson, January 22, 1786, in *The Papers of James Madison*, eds. Robert A. Rutland, William M. E. Rachal, Barbara D. Ripel, and Fredrika J. Teute, vol. 8, *10 March 1784–28 March 1786* (Chicago: University of Chicago Press, 1973), 474.

3. Bryan's Station is sometimes referred to as Bryant's Station.

4. Bryan's Station Baptist Church Records, Fayette Co., KY, 1786, July 1787, KHS; Craig Thompson Friend, *Along the Maysville Road: The Early American Republic in the Trans-Appalachian West* (Knoxville: University of Tennessee Press, 2005), 9 (quote), 29–30; Craig Thompson Friend, *Kentucke's Frontiers* (Bloomington: Indiana University Press, 2010), 99–101; John H. Spencer, *A History of Kentucky Baptists, from 1769 to 1885, including more than 1800 biographical sketches*, vol. 1 (Cincinnati: J.R. Baumes, 1886), 112.

5. Morgan Edwards, *The Customs of Primitive Churches, or, A set of propositions relative to the name, materials, constitution, power, officers, ordinances, rites, business, worship, discipline, government, &c. of a church; to which are added their proofs from scripture; and historical narratives of the manner in which most of them have been reduced to practice* (Philadelphia: 1768), 61, LCP.

6. Bryan's Station Baptist Church Records, November 1786, July 1787, KHS.

7. Jean E. Friedman, *The Enclosed Garden: Women and Community in the Evangelical South*, 1830–1900 (Chapel Hill: University of North Carolina Press, 1985).

8. Ellen Eslinger, *Citizens of Zion: The Social Origins of Camp Meeting Revivalism* (Knoxville: University of Tennessee Press, 1999), 95–96.

9. Mount Pleasant Baptist Church Records, folder 1, July–September 1799, KHS.

10. Buffalo Lick Baptist Church Minutes, November 1813, Filson Historical Society, Louisville, KY (hereafter FHS).

11. Bryan's Station Baptist Church Records, August 1792, December 1793, KHS.

12. George W. Ranck, *"The Travelling Church": An Account of the Baptist Exodus from Virginia to Kentucky in 1781 under the Leadership of Rev. Lewis Craig and Capt. William Ellis* (Louisville: Press of the Baptist Book Concern, 1891), 9–13. For a description of Craig, see Spencer, *A History of Kentucky Baptists*, vol. 1, 32.

13. Thomas E. Buckley, *Establishing Religious Freedom: Jefferson's Statute in Virginia* (Charlottesville: University of Virginia Press, 2013), 40.

14. Robert Baylor Semple, *A History of the Rise and Progress of the Baptists in Virginia* (Richmond: Published by the Author. John O'Lynch, Printer, 1810), 15.

15. Ranck, "*The Travelling Church*," 10.

16. For more on Harris, see Semple, *A History of the Rise and Progress of the Baptists in Virginia*, 377–385.

17. Jewel L. Spangler, *Virginians Reborn: Anglican Monopoly, Evangelical Dissent, and the Rise of the Baptists in the Late Eighteenth Century* (Charlottesville: University of Virginia Press, 2008), 79–83; Spencer, *A History of Kentucky Baptists*, vol. 1, 107; Semple, *A History of the Rise and Progress of the Baptists in Virginia*, 17–18.

18. Buckley, *Establishing Religious Freedom*, 40–41.

19. Buckley, *Establishing Religious Freedom*, 51–58; quotes are from p. 53.

20. James Madison to Thomas Jefferson, January 22, 1786, *The Papers of James Madison*, vol. 8, 473.

21. Buckley, *Establishing Religious Freedom*, 58–80. Thanks to the dissenters' petition campaign in 1786, the assembly also repealed the Incorporation Act; see Buckley, chap. 6.

22. See in general Ranck, "*The Travelling Church*."

23. Stephen F. Aron, *How the West Was Lost: The Transformation of Kentucky from Daniel Boone to Henry Clay* (Baltimore: Johns Hopkins University Press, 1996), 3.

24. For this brief history of Native peoples, I have relied on Craig Thompson Friend's *Kentucke's Frontiers*, 3–10.

25. Friend, *Kentucke's Frontiers*, 10–17.

26. Friend, *Kentucke's Frontiers*, 27–31, 39.

27. Friend, *Kentucke's Frontiers*, 39–56.

28. Friend, *Kentucke's Frontiers*, 56–57; Aron, *How the West Was Lost*, 30.

29. Friend, *Along the Maysville Road*, 4–5, 20–23.

30. Aron, *How the West Was Lost*, 35, 40–41, 47–48; Craig, *Along the Maysville Road*, 15–16.

31. Malcolm J. Rohrbough, *Trans-Appalachian Frontier: People, Societies, and Institutions, 1775–1850* (Bloomington: Indiana University Press, 2008), 58–59.

32. The Transylvania Land Company was a speculative scheme hatched by North Carolinian Richard Henderson to secure large tracts of land leased from Natives in the trans-Appalachian West. Henderson's plans failed owing to high land prices and quitrent. Instead of giving up on the West, however, Henderson redirected his efforts south to the Cumberland River Valley of Tennessee; see Rohrbough, *Trans-Appalachian Frontier*, 26, 46. See also Lowell H. Harrison, *Kentucky's Road to Statehood* (Lexington: University Press of Kentucky, 1992), 2–3; John R. Finger, *Tennessee Frontiers: Three Regions in Transition* (Bloomington: Indiana University Press, 2001), 51–52. As James Willard Hurst notes in *Law and the Conditions of Freedom* (Madison: University of Wisconsin Press, 1956), 5, "Often unlawful in origin, settlement nevertheless quickly brought effective demand for law."

33. Quoted in Friend, *Along the Maysville Road*, 23; see also Eslinger, *Citizens of Zion*, 89.

34. Aron, *How the West Was Lost*, 48.

35. Ranck, "*The Travelling Church*," 27–32.

36. Eslinger, *Citizens of Zion*, 163.

37. Spencer, *A History of Kentucky Baptists*, vol. 1, 31, 33, 136–137, 162.

38. Spencer, *A History of Kentucky Baptists*, vol. 1, 42, 54–56, 85.

39. It later became Boone County.

40. John Taylor, *A History of Ten Baptist Churches, of Which the Author has been Alternatively a Member* (Frankfort, KY: J.H. Holeman, 1823), 81.

41. "Bullittsburg Baptist Church Book, 1795–1800," Baptist History Homepage, accessed December 7, 2016, http://baptisthistoryhomepage.com/bullittsbrg.minutes.95-00.html.

42. Friend, *Along the Maysville Road*, 26–27, 70–71.

43. Friend, *Kentucke's Frontiers*, 179–184.

44. Taylor, *A History of Ten Baptist Churches*, 83, 95–97.

45. Richard R. Beeman and Rhys Isaac, "Cultural Conflict and Social Change in the Revolutionary South: Lunenburg County, Virginia," *Journal of Southern History* 46, no. 4 (November 1980): 530.

46. Rhys Isaac, *The Transformation of Virginia, 1740–1790* (Chapel Hill: University of North Carolina Press, 1982), 58, 157; Monica Najar, *Evangelizing the South: A Social History of Church and State in Early America* (New York: Oxford University Press, 2008), 90–92.

47. The Regular Baptist Association in Philadelphia adopted a confession of faith in 1742—a slightly revised version of the Second London Confession of Faith of 1677—and this doctrinal articulation became standard, with slight modifications by some churches, for Baptists throughout the Southern and Western United States. See Albert W. Wardin Jr., *Tennessee Baptists: A Comprehensive History, 1779–1999* (Brentwood: Tennessee Baptist Convention, 1999), 34–37. For instance, upon its formation in June 1794, the Bullittsburg Church adopted the Philadelphia Confession of Faith "as received by the Elkhorn Association"; "Bullittsburg Baptist Church Book, 1795–1800."

48. For Noel quote, see Records of the Franklin Association of Baptists, 1826, p. 8, Archives and Special Collections, James P. Boyce Centennial Library, Southern Baptist Theological Library, Louisville, KY (hereafter SBTL).

49. Taylor, *A History of Ten Baptist Churches*, 5, 7.

50. Friend, *Kentucke's Frontiers*, 168; Najar, *Evangelizing the South*, 7; Spangler, *Virginians Reborn*, 77–79.

51. Taylor, *A History of Ten Baptist Churches*, 74.

52. "Deposition of James Fishback," in *Bennett et al. Trustees of the Mt. Vernon Church v. Curd et al.* (1836), folder 1, box 69, case no. 7914, Court of Justice, Woodford Circuit Case Files, 1833–1837 (hereafter CJWCC), Kentucky Department of Library and Archives, Frankfort, KY (hereafter KDLA).

53. "Bullitsburg Baptist Church Book, 1795–1800"; "Bullittsburg Baptist Church Book, 1801–1802," Baptist History Homepage, accessed December 12, 2016, http://baptisthistoryhomepage.com/bullittsbrg.minutes.01-02.html.

54. Bryan's Station Baptist Church Records, May 1794, KHS.

55. Samuel Jones, *A Treatise of Church Discipline and a Directory. Done by Appointment of the Philadelphia Baptist Association* (Lexington: Printed by T. Anderson at the Gazetteer Office, 1805), 26, LCP.

56. Jones, *A Treatise of Church Discipline*, 26; Friend, *Kentucke's Frontiers*, 199.

57. Thomas Hooker, *A Survey of the Summe [sic] of Church-Discipline* (London, 1648), part I, 13–14, LCP; emphasis in original.

58. Eleazer Savage, *Manual of Church Discipline* (Rochester: Sage & Brother, 1844), 80, 80n; emphasis in original.

59. See in general William Collins, *Narrative: Containing a Statement of Facts in Relation to the Exclusion of William Collins and William Anderson from the Elizabeth Church of Particular Baptists in Bourbon County* (Frankfort, KY: Hodges, Todd & Pruett—Printers, 1843) in *Baptists in Kentucky: Pamphlets from the Durrett Collection* (1843), University of Chicago Library.

60. Wardin, *Tennessee Baptists*, 97–100. For quote, see South Elkhorn Baptist Church Records, May 1821, KHS.

61. Book of the Records of Long Run Association, Typescript, September-1823, -1824, -1825, SBTL.

62. Book of the Records of Long Run Association, Typescript, September-1803, -1804, -1805, SBTL.

63. Jacob Creath, *Biographical sketches of Elder William Creath, a Calvinist Minister of Mecklenburg County, Virginia and his family, by his son, Jacob Creath, of Palmyra, MO* (St. Louis: T. W. Ustick, Printer, 1866), 28.

64. "Help for the Churches: A Brief Treatise on the Form and Discipline of a Gospel Church," 1, no date, William A. Baker Papers, folder: "Help for the Churches," Virginia Historical Society, Richmond, VA (hereafter VHS).

65. First Baptist of Nashville Records, January 27, 1833, Southern Baptist Library and Archive, Nashville, TN (hereafter SBLA); Records of the Franklin Association of Baptists, 1827, p. 6, SBTL.

66. Pleasant Grove Baptist Church Records, September 1814, FHS.

67. William Warren Sweet, *Religion on the American Frontier: The Baptists, 1783–1830* (New York: Cooper Square Publishers, 1964), 24–26; Eslinger, *Citizens of Zion*, 166.

68. Carter Tarrant Letter, June 27, 1808, KHS.

69. Taylor, *A History of Ten Baptist Churches*, 144.

70. Mt. Olivet Church Records, June 1866, SBLA; Alexander Campbell, "A Restoration of the Ancient Order of Things, No. XXVI, On the Discipline of the Church, No. III," *Christian Baptist* 6 (August 4, 1828): 471; *Reply of the Committees of the Washington & Lewisburg Baptist Churches, to the Proceedings of the Mayslick Church, and Council, held in Mayslick, December, 1845, and published in the Baptist Banner in January, 1846* (Maysville, KY: Maysville Eagle Office, 1846), 11, in *Baptists in Kentucky*.

71. Collins, *Narrative*, 25.

72. "Help for the Churches," VHS.

73. Pleasant Grove Baptist Church Records, July–August 1825, FHS.

74. Red River Church Minute Book, September 1808, June 1809, SBLA; Robert B. McAfee Journals, 1796–1800, folder 1, p. 61, KHS; *Reply of the Washington Church to the Proceedings of the Bracken Association held in Millersburg, Bourbon Co. Ky., September 1847* (Maysville, KY: J. Sprigg Chambers, Printer, 1847), 17, 22–25, in *Baptists in Kentucky.*

75. Eslinger, *Citizens of Zion*, 109.

76. Bryan's Station Baptist Church Records, November 1803, KHS.

77. Aron, *How the West Was Lost*, 188.

78. John B. Boles, *Religion in Antebellum Kentucky* (Lexington: University Press of Kentucky, 1976), 16–20. See also Amanda Porterfield, *Conceived in Doubt: Religion and Politics in the New American Nation* (Chicago: University of Chicago Press, 2012); Eric R. Schlereth, *An Age of Infidels: The Politics of Religious Controversy in the Early United States* (Philadelphia: University of Pennsylvania Press, 2013).

79. See the circular letter in "Minutes of the Philadelphia Baptist Association, held at Philadelphia, October 4th, 5th, & 6th, 1796," 5, LCP.

80. "Copy of the Diary of David Barrow, Baptist Minister, 1795," 26, FHS; Smith quoted in John B. Boles, *The Great Revival: Beginnings of the Bible Belt* (Lexington: University Press of Kentucky, 1996), 26.

81. Spencer, *History of Kentucky Baptists*, vol. 1, 142, 540–541, 642.

82. See tables 1 and 2 in the appendix for the frequency of all charges between 1786 and 1845.

83. Bryan's Station Baptist Church Records, May 1809, KHS.

Chapter 2 · Churches' "Perplexing Difficulties"

1. John Taylor, *A History of Ten Baptist Churches, of Which the Author has been Alternatively a Member* (Frankfort, KY: J.H. Holeman, 1823), 81, 176–177. For the quote that opens this chapter, see Pleasant Grove Baptist Church Records, March 1846, Filson Historical Society, Louisville, KY (hereafter FHS).

2. Christine Leigh Heyrman, *Southern Cross: The Beginnings of the Bible Belt* (Chapel Hill: University of North Carolina Press, 1998), chap. 3.

3. Monica Najar, *Evangelizing the South: A Social History of Church and State in Early America* (New York: Oxford University Press, 2008), 36–37; Blair A. Pogue, "'I Cannot Believe the Gospel That Is So Much Preached': Gender, Belief, and Discipline in Baptist Religious Culture," in *The Buzzel about Kentuck: Settling the Promised Land*, ed. Craig Thompson Friend (Lexington: University Press of Kentucky, 1999), 217–240.

4. Quotation is from Craig Thompson Friend, *Kentucke's Frontiers* (Bloomington: Indiana University Press, 2010), 170. In their 1826 circular letter, the Elkhorn Association of Baptists equated the use of "the appellation of Mr. and Mrs. instead of the scriptural style of brother and sister" with a "conformity to the world." See Records of the Elkhorn Association of Baptists, 1826, 7, Archives and Special Collections, James P. Boyce Centennial Library, Southern Baptist Theological Library, Louisville, KY (hereafter SBTL).

5. For "children of the same Father," see Records of the Elkhorn Association of Baptists, 1830, 5–6, SBTL. For Jesus as head of household, see "The Pulpit: The Duty of Family Worship," *Tennessee Baptist* (Nashville, TN), November 8, 1851.

6. Heyrman, *Southern Cross*, 137–138.

7. Records of the Elkhorn Association of Baptists, 1826, 5–7, SBTL. For a similar example emanating from a local Baptist church, see Harrod's Creek Baptist Church Records, vol. 1, February 1820, SBTL.

8. Records of the Elkhorn Association of Baptists, 1831, 7, SBTL.

9. Heyrman, *Southern Cross*, 158–159.

10. Letter from Absalom Bainbridge to Norborne Beall, ca. August 1809, and letter from Absalom Bainbridge to Juliet [Bainbridge], ca. August 1809, Beall-Booth Family Papers, folder 45, Norborne Beall Correspondence, 1809, FHS.

11. Bainbridge to Beall Notice, September 25, 1809, Beall-Booth Family Papers, folder 117, Norborne Beall Papers, Business Records: Agreements, 1803–1820, FHS.

12. Letter from Absalom Bainbridge to Mrs. [Eliza] Bainbridge, December 4, 1809, Beall-Booth Family Papers, folder 45, FHS.

13. Friend, *Kentucke's Frontiers*, xxii.

14. Cynthia Cumfer, *Separate Peoples, One Land: The Minds of Cherokees, Blacks, and Whites on the Tennessee Frontier* (Chapel Hill: University of North Carolina Press, 2007), 159–160.

15. Honor Sachs, *Home Rule: Households, Manhood, and National Expansion on the Eighteenth-Century Kentucky Frontier* (New Haven: Yale University Press, 2015), 21–22; Friend, *Kentucke's Frontiers*, 120.

16. Craig Thompson Friend, *Along the Maysville Road: The Early American Republic in the Trans-Appalachian West* (Knoxville: University of Tennessee Press, 2005), 4.

17. Cumfer, *Separate Peoples, One Land*, 156–157.

18. Sachs, *Home Rule*, 142.

19. Cumfer, *Separate Peoples, One Land*, 169; Laura F. Edwards, *The People and Their Peace: Legal Culture and the Transformation of Inequality in the Post-Revolutionary South* (Chapel Hill: University of North Carolina Press, 2009), 7–8.

20. Linda K. Kerber, *Women of the Republic: Intellect and Ideology in Revolutionary America* (Chapel Hill: University of North Carolina Press, 1980), 10.

21. David's Fork Baptist Church Records, March 1803, David's Fork Baptist Church, accessed March 2, 2015, http://davidsfork.org/images/David_s_Fork_minutes_1802-1850_PDF.pdf.

22. Records of the Elkhorn Association of Baptists, 1831, 6–7, 1832, 4, SBTL.

23. Najar, *Evangelizing the South*, 73.

24. Pleasant Grove Baptist Church Records (formerly Flat Rock), May 1822, June/July 1823, FHS.

25. Elk Lick Primitive Baptist Church, vol. 1, August 1812, Kentucky Historical Society, Frankfort, KY (hereafter KHS).

26. Red River Baptist Church Records, October 1823, Southern Baptist Library and Archive, Nashville, TN (hereafter SBLA).

27. Mayslick Baptist Church, November 1799, University of Kentucky Special Collections Research Center, Lexington, KY (hereafter UKSCRC).

28. "Bullittsburg Baptist Church Book, 1809–1812," April–May 1812, Baptist History Homepage, accessed July 23, 2020, http://baptisthistoryhomepage.com/bullittsbrg.minutes.09-12.html.

29. Mount Pleasant Baptist Church, vol. 2, July 1831, UKSCRC.

30. Mount Pleasant Baptist Church, vol. 1, April 1806, UKSCRC.

31. Church Records of the Long Run Baptist Church, vol. 2, October 1841, SBTL.

32. Harrod's Creek Baptist Church Records, vol. 1, October 1820, January–February 1821, March 1823, SBTL.

33. Bryan's Station Baptist Church Records, Nov. 1828–March 1829, KHS.

34. Nancy F. Cott, *Public Vows: A History of Marriage and the Nation* (Cambridge: Harvard University Press, 2000), 29; Najar, *Evangelizing the South*, 70–71.

35. Pleasant Grove Baptist Church Records (formerly Flat Rock), April 1813, FHS; Tick Creek Bethel Church Records, January 1810, FHS.

36. David's Fork Baptist Church Records, May–June 1805.

37. Old Mill Creek Baptist Church Session Book, January 1825, KHS.

38. Pleasant Grove Baptist Church Records (formerly Flat Rock), August 1822, FHS; "Bullitsburg Baptist Church Book, 1813–1817," Baptist History Homepage, November 1813, accessed July 17, 2020, http://baptisthistoryhomepage.com/bullittsbrg.minutes.13-17.html.

39. Mayslick Baptist Church, September 1804, August 1821, July–August 1822, UKSCRC.

40. See tables 3, 4, and 5 in the appendix.

41. Najar, *Evangelizing the South*, 84.

42. Harrod's Creek Baptist Church, Crestwood, KY, August 1819, SBTL.

43. Bryan's Station Baptist Church Records, November 1804, KHS. For Tompson as sheriff, see Robert M. Ireland, *The County Courts in Antebellum Kentucky* (Lexington: University Press of Kentucky, 1979), 31.

44. Harrod's Creek Baptist Church Records, vol. 1, January 1820, SBTL.

45. Red River Church Minute Book, October 1814–April 1815, SBLA.

46. David's Fork Baptist Church Records, July–August 1824.

47. Bryan's Station Baptist Church Records, September 1791, July 1792, October 1795, 1786–1860, KHS.

48. Mayslick United Baptist Church Records, February 1805, UKSCRC.

49. Book of Records of the Long Run Association (typescript), September 1825, p. 144, SBTL.

50. Quotes are from "Divorces in Kentucky," *New York Evangelist*, March 9, 1848, and are attributed to the *Baptist Banner*, which claimed that "an unusual number of divorces [had] already been granted by our Legislature, and that still its time is mainly taken up with applications yet undecided upon."

51. William Littell, *The Statute Law of Kentucky, 1798–1801*, vol. 2 (Frankfort: Johnson & Pleasants, 1810), 409–410. In 1812 the Kentucky General Assembly broadened the conditions for a wife's gaining alimony, enacting "An Act concerning Alimony and separate maintenance of Wives and Children abandoned by their Husbands and Fathers." This measure was aimed at men who affiliated themselves with unorthodox religious sects, particularly the Shakers. "That were any man united in lawful marriage," the act stated, "hath or hereafter shall renounce the marriage covenant, by refusing to live with his wife in the conjugal relation, by uniting himself to any sect, whose creed, rules or doctrines require a renunciation of the marriage covenant, or forbid a man and wife to dwell and cohabit together, according to the true spirit and object of marriage, the person so offending shall subject himself to recovery of alimony or separate maintenance by the wife aggrieved thereby." The act also stipulated that any conveyance of real or personal property by the husband to the particular sect was subject to the decrees of the court in an alimony proceeding. In 1831 the assembly did away with jury decisions in alimony cases, placing the decisions in the hands of the chancellor. See C. S. Moreheard and Mason Brown, *A Digest of the Statute Laws of Kentucky, of a Public and Permanent Nature, From the Commencement of the Government to the Session of the Legislature, Ending on the 24th February, 1834, with References to Judicial Decisions, in Two Volumes*, vol. 1 (Frankfort, KY: Albert G. Hodges, 1834), 124–126.

52. William Littell, *The Statute Law of Kentucky, 1808–1811*, vol. 4 (Frankfort, KY: Printed for William Hunter by Robert Johnston, 1814), 19–20. Although this law granted authority to circuit courts to hear divorce petitions, the state assembly issued divorces through this period. In 1816 the assembly passed "An Act to amend the law concerning writs of error," which forbade the Court of Appeals from reversing "the decree of any court of equity hereafter obtained, granting a divorce from the marriage contract" if brought on a writ of error. This did not stop the Court of Appeals from taking up cases where the lower court granted a divorce and a division of the couple's estate in the same decree, though their actions

were limited to judging the latter and not the former issue. For example, see *Thornberry v. Thornberry*, 14 Ky. 251 (1823). Nor did it stop the Court of Appeals from ruling on cases brought by a party "aggrieved by an erroneous decree" by a lower court, such as a dismissal without prejudice. See *Boggess against Boggess*, 34 Ky. 307, Lexis 71 (1836). For the 1816 law, see *Acts Passed at the First Session of the Twenty-Fourth General Assembly, For the Commonwealth of Kentucky, Begun and Held in the Town of Frankfort, on Monday the Fourth day of December, One Thousand Eight Hundred and Fifteen, and of the Commonwealth the Twenty-Fourth* (Frankfort, KY: Gerard & Berry—Printers for the Commonwealth, 1816), 572–573. Although section 6 of the 1809 divorce law was overturned by the 1843 act, in 1847 Judge Breck upheld the decision of a chancery court that claimed a second marriage by the injured party, coming only months after she was granted a divorce decree, was not valid either de jure or de facto. See *Cox and Wife, &c. v. Combs*, 47 Ky. 231, Lexis 160 (1847); For the 1843 law, see "An Act to amend an act, entitled, an act regulating divorces in this Commonwealth, approved 31st January, 1809," in *Acts of the General Assembly of the Commonwealth of Kentucky: Passed at the December Session, 1842* (Frankfort: A.G. Hodges, State Printer, 1843), 29.

53. *Logan v. Logan*, 41 Ky. 142, 146–147, Lexis 113 (1841); italics in original.

54. Cott, *Public Vows*, 11. As Norma Basch puts it, as the "source of harmony and stability in a shifting, competitive world, [marriage] was the irrevocable contract that made all other contracts possible." Divorce, however, "took away marriage's irrevocability, bringing it closer to other contracts." Norma Basch, *Framing American Divorce: From the Revolutionary Generation to the Victorians* (Los Angeles: University of California Press, 1999), 3.

55. Alexander Campbell, "Queries—Answered," *Christian Baptist*, vol. 6 (1828), 539. Still, Baptists and Methodists expected members to marry only other converted believers. The latter group, especially, relied upon excommunication to enforce the stricture. Evangelicals largely gave up on this insistence by the turn of the nineteenth century. See Heyrman, *Southern Cross*, 139–140, 156.

56. Fidus, "No. XII—Dr. Bythewood's Opinion and J.S. Waller Contrasted," *Tennessee Baptist*, March 1, 1849.

57. Frankfort Baptist Church Records, vol. 1, January–March 1828, KHS.

58. Elk Lick Primitive Baptist Church Records, vol. 1, August–September 1846, KHS.

59. Cott, *Public Vows*, 35.

60. Tick Creek Bethel Church Records, July and September 1810, FHS.

61. Minute Books of Eminence, KY Baptist Church (formerly Fox Run), vol. 1, August–October 1824, SBTL.

62. For queries to the Elkhorn Association, see "The Elkhorn Baptist Association," Baptist History Homepage, accessed October 17, 2020, http://baptisthistoryhomepage.com/elkhorn.query.const.html. The association advised churches not to accept any more members affected by this circumstance and referred the query to the next gathering, yet it does not appear they revisited the issue.

63. Book of the Records of the Long Run Association (typescript), 1812, p. 56, SBTL. The Red River Church of Robertson County, Tennessee, sent a similar query to their association in September 1801, asking "whether a negro that was sold from his wife in some of the Eastern States & brought to this country and has taken another wife can be rec'd into fellowship?" See Red River Church Minute Book, September 1801, SBLA.

64. Onesimus, "Marriage and Divorce," *Columbian Star and Christian Index* (Atlanta, GA) 3, no. 6 (August 7, 1830).

65. One has to wonder about the underlying economic incentives in allowing enslaved people to remarry after separation.

66. Corinthinus, "Marriage and Divorce," *Christian Index* (Atlanta, GA) 4, no. 1 (January 1, 1831).

67. For all charges, see David's Fork Baptist Church Records, 1803–1860.

68. Mayslick, Ky. United Baptist Church Records, vol. 1, May–June 1818, UKSCRC.

69. Mayslick, Ky. United Baptist Church Records, vol. 1, July 1805, July 1809, UKSCRC.

70. Najar, *Evangelizing the South*, 150–159.

71. John H. Spencer, *A History of Kentucky Baptists from 1769 to 1885, Including more than 1800 Biographical Sketches*, vol. 1 (Cincinnati: J.R. Baumes, 1886), 186.

72. Najar, *Evangelizing the South*, 154–157.

73. Mayslick, Ky. United Baptist Church Records, vol. 1, September 1813, UKSCRC.

74. Najar, *Evangelizing the South*, 161, 138–139. For the persistent strains of antislavery activism among evangelicals through the antebellum era, see Luke E. Harlow, *Race, Religion, and the Making of Confederate Kentucky, 1830–1880* (New York: Cambridge University Press, 2014).

75. On how enslaved people in the courtroom forced whites to confront them as persons and property, see Ariela J. Gross, *Double Character: Slavery and Mastery in the Antebellum Southern Courtroom* (Athens: University of Georgia Press, 1998).

76. On the region's hardening racial hierarchy, see Friend, *Kentucke's Frontiers*, xxii.

77. Red River Church Minute Book, March 1798, June 1799, SBLA.

78. Bryan's Station Baptist Church Records, July–September 1792, KHS.

79. Mount Pleasant Baptist Church Records, folder 1, November 1795, KHS. The Mount Gomer Church changed its name to Mount Pleasant in 1801.

80. Buffalo Lick Baptist Church Records, July 1809, FHS.

81. Buffalo Lick Baptist Church Records, July 1809, December 1810, January 1811, February 1811, May 1811, October 1811, FHS.

82. Tick Creek Bethel Church Records, September/October 1814, FHS.

83. Bryan's Station Baptist Church Records, August 1801, February 1802, KHS.

84. Beech Creek Church Records, January 1826, FHS.

85. Little Cedar Lick Baptist Church Records, April 1842, May 1845, SBLA.

86. Bryan's Station Baptist Church Records, June 1843, KHS.

87. *Commonwealth v. Humphrey and Sam* (1813), box 31, drawer 271, Fayette County Courts of Justice, Kentucky Department of Library and Archives, Frankfort, KY (hereafter KDLA).

88. David's Fork Baptist Church Records, April/May 1814.

89. *Commonwealth v. Jim* (1813), Fayette County Circuit Case Files, Chancery Court Decided Cases, box 31, drawer 271, KDLA.

90. Dylan C. Penningroth, *Claims of Kinfolk: African American Property and Community in the Nineteenth-Century South* (Chapel Hill: University of North Carolina Press, 2003), 6.

91. Bryan's Station Baptist Church Records, July–October 1805, KHS.

92. Penningroth mentions that churches "served as forums for settling disputes amongst enslaved people" but looks only briefly at cases taken up by an all-Black church in Richmond, Virginia, in the 1840s and not at cases of the theft and property disputes of enslaved people within biracial churches. Penningroth notes, too, that churches served as sites for enslaved members to secure their property. "Recognition of the Sabbath," he insists, "was intertwined with the informal system of display and acknowledgment that secured slaves' ownership of property." Penningroth, *Claims of Kinfolk*, 100–101.

93. Stephen Aron, *How the West Was Lost: The Transformation of Kentucky from Daniel Boone to Henry Clay* (Baltimore: Johns Hopkins University Press, 1996), 147.

94. Bibb quoted in Walter Johnson, *River of Dark Dreams: Slavery and Empire in the Cotton Kingdom* (Cambridge: Harvard University Press, 2013), 213.

95. Edward L. Ayers, *Vengeance and Justice: Crime and Punishment in the Nineteenth-Century American South* (New York: Oxford University Press, 1984), 125.

96. Red River Church Minute Book, February 1811, SBLA; Mt. Olivet Baptist Church (formerly Big Cedar Lick), July 1814, SBLA; Bryan's Station Baptist Church, May 1836, KHS. The church excluded Peter in July 1836.

97. Friend, *Along the Maysville Road*, 206–208.

98. Friend, *Along the Maysville Road*, 35.

99. Friend, *Along the Maysville Road*, 84–85. For the 1798 code, see C. S. Morehead and Mason Brown, *A digest of the statute laws of Kentucky, of a public and permanent nature: from the commencement of the government to the session of the Legislature, ending on the 24th February, 1834: with references to judicial decisions*, vol. 2 (Frankfort, KY: A.G. Hodges, 1834), 1471–1480.

100. Friend, *Along the Maysville Road*, 85.

101. Friend, *Kentucke's Frontier*, xxii.

102. See table 7 in the appendix.

103. Heyrman, *Southern Cross*, 137–138.

104. Pleasant Grove Baptist Church Records, 1846–1860, FHS.

Chapter 3 · A "Habitation of Justice?"

1. For background on the dispute, see Jacob Creath Jr., *A History of Facts*, and Foster's declaration to the court, both in *Foster et al. v. Creath et al.*, box 91, drawer 811, case 60, Fayette County Courts of Justice (hereafter FCCJ), Kentucky Department of Library and Archives, Frankfort, KY (hereafter KDLA); quote on p. 15. For the quote that opens this chapter, see Mount Pleasant Baptist Church Records, August 1795, Kentucky Historical Society, Frankfort, KY (hereafter KHS).

2. Creath, *A History of Facts*, 10–11.

3. Christine Heyrman, *Southern Cross: The Beginnings of the Bible Belt* (Chapel Hill: University of North Carolina Press, 1997), 155; Randy J. Sparks, *On Jordan's Stormy Banks: Evangelicalism in Mississippi, 1773–1876* (Athens: University of Georgia Press, 1994), 151; Christopher Waldrep, "'So Much Sin': The Decline of Religious Discipline and the 'Tidal Wave of Crime,'" *Journal of Social History* 23, no. 3 (Spring 1990): 535–536; Gregory A. Wills, *Democratic Religion: Freedom, Authority, and Church Discipline in the Baptist South, 1785–1900* (New York: Oxford University Press, 1997), 9–10. Wills, primarily focused on Baptists in Georgia, notes on page 117 that the 1840s was the beginning of the disciplinary decline among southern Baptists, with the real diminishment taking place after the Civil War. Randolph Roth, *The Democratic Dilemma: Religion, Reform, and the Social Order in the Connecticut River Valley of Vermont, 1791–1850* (New York: Cambridge University Press, 1987), 282–283. For a shift in focus, especially on disputes over debt and commerce, see Robert Elder, *The Sacred Mirror: Evangelicalism, Honor, and Identity in the Deep South* (Chapel Hill: University of North Carolina Press, 2016), 56–62.

4. Bruce H. Mann, *Republic of Debtors: Bankruptcy in the Age of American Independence* (Cambridge: Harvard University Press, 2002), 4–5.

5. Mark D. McGarvie, *One Nation under Law: America's Early National Struggles to Separate Church and State* (Dekalb: Northern Illinois University Press, 2004), 11.

6. See, in general, Laura F. Edwards, *The People and Their Peace: Legal Culture and the Transformation of Inequality in the Post-Revolutionary South* (Chapel Hill: University of North Carolina Press, 2009).

7. Mark A. Noll, "Protestants, Money, and the Market, 1790–1860," in *God and Mammon*, ed. Mark A. Noll (New York: Oxford University Press, 2001), 270.

8. That is not to say that state law was neutral in its workings, but, legal historian Morton Horwitz claims, legal thinkers during the antebellum period saw "major advantages in creating an intellectual system which gave common law rules the appearance of being self-contained, apolitical, and inexorable." See Horwitz, *The Transformation of American Law, 1780–1860* (Cambridge: Harvard University Press, 1977), 254.

9. Robert Baylor Semple, *A History of the Rise and Progress of the Baptists in Virginia* (Richmond: John O'Lynch, Printer, 1810), 380, 383–384.

10. See the Circular Letter, p. 3, in Records of the Long Run Association, 1818, Archives and Special Collections, James P. Boyce Centennial Library, Southern Baptist Theological Library, Louisville, KY (hereafter SBTL).

11. Mount Pleasant Baptist Church Records, January 1806, KHS; Church Records of the Long Run Baptist Church, vol. 1, November 1806, SBTL; Stamping Ground Baptist Church Records, December 1805, University of Kentucky Special Collections Research Center, Lexington, KY (hereafter UKSCRC); Mss. C C Church Records, Minute Books, 1815, Filson Historical Society, Louisville, KY (hereafter FHS).

12. Stephen Aron, *How the West Was Lost: The Transformation of Kentucky from Daniel Boone to Henry Clay* (Baltimore: Johns Hopkins University Press, 1996), 82–84.

13. Horwitz, *The Transformation of American Law*, 147–154.

14. Aron, *How the West Was Lost*, 82.

15. Carli N. Conklin, "Transformed, Not Transcended: The Role of Extrajudicial Dispute Resolution in Antebellum Kentucky and New Jersey," *American Journal of Legal History* 48, no. 1 (January 2006): 48–51. Disputing parties in Kentucky could resort to extrajudicial arbitration if they agreed upon referees, who would then be empowered by the court to subpoena witnesses and decide on the case. Their decision was sent to the court, which took it as its own decree. Furthermore, the decision could not be overturned or appealed unless there was evidence of the arbitrators' partiality toward one party. See "An Act Concerning Awards," in C. S. Moreheard and Mason Brown, *A Digest of the Statute Laws of Kentucky, of a Public and Permanent nature, From the Commencement of the Government to the Session of the Legislature, Ending on the 24th February, 1834, with References to Judicial Decisions, in Two Volumes* (Frankfort: Albert G. Hodges, 1834), 143–148.

16. In *How the West Was Lost*, 86–87, Aron notes that "Baptists, and to a lesser extent members of other evangelical churches, relied on lay referees to mediate between complainants and ensure that squabbles did not cause a 'breach of fellowship.'"

17. Mount Pleasant Baptist Church Records, folder 1, June–September 1799, KHS; emphasis added.

18. Stamping Ground Baptist Church Records, First Minute Book, 1795–1842, December 1805, UKSCRC.

19. Harrod's Creek Baptist Church Records, September 1819, SBTL.

20. Tick Creek Bethel Baptist Church Records, August 1815–August 1816, FHS.

21. Buffalo Lick Baptist Church Minutes, September–October 1811, FHS.

22. Monica Najar, *Evangelizing the South: A Social History of Church and State* (New York: Oxford University Press, 2008), 105.

23. David's Fork Baptist Church Records, David's Fork Baptist Church, September 1819, accessed March 2, 2015, http://davidsfork.org/images/David_s_Fork_minutes_1802-1850_PDF.pdf.

24. Red River Church Minute Book, Adams, Tennessee, Robertson County, April–June 1823, Southern Baptist Library and Archive, Nashville, TN (hereafter SBLA).

25. Mayslick, Ky. United Baptist Church Records, vol. 1, February–March 1805, UKSCRC.

26. Red River Church Minute Book, July 1808, SBLA.

27. "Bullittsburg Baptist Churchbook, 1795–1800," Baptist History Homepage, January 1800, accessed January 6, 2019, http://baptisthistoryhomepage.com/bullittsbrg.minutes.95-00.html.

28. "Bullittsburg Baptist Churchbook, 1803–1805," Baptist History Homepage, January 1803, accessed January 6, 2019, http://baptisthistoryhomepage.com/bullittsbrg.minutes.03-05.html.

29. Mount Pleasant Baptist Church, Record Books, vol. 1, November 1819, April 1820, UKSCRC. For the various other charges mentioned, see Mount Pleasant Baptist Church, Record Books, vol. 1, November 1819–December 1820, UKSCRC.

30. John Lauritz Larson, *The Market Revolution in America: Liberty, Ambition, and the Eclipse of the Common Good* (New York: Cambridge University Press, 2010), 3.

31. Craig Thompson Friend, *Along the Maysville Road: The Early American Republic in the Trans-Appalachian West* (Knoxville: University of Tennessee Press, 2005), 220.

32. Friend, *Along the Maysville Road*, 193.

33. Friend, *Along the Maysville Road*, 223, 120.

34. Stamping Ground Baptist Church Records, First Minute Book, May–June 1810, UKSCRC; Pleasant Grove Baptist Church Records, September–October 1815, FHS; Fox Run Baptist Church Records, September 1820, SBTL; Mayslick, Ky. United Baptist Church Records, vol. 1, January 1808, UKSCRC.

35. Larson, *The Market Revolution in America*, 39–41.

36. Friend, *Along the Maysville Road*, 232–236.

37. Larson, *The Market Revolution in America*, 88–89.

38. Friend, *Along the Maysville Road*, 236, 248–249, 281.

39. David Rice, *An Outline of the History of the Church in the State of Kentucky, during a Period of Forty Years: Containing the Memoirs of David Rice* (Lexington, 1824), 79.

40. Minutes of the Long Run Association of Baptists, 1820, SBTL.

41. Mount Pleasant Baptist Church, Record Books, vol. 1, March 1821, UKSCRC; "Bullittsburg Baptist Churchbook, 1818–1822," Baptist History Homepage, May 1820, accessed May 20, 2020, http://baptisthistoryhomepage.com/bullittsbrg.minutes.18-22.html; Mayslick, Ky. United Baptist Church Records, vol. 1, August 1821, UKSCRC.

42. David's Fork Baptist Church Minutes, September 1819.

43. Old Mill Creek Baptist Church Session Book, book 1, November–December 1816, January–February 1817, June 1818, September–November 1819, KHS.

44. Mount Pleasant Baptist Church, Record Books, vol. 1, January 1824–February 1827, UKSCRC; Bryan's Station Baptist Church Records, April 1826, KHS.

45. Elder, *The Sacred Mirror*, 56–57, 60–62.

46. Mann, *Republic of Debtors*, 2–4.

47. Bryan's Station Baptist Church Records, May 1792, KHS.

48. Alexander Campbell, "A Restoration of the Ancient Order of Things. No. XXVII. On the Discipline of the Church—No. IV," *Christian Baptist*, vol. 6 (1828), 486.

49. Rev. John T. Brooke, *Debt: or The Morality of the Credit System. A Sermon* (Cincinnati: Published by Weed & Wilson, 1841), 3, 4–7, 10–13, Library Company of Philadelphia, Philadelphia, PA (hereafter LCP).

50. Stamping Ground Baptist Church Records, First Minute Book, May–July 1797, UKSCRC.

51. Orville Dewey, *Moral Views of Commerce, Society and Politics, in Twelve Discourses* (New York: David & Co., 1838), 9, 27–28, LCP.

52. See in general Jessica M. Lepler, *The Many Panics of 1837: People, Politics, and the Creation of a Transatlantic Financial Crisis* (New York: Cambridge University Press, 2013).

53. Larson, *The Market Revolution in America*, 92, 93.

54. See tables 8 and 9 in the appendix for a breakdown of charges by race.

55. Eleazer Savage, *Manual of Church Discipline* (Rochester: Sage & Brother, 1844), 50–51.

56. Horwitz, *Transformation of American Law*, 255.

57. Frankfort Baptist Church Records, "Letter to the Franklin Association," August 1823, KHS.

58. Savage, *Manual of Church Discipline*, v.

59. Warham Walker, *Church Discipline: An Exposition of the Scripture Doctrine of Church Order and Government* (Boston: Gould, Kendall and Lincoln, 1844), 153–154, 156.

60. See the preface in William Crowell, *The Church Member's Manual, of Ecclesiastical Principles, Doctrine, and Discipline: Presenting a Systematic View of the Structure, Polity, Doctrines, and Practices of Christian Churches, as Taught in the Scriptures* (Cincinnati: Geo. S. Blanchard, 1873); published also in New York and Boston. William Crowell, *The Church Member's Hand-book: A Guide to the Doctrines and Practice of Baptist Churches* (Boston: Gould, Kendall and Lincoln, 1850). He notes that this latter publication's chapter on discipline "is substantially from" the 1847 manual.

61. Crowell, *The Church Member's Hand-book*, 109, 110–115.

62. Thomas Hume, "The Decline of Spirituality in the Church," *Baptist Preacher* (Richmond, VA) 3, no. 9 (September 1844).

63. Horwitz, *Transformation of American Law*, 258.

64. James Kent, *Commentaries on American Law*, vol. 1 (New York: G. F. Hopkins & Son, 1826), 443.

65. Edwards, *The People and Their Peace*, 289–290.

66. Creath, *A History of Facts*, 8; emphasis in original.

67. Creath, *A History of Facts*, 12–14.

68. Creath, *A History of Facts*, 15.

69. Following the church's ruling in 1839, and Creath's pamphlet of 1840, Henry Foster and other church members responded with a publication accusing Creath of slander. Both parties agreed to submit the case to Alexander Campbell—the leader of the Reformation movement—for mediation. In an 1845 letter to Creath's uncle, Jacob Creath Sr., Campbell denounced both pamphlets, lamenting the damage done to the cause of religion and brotherly affection in the area. Four months later, in the spring of 1846, Campbell again wrote to Creath Sr. about the matter. Having considered "all the evidence in the case, printed, and written, and oral," he insisted that the David's Fork Church should "recall the libel" published against Creath Jr. and release "his land, as well as his character" from all liability. The church, as both individuals and communities were wont to do, had erred "in judgment and in heart." Other churches, too, had gone similarly astray, as Campbell noted that he had numerous cases "on my immense file of documents, which, indeed, is now like the docket of the court of chancery, some ten years behind the age." Peter Donan, *Memoir of Jacob Creath, Jr.* (Cincinnati: R. W. Carroll & Co., 1872), 122. For the full text of both letters see, pp. 116–123. Creath remarked that meddling with Campbell's decision "would seem to me a little like tampering with a judgment of the Supreme Court" (p. 125).

70. William Collins, *Narrative: Containing a Statement of Facts in Relation to the Exclusion of William Collins and William Anderson from the Elizabeth Church of Particular Baptists in Bourbon County* (Frankfort: Hodges, Todd & Pruett, 1843), 3–5, in *Baptists in Kentucky: Pamphlets from the Durrett Collection* (1843), University of Chicago Library.

71. Collins, *Narrative*, 8–12.

72. Collins, *Narrative*, 14. "I told him," Collins reported, "that of all men I ever had any dealings with, he was the most difficult; and if I ever got clear of him, I would keep so, so help me God. (And if I lie in these expressions, then let civil and religious society renounce me forever.)"

73. Collins, *Narrative*, 17–24.

74. Collins, *Narrative*, 24–27.

75. Collins, *Narrative*, 3, 7, 16, 20, 27.

76. *Reply of the Washington Church, to the Proceedings of the Bracken Association, Held in Millersburg, Bourbon Co. KY., September 1847* (Maysville, KY: J. Sprigg Chambers, 1847), 3, in *Baptists in Kentucky*.

77. *Reply of the Washington Church*, 8. It appears confusion arose in December 1841, when Mason intimated that he had preached for the Mayslick church for many years and had not received a Christmas gift. He asked members who were able to bring one dollar to the next

meeting, and there he would tell them what he planned to do with the donations. Depending on the witness, Mason claimed either in December or at the next meeting that the money was for Georgetown College. He donated the money to that institution, but it may have been to fulfill a personal pledge he had previously made. See Judge A. Beatty's 1846 letter on the subject in *Reply of the Washington Church*, 19–22. Beatty claimed that Mason's error was unintentional, not criminal, and it should have been judged as such.

78. *Reply of the Washington Church*, 10. The Washington church claimed that Mason had already answered and made satisfaction for the other two charges while still under the jurisdiction of the Mayslick church, and therefore no more investigation was needed.

79. *Reply of the Committees of the Washington & Lewisburg Baptist Churches, To the Proceedings of the Mayslick Church, and Council, held in Mayslick, December, 1845, and published in the Baptist Banner in January, 1846* (Maysville: Maysville Eagle Office, 1846), 11, in *Baptists in Kentucky*.

80. *Reply of the Committees*, 12–14; emphasis in original.

81. *Reply of the Washington Church*, 28.

82. *Reply of the Washington Church*, 25, 28, 3.

83. *Reply of the Washington Church*, 9–10, 11; emphasis added. For "lawless power" reference, see p. 3.

84. Collins, *Narrative*, 27–28.

Chapter 4 · "The Putrid Carnage of Contention"

1. Minute Books of Eminence, KY Baptist Church (formerly Fox Run), April/May 1831, Archives and Special Collections, James P. Boyce Centennial Library, Southern Baptist Theological Library, Louisville, KY (hereafter SBTL). For the marriage of Elizabeth Drane and Jeptha Brite, see Jordan Dodd, Kentucky Marriages, 1802–1850 [database online] Provo, UT. In the June 1831 records of the Fox Run Baptist Church, a letter from the Dranes and Brites mentions that a "Creath" preached in the Brite home. Jacob Creath Jr. "was the most active and turbulent advocate of Campbellism in the state," while his uncle, Jacob Creath Sr., "was among the first converts to Campbellism." See John H. Spencer, *A History of Kentucky Baptists from 1769 to 1885, including more than 1800 biographical Sketches*, vol. 1 (Cincinnati: J.R. Baumes, 1886), 204, 312. For the quotes that open this chapter, see John Taylor, *The History of Clear Creek Church; and Campbellism Exposed* (Frankfort, KY: A.G. Hodges, 1830), 26.

2. Nathan O. Hatch, *The Democratization of American Christianity* (New Haven: Yale University Press, 1989), 3–6.

3. Sam Haselby, *The Origins of American Religious Nationalism* (New York: Oxford University Press, 2015), 200.

4. David Sehat, *The Myth of American Religious Freedom* (New York: Oxford University Press, 2011). As historian William R. Sutton notes, what emerged during these decades "was a hybrid Protestant theology that deemphasized or rejected predestination in order to assert through Arminianism the innate power of individuals to choose salvation, to strive for moral perfection, and to create a society ready to become the millennial Kingdom of God on earth." See Sutton, *Journeymen for Jesus: Evangelical Artisans Confront Capitalism in Jacksonian Baltimore* (University Park: Pennsylvania State University Press, 1998), 4.

5. In this book I refer to it as the Reformation, which is the term most commonly used in the primary sources.

6. Barton W. Stone, *An Address to the Christian Churches in Kentucky, Tennessee, & Ohio, on Several Important Doctrines of Religion* (Nashville: Printed by M. & J. Norvell, 1814), 6–7; italics in original.

7. John B. Boles, *The Great Revival: Beginnings of the Bible Belt* (Lexington: University Press of Kentucky, 1996), 68.

8. Hatch, *The Democratization of American Christianity*, 49–62. For a critique of Hatch's "democratization" thesis, see Amanda Porterfield, *Conceived in Doubt: Religion and Politics in the New American Nation* (Chicago: University of Chicago Press, 2012).

9. On the General Union and its theological points, see Richard C. Traylor, *Born of Water and Spirit: The Baptist Impulse in Kentucky, 1776–1860* (Knoxville: University of Tennessee Press, 2015), 115–116. On James Garrard, see Ira V. Birdwhistell, *The Baptists of the Bluegrass: A History of the Elkhorn Baptist Association, 1785–1985* (Berea, KY: Berea College Press, 1986), 48.

10. John B. Boles, *Religion in Antebellum Kentucky* (Lexington: University Press of Kentucky, 1995), 29.

11. Ira V. Birdwhistell, *Gathered at the River: A Narrative History of the Long Run Baptist Association* (Louisville: Long Run Baptist Association, 1978), 9; Christopher Waldrep, "The Making of a Border State Society: James McGready, the Great Revival, and the Prosecution of Profanity in Kentucky," *American Historical Review* 99, no. 3 (June 1994): 772.

12. Spencer, *A History of Kentucky Baptists*, vol. 1, 553–554.

13. John F. Schermerhorn and Samuel J. Mills, *A Correct View of that Part of the United States which Lies West of the Alleghany Mountains, with Regard to Religion and Morals* (Hartford: Peter B. Gleason & Co. Printers, 1814), 19–20, 48, Library Company of Philadelphia, Philadelphia, PA (hereafter LCP).

14. Schermerhorn and Mills, *A Correct View*, 20–22, LCP.

15. Traylor, *Born of Water and Spirit*, 104–105; George Washington Doane, *The Missionary Bishop: The Sermon at the Consecration of the Right Reverend Jackson Kemper, D.D., Missionary Bishop for Missouri and Indiana; in St. Peter's Church, Philadelphia, September 25, 1835* (Burlington, NJ: J. L. Powell: Missionary Press, 1835), 12, LCP.

16. *Proceedings of the Baptist Convention for Missionary Purposes; held in Philadelphia, in May, 1814* (Philadelphia: Printed for the Convention, by Ann Coles, 1814), 13, 27–33, LCP.

17. In 1812 Kentucky Baptists witnessed two short-lived periodicals devoted to missionary activities: Noel's *Gospel Herald*, which succeeded Stark Dupuy's *Kentucky Missionary and Theological Magazine*. Spencer, *A History of Kentucky Baptists*, vol. 1, 567–568.

18. On Rice at the Elkhorn Association and related quotes, see Birdwhistell, *The Baptists of the Bluegrass*, 54; Mayslick, Ky. United Baptist Church Records, vol. 1, University of Kentucky Special Collections Research Center, Lexington, KY (hereafter UKSCRC).

19. Spencer, *A History of Kentucky Baptists*, vol. 1, 578–579; Birdwhistell, *Gathered at the River*, 15.

20. John Taylor, "Thoughts on Missions," Baptist History Homepage, accessed February 14, 2021, http://baptisthistoryhomepage.com/j.taylor.miss.html.

21. *Proceedings of the Baptist Convention*, 42, 3; Jeffrey Wayne Taylor, *The Formation of the Primitive Baptist Movement* (Kitchener, ON: Pandora Press, 2004).

22. "Elder Daniel Parker," *Baptist Chronicle and Literary Register* (November 1830), 172; William Warren Sweet, *Religion on the American Frontier: The Baptists, 1783–1830* (New York: Cooper Square Publishers, 1964), 69–75.

23. John Taylor, *History of Clear Creek Church and Campbellism Exposed* (Frankfort: A.G. Hodges, 1830), 8–9.

24. Taylor, "Thoughts on Missions," emphasis in original; Sweet, *Religion on the American Frontier*, 67–68; Elkhorn's actions quoted in Birdwhistell, *The Baptists of the Bluegrass*, 60.

25. Taylor, "Thoughts on Missions."

26. For Taylor on associations, see *Reply of the Washington Church, to the Proceedings of the Bracken Association, Held in Millersburg, Bourbon Co. KY., September 1847* (Maysville, KY: J. Sprigg Chambers, 1847), 4–5, in *Baptists in Kentucky: Pamphlets from the Durrett Collection*, University of Chicago Library.

27. Peter S. Gayle, "Communication—For the Baptist," *The Baptist* (Nashville) 1, no. 1 (January 1835), 3–4.

28. South Elkhorn Baptist Church Records, May 1821, Kentucky Historical Society, Frankfort, KY (hereafter KHS).

29. Alexander Campbell, *Christian Baptist* 1, no. 1 (August 1823), 19–20, dedication page, Hathi Trust, accessed February 14, 2021, https://hdl.handle.net/2027/umn.31951001892486s; Hatch, *The Democratization of American Christianity*, 167–168.

30. Douglas A. Foster, Paul M. Blowers, Anthony L. Dunnavant, and D. Newell Williams, eds. *The Encyclopedia of the Stone-Campbell Movement* (Grand Rapids: William B. Eerdmans, 2004), 116–119.

31. Foster et al., *The Encyclopedia of the Stone-Campbell Movement*, 716.

32. Campbell quoted in Bridwhistell, *The Baptists of the Bluegrass*, 62.

33. The *Baptist Recorder* was superseded by U. B. Chamber's *Baptist Chronicle and Literary Register*, published in Georgetown, KY, in 1830. See Gaylord P. Albaugh, *History and Annotated Bibliography of American Religious Periodicals and Newspapers: Established from 1730 through 1830*, vol. 1 (Worcester, MA: American Antiquarian Society, 1994), 69. For quote, see "The Millennial Harbinger," *Baptist Chronicle and Literary Register*, February 1, 1830, 21.

34. Birdwhistell, *Gathered at the River*, 23–35; unsigned letter, September 1, 1830, Bush-Beauchamp Family Papers, folder 44, James E. Stone Sermons, Religious Writings, and Prayers, 1820–1866, Filson Historical Society, Louisville, KY (hereafter FHS); see also in general, Traylor, *Born of Water and Spirit*, chap. 4.

35. "Deposition of Jasper J. Morris," in *Cahill v. Bigger* (1844), Nicholas County Circuit Court, Civil Case Files (hereafter NCCCF), box 24, bundle 240, Kentucky Department of Libraries and Archives (hereafter KDLA); "Deposition of James Ingels" and "Deposition of Nancy Pierce," in *Trustees of Church of Bethlehem v. Benjamin Howe & John Curle* (1847), Bourbon County Case Files, Court of Justice (hereafter BCCCJ), box 142, case no. 21645, KDLA.

36. Unsigned, untitled article, *Baptist Banner* (Louisville, KY), December 12, 1835.

37. For information on the Waller family, see Spencer, *A History of Kentucky Baptists*, vol. 1, 28–29, 43, 445.

38. Minutes of the Franklin Association of Baptists, 1830, 6; "Complainants Bill" in *Cahill v. Bigger* (1844), NCCCF, KDLA; R. B. C. Howell, *A Memorial of the First Baptist Church Nashville, Tennessee, from 1820–1863, by a member of the church*, vol. 1 (Nashville, 1863), 76, Southern Baptist Library and Archives, Nashville, TN (hereafter SBLA); underlining in original.

39. Birdwhistell, *The Baptists of the Bluegrass*, 71–73.

40. Taylor, *History of Clear Creek Church*, 13, 49; "Deposition of Roadham Rout" and "Deposition of Spencer Anderson," in *Bennett et al. Trustees of the Mt. Vernon Church v. Curd et al.* (1836), folder 1, box 69, case 7914, Court of Justice, Woodford Circuit Case files, 1833–1837 (hereafter CJWCC), KDLA.

41. Numbers from Basil Manly Jr.'s *Sketches of the History of the Elkhorn Association, Kentucky* (1876), Baptist History Homepage, accessed March 12, 2017, http://baptisthistory homepage.com/elkhorn.assoc.his1.manly.html.

42. For average, see Records of the Elkhorn Association of Baptists, 1826–1840, SBTL; on the history of the association in general, see Birdwhistell, *The Baptists of the Bluegrass*.

43. Birdwhistell, *Gathered at the River*, 9–11; Spencer, *History of Kentucky Baptists*, vol. 1, 566. For averages, see Book of the Records of Long Run Association (typescript), vol. 1, SBTL.

44. Records of the Franklin Association of Baptists, 1815–1830, SBTL.

45. Minutes of the Long Run Association, September 1825 and 1826, SBTL. The exclusionary rate is based on Long Run's affiliated churches' membership totals and their reported exclusions

for the previous year. In 1805 the exclusionary rate was 4.68%. To place the 1826 percentage in context, from 1814 to 1825, it never reached 2% and averaged only 1.47%. One can conclude that the queries to the churches had some effect and led to this drastic increase in excommunications.

46. Records of the Elkhorn Association of Baptists, 1827, SBTL.

47. Minutes of the Franklin Association of Baptists, 1825–1827, SBTL; emphasis in original.

48. Spencer, *History of Kentucky Baptists,* vol. 1, 598–599; Records of the Elkhorn Association of Baptists, 1827–1828, SBTL.

49. Records of the Elkhorn Association of Baptists, 1829–1830, SBTL; Records of the Franklin Association of Baptists, 1828–1830, SBTL; Book of Records of the Long Run Association (typescript), September 1830, 176–177, SBTL.

50. For numbers, see Book of Records of the Long Run Association, 1829–1831, SBTL; Records of the Elkhorn Association of Baptists, 1829–1831, SBTL. The Franklin Association's membership losses were less severe. Between 1829 and 1833, for instance, its membership totals dropped by only 268 persons, from 1,860 to 1,592. Nonetheless, the association's reaction to Campbell was as vehement as that of their counterparts at Long Run and Elkhorn. For losses in the state overall, see Birdwhistell, *Gathered at the River,* 29–31.

51. Spencer, *History of Kentucky Baptists,* vol. 1, 646.

52. "For the Baptist Chronicle," *Baptist Chronicle and Literary Register,* May 1830, 74.

53. "Extract from the Rev. Andrew Nuckols," *Baptist Chronicle and Literary Register,* December 1830, 189.

54. "Associations," *Baptist Chronicle and Literary Register,* September 1830, 140.

55. Records of the Elkhorn Association of Baptists, 1829, SBTL.

56. This does not mean that the church charged 5.5% of the membership with a transgression, as one individual could be subject to multiple charges.

57. For quotes from church letter, see Pleasant Grove Baptist Church Records (formerly Flat Rock), August 1831, FHS; emphasis added. For all other charges, see Pleasant Grove Baptist Church Records (formerly Flat Rock), 1815–1836, FHS.

58. For membership numbers, see Records of the Elkhorn Association of Baptists, 1824, 1826–1840, SBTL. For all charges, see David's Fork Baptist Church Records, 1802–1860, David Fork's Baptist Church, accessed September 17, 2018, http://baptisthistoryhomepage.com/Davidsfork.Baptist.Churchbooks.pdf. The church charged ten whites for non-attendance at meetings and eight whites for joining or interacting with another religious group.

59. For the quote on the Mount Pleasant Church's prosperity, see Spencer, *History of Kentucky Baptists,* vol. 1, 209. On Smith, Stone, and Campbell, see Records of the Franklin Association of Baptists, 1827, SBTL. For all disciplinary activity, see Mount Pleasant Baptist Church Records, 1819–1828, KHS. Mount Pleasant's record book ends abruptly in December 1828. Several pages, perhaps as many as sixty, were ripped out after that date. There is evidence that churches other than those noted here witnessed similar declines in disciplinary activity. The Harrod's Creek Church divided over Campbell's doctrine in 1831. From 1819 to 1824, the church recorded one charge for every 3.8% of the membership body. In contrast, from 1825 to 1830, that average dipped to 2.3%. Unfortunately, in 1831, after most of the church joined the Campbellites, the record book becomes sloppy and jumps over most of 1832 before picking back up in 1837. Yet even from that point, when entries became more consistent, the church documented no charges for three years until recording one in May 1840. See the Harrod's Creek Baptist Church, Crestwood, K.Y., 1819–1840, vol. 1, SBTL. On the schism, see Spencer, *History of Kentucky Baptists,* vol. 1, 348–349. Likewise, the Buffalo Lick Baptist Church did not suffer a schism, but it did see a drastic cut in its disciplinary rates as dissension over the Stone-Campbell movement saturated the Franklin Association. From 1815 to 1825, the church leveled one charge for every 5.64% of the membership body. Over the next decade (1826–1836), that rate fell to just 1.86%. Narrowing the period to 1826 (when the

Franklin Association published its letter against anti-creedists) through the association's 1833 exclusion of the Hopewell Church for adhering to the Reformation doctrine, Buffalo Lick's disciplinary rate was only 1.49%. For averages, see membership numbers reported to the Long Run Association, 1815–1817, and the Franklin Association, 1820–1836, SBTL. For charges, see Buffalo Lick Baptist Church Records, FHS. Buffalo Lick's membership totals for 1818–1819 are unknown. However, the church reported sixty-one members in 1816, sixty in 1817, and sixty in 1820. Thus, I assumed sixty for both 1818 and 1819. Similarly, membership in 1836 is unknown, but the church reported eighty-three members in 1835 and eighty-five in 1837, which led me to postulate eighty-four members for the intervening year.

60. Geo. C. Sedgwick, "How to Deal with Campbellites when they first appear in an Orthodox Church," *Baptist Chronicle and Literary Register*, December 1830, 189. Sedgwick's article first appeared in the *Regular Baptist Miscellany* published in Zanesville, OH.

61. Hatch, *Democratization of American Christianity*, 63.

62. Henry Grew, *A Narrative of Proceedings in the Bank Street Church, Philadelphia, Relative to the Reception of an Adhering Free Mason; With an Examination of Masonic Oaths, and of the Principles of Discipline Adopted by Said Church* (Philadelphia, 1836), 4, 12–13, LCP.

63. Grew, *Narrative of Proceedings*, 17–18.

64. Grew, *Narrative of Proceedings*, 21–26.

65. Taylor, *History of Clear Creek Church*, 5.

66. M. A. Crute to Sarah G. Woodfin, 1844, Bodley Family Papers, folder 31: Correspondence, 19 January 1844 to 31 November 1844, FHS.

67. *Proceedings of the General Meeting of Western Baptists, at Cincinnati, Commencing on the Sixth of November, 1833* (Cincinnati: N.S. Johnson, 1834), 12, LCP.

68. *Proceedings of the General Meeting*, 13–14, 19.

69. Traylor, *Born of Water and Spirit*, 114.

70. For Clack's proposition, see "Bloomfield, Ky. Nov. 24, 1831," *Baptist Chronicle and Literary Register*, December 1831, 187; "Letter from J.S. Wilson to Elder Clack," *Baptist Chronicle and Literary Register*, January 1832, 8.

71. "Bloomfield, Ky. Nov. 24, 1831," *Baptist Chronicle and Literary Register*, December 1831, 187; "Letter from J.S. Wilson to Elder Clack," *Baptist Chronicle and Literary Register*, January 1832, 8; "State Convention. Highly Important!" *Baptist Chronicle and Literary Register*, January 1832, 6; A Baptist, "Baptist State Convention," *Baptist Chronicle and Literary Register*, February 1832, 28.

72. Buffalo Lick Baptist Church Minutes, November 1832, FHS.

73. Traylor, *Born of Water and Spirit*, 118–121, 122 (quote), 181–185.

74. Rev. Thomas Hume, "The Decline of Spirituality in the Church," *Baptist Preacher* (Richmond, VA) 3, no. 9 (September 1844).

75. Elliot, *Letters on the General Structure, Government, Laws and Discipline of the Church*, 85–87, and "Letter V" in general, LCP. Elliot went on to claim that if churches did not interpret "the laws and instructions of the Saviour," it would handicap their ability to retain their purity. The result would be "that every man who may choose to enter the sacred enclosure of christian ordinances, must be admitted, and retained, irrespective of religious, or moral character; and thus, the church will be converted into a vast theatre, on which conflicting views, and multifarious and adverse forms of religion, and profligacy, will be exhibited, in motley assemblage, before the world" (p. 101). It seems his fear was that the enclosed gardens of fellowship would resemble the chaotic world beyond their gates.

76. From the records of the Russell's Creek Association meeting held in Green County; see "Associations," *Baptist Chronicle and Literary Messenger*, November 1830, 167.

77. Geo. L. Willis Sr., *History of Shelby County, Kentucky* (Shelby County Genealogical-Historical Society's Committee on Printing, 1929), 59–60.

78. Taylor, *History of Clear Creek Church*, 35.

79. Records of the Elkhorn Association, 1827–1831, quote from 1830, STBL. For Taylor on the Clear Creek division, see John Taylor, "For the Baptist Chronicle," *Baptist Chronicle and Literary Register*, November 1830, 166. On the Bracken Association, see "Deposition of Jasper L. Morris," in *Cahill v. Bigger*, NCCCF, KDLA.

80. Five of the seven charges brought before the church from 1826 to 1830 were against Black members. For all charges and those against Bro. Thomas, see Minute Books of Eminence, KY Baptist Church (formerly Fox Run), 1820–1830, August 1829, SBTL. Membership totals are from Book of Records of the Long Run Association, 1820–1830, SBTL.

81. Recall that at that 1830 meeting the Long Run Association insisted that member churches "discountenance those writing and all those who support [Campbell's] course of rebellion against the principles of our Associational existence."

82. Minute Books of Eminence, June 1831, SBTL.

83. Minute Books of Eminence, June 1831, SBTL.

84. Willis, *History of Shelby County*, 79; not to be confused with the Clear Creek Baptist Church of Woodford County.

85. Eleazer Savage, *Manual of Church Discipline* (Rochester: Sage & Brother, 1844), 72; Silas J. Evans, *A History of Persecution for Truth's Sake in Louisville, Ky.* (Louisville: Printed for the Author, 1858), in *Baptists in Kentucky*.

86. Taylor, *History of Clear Creek Church*, 51; James Fishback, "For the Baptist Banner, No. 1," *Baptist Banner*, July 30, 1836.

Chapter 5 • "A Great Curse to the Neighborhood"

1. "Deposition of James Fishback," pp. 23–26, in *Bennett et al. Trustees of the Mt. Vernon Church v. Curd et al.* (1836), folder 1, box 69, case 7914, Court of Justice, Woodford Circuit Case Files, 1833–1837 (hereafter CJWCC), Kentucky Department of Library and Archives, Frankfort, KY (hereafter KDLA). For the quote that opens this chapter, see "Deposition of Roadham Rout" in same case file.

2. "Remonstrance," *Bennett et al. v. Curd et al.*, folder 2, CJWCC, KDLA.

3. "Deposition of James Fishback," pp. 23, 30–32. On the new church, see the complainants' declaration to the court, 9, *Bennett et al. v. Curd et al.*, folder 1, CJWCC, KDLA.

4. *Watson v. Jones*, 80 U.S. 679, Lexis 1383 (1871).

5. *Jones v. Wolf*, 443 U.S. 595, Lexis 16 (1979).

6. The deference rule "prohibited inquiry into doctrine because civil courts were required to defer to the determination of the ecclesiastical court" whenever matters of discipline, faith, or church rules or custom came before the courts. See Brian Schmalzbach, "Confusion and Coercion in Church Property Litigation," *Virginia Law Review*, 96 no. 2 (April 2010): 446–447. In 1979, without overturning this approach, the U.S. Supreme Court put forth the neutral principle framework, indicating "that civil courts need not defer to higher church authorities if they instead rely on authoritative documents," such as express trusts, deeds, or corporate charters, "that can be interpreted without invoking religious understandings." See Kent Greenwalt, "Hands Off! Civil Court Involvement in Conflicts over Religious Property," *Columbia Law Review* 98, no. 8 (December 1998): 1859. See also Kathleen E. Reeder, "Whose Church Is It, Anyway? Property Disputes and Episcopal Church Splits," *Columbia Journal of Law and Social Problems* 40, no. 2 (Winter 2006): 125; Justin M. Gardner, "Ecclesiastical Divorce in Hierarchical Denominations and the Resulting Custody Battle over Church Property: How the Supreme Court Has Needlessly Rendered Church Property Trusts Ineffectual," *Ave Maria Law Review* 6, no. 1 (Fall 2007): 235.

7. For a recent investigation of church property issues in the early republic and antebellum periods, see Sarah Barringer Gordon, "The First Disestablishment: Limits on Church Power and Property before the Civil War," *University of Pennsylvania Law Review* 162, no. 2

(January 2014): 307–372; and Sarah Barringer Gordon, "The Landscape of Faith: Religious Property and Confiscation in the Early Republic," in *Making Legal History: Essays in Honor of William E. Nelson*, eds. Daniel J. Hulsebosch and R. B. Bernstein (New York: New York University, 2013). For a focus on property issues in Virginia, see Thomas E. Buckley, *Establishing Religious Freedom: Jefferson's Statute in Virginia* (Charlottesville: University of Virginia Press, 2013), especially chaps. 4 and 5. For disputes resulting from the sectional crisis, see Lucas Volkman, *Houses Divided: Evangelical Schisms and the Crisis of the Union in Missouri* (New York: Oxford University Press, 2018), especially chaps. 2 and 3.

8. Quote is from Kentucky Court of Appeals Judge J. R. Underwood in his dissent in *Gass v. Wilhite* 32 Ky. 170, 203, Lexis 55 (1834).

9. Nathan O. Hatch, *The Democratization of American Christianity* (New Haven, CT: Yale University Press, 1989). Quote is from Gordon, "The First Disestablishment," 320. On the process of disestablishment in the nineteenth century, with a particular focus on legislative enactments, see Steven K. Green, *The Second Disestablishment: Church and State in Nineteenth-Century America* (New York: Oxford University Press, 2010); and Mark D. McGarvie, *One Nation under Law: America's Early National Struggles to Separate Church and State* (DeKalb: Northern Illinois University Press).

10. Belden C. Lane, *Landscapes of the Sacred: Geography and Narrative in American Spirituality* (Baltimore: Johns Hopkins University Press, 2001), 32, chap. 1 in general.

11. See David Chidester and Edward T. Linenthal's "Introduction" to their edited volume, *American Sacred Space* (Bloomington: Indiana University Press, 1995), 8.

12. Chidester and Linenthal, "Introduction," 8. For a look at how property and religious pluralism interact in contemporary American culture, see Bret E. Carroll, "Worlds in Space: American Religious Pluralism in Geographic Perspective," in *Gods in America: Religious Pluralism in the United States*, eds. Charles L. Cohen and Ronald L. Numbers (New York: Oxford University Press, 2013), 56–102. Carroll insists that any attempt to understand the "complex dynamic" that is American religious pluralism "must begin by recognizing that it is fundamentally spatial" (p. 60).

13. *Shannon v. Frost*, 42 Ky. 253, 259, Lexis 151 (1842).

14. Craig Thompson Friend, *Kentucke's Frontiers* (Bloomington: Indiana University Press, 2010), 231.

15. Frank Stone to James E. Stone Jr., October 8, 1863, Stone and Lewis Families Correspondence, 1832–1887, Bush Beauchamp Family Papers, 1835–1982, Filson Historical Society, Louisville, KY (hereafter FHS).

16. Anne C. Loveland and Otis B. Wheeler, *From Meetinghouse to Megachurch: A Material and Cultural History* (Columbia: University of Missouri Press, 2003), 14–15, 20–21. On the laity's role in crafting a region's religious geography, see Shelby M. Balik, *Rally the Scattered Believers: Northern New England's Religious Geography* (Bloomington: Indiana University Press, 2014), especially chap. 4.

17. Frankfort Baptist Church Records, March–May 1816, Kentucky Historical Society, Frankfort, KY (hereafter KHS). Remembering his time with the Frankfort Church in the late 1810s, soon after its organization, John Taylor claimed that when he set out from home for the monthly meeting, "it was often unknown where it would be held, till we got to Frankfort—sometimes in the Assembly Hall, Senate Chamber, or Courthouse; and sometimes neither of the places could be gotten. Then we had to seek a bye-corner somewhere else." See John Taylor, *A History of Ten Baptist Churches, of Which the Author has been Alternatively a Member* (Frankfort, KY: J.H. Holeman, 1823), 134.

18. R. B. C. Howell, *A Memorial of the First Baptist Church at Nashville, Tennessee from 1820 to 1863 by a Member of the Church* (1863), 67. Typescript available at the Southern Baptist Library and Archive, Nashville, TN (hereafter SBLA).

19. Loveland and Wheeler, *From Meetinghouse to Megachurch*, 21, quote on 22.

20. "Deposition of Nancy Pierce," in *Trustees of Church of Bethlehem v. Benjamin Howe & John Curle* (1847) Bourbon County Case Files, Court of Justice (hereafter BCCFCJ), box 142, case #21645, KDLA.

21. "Deposition of John Kenny," in *Trustees of Church of Bethlehem v. Howe & Curle*, BCCFCJ, KDLA.

22. "Remonstrance," *Bennett et al. v. Curd et al.*, folder 2, CJWCCC, KDLA.

23. Quoted in Loveland and Wheeler, *From Meetinghouse to Megachurch*, 7.

24. Kevin M. Sweeney, "Meetinghouses, Town Houses, and Churches: Changing Perceptions of Sacred and Secular Space in Southern New England, 1720–1850," *Winterthur Portfolio* 28, no. 1 (Spring 1993): 59–60.

25. Rhys Isaac, *The Transformation of Virginia, 1740–1790* (Chapel Hill: University of North Carolina Press, 1982), 58–61.

26. Ellen Eslinger, *Citizens of Zion: The Social Origins of Camp Meeting Revivalism* (Knoxville: University of Tennessee Press, 1999), 132–133.

27. "Deposition of Bee Salter," in *Baptist Church of Lancaster v. Presbyterian Church of Lancaster* (1855), Garrard County Circuit Court, Chancery / Equity Case Files (hereafter GCCCE), box 76, bundle 308, case #24-28, KDLA.

28. Frankfort Baptist Church Records, vol. 1, September 1822, KHS.

29. "Exhibit A," *Cahill v. Bigger* (1844), Nicholas County Circuit Court, Civil Case Files (hereafter NCCCF), box 24, bundle 240, KDLA.

30. Record of the Elkhorn Association of Baptists, 1829, Archives and Special Collections, James P. Boyce Centennial Library, Southern Baptist Theological Library, Louisville, KY (hereafter SBTL).

31. "Deposition of James Fishback," 5, in *Bennett et al. v. Curd et al.*, CJWCC, KDLA; underlining in original. For an example of property deeded specifically for a "Republican Meetinghouse" see the 1830 deed from Michael Mitchel to trustees of the Glenns Creek Republican Meeting house, Woodford County Deed Book M, 279–280, KDLA.

32. "Deposition of JC Bryant," in *Baptist Church of Lancaster v. Presbyterian Church of Lancaster*, GCCCE, KDLA.

33. "Separate Answer of John Curle to the Amended Bill," *Trustees of Church of Bethlehem v. Howe & Curle*, BCCFCJ, KDLA; "Deposition of Jacob Robinson," and the "Deposition of William Huffman, Sr." in *Baptist Church of Lancaster v. Presbyterian Church of Lancaster*, GCCCE, KDLA. Despite their apparent ecumenical foundations, individuals and communities restricted access to these "republican meetinghouses" to mainline religious groups. For instance, Col. Thomas Buford, along with numerous other deponents, insisted that the Lancaster meetinghouse was "free to all sects except Roman Catholics and Shaking Quakers."

34. James Whitsitt, "Article 3—No Title," *Nashville Republican*, July 25, 1835.

35. "Deposition of Thomas Buford," in *Baptist Church of Lancaster v. Presbyterian Church of Lancaster*, GCCCE, KDLA.

36. "Exhibit [x]: Original Article for Building Meeting House," in *Bennett et al. v. Curd et al.*, folder 2, CJWCC, KDLA. They further agreed to pay half the sum "when the bricks are made or stone, at the building and the foundation above the ground." The other half "when the house shall be completed."

37. "Respondent's Bill," 5, *Bennett et al. v. Curd et al.*, folder 1, CJWCC, KDLA. Fishback also claimed that when the Mount Vernon Church was constituted in June 1822, "there were it is believed fewer professors of religion immediately in the neighborhood, of any denomination of Christians, in proportion to the actual population of it than in any a neighborhood" that he knew of in the state; see "Deposition of James Fishback," 13.

38. On December 7, 1835, the trustees of the meetinghouse filed an injunction and restraining order against the opposition church; see "Wallace &c. to Curd, injunction bond," and "Summons and restraining order." On January 30, 1836, the defendants filed a demurrer with the court, which was overruled; see "Curd &c. v. Wallace &c. Demurrer." All are in *Bennett et al. v. Curd et al.*, folder 2, CJWCC, KDLA.

39. "Article 2—No Title," *Nashville Republican*, July 16, 1835, 2. Even before the Campbellite divisions in the region, opposing factions often shared meetinghouses following schisms. After a number of members left the Versailles Baptist Church in the early 1820s to join a newly constituted Particular Baptist church, each body worshipped in the Regular Baptists' meetinghouse. "The reason I understood for using this freedom is," John Taylor wrote, "some of the members with [the new church], have paid very liberally for building the meeting house . . . and it is more to be lamented that this is not the only case in Kentucky." Taylor, *A History of Ten Baptist Churches*, 184.

40. "Deposition of James McKee," in *Baptist Church of Lancaster v. Presbyterian Church of Lancaster*, GCCCE, KDLA.

41. Chris Beneke, *Beyond Toleration: The Religious Origins of American Pluralism* (New York: Oxford University Press, 2006), 7.

42. "Deposition of JC Bryant," in *Baptist Church of Lancaster v. Presbyterian Church of Lancaster*, GCCCE, KDLA. Bryant's deposition was in 1855, but he spoke about the subscribing to the meetinghouse in 1815.

43. "Deposition of Bee Salter," in *Baptist Church of Lancaster v. Presbyterian Church of Lancaster*, GCCCE, KDLA.

44. See, for example, "Deposition of Polly Wilmot," "Deposition of Thomas Buford," and "Deposition of James McKee," in *Baptist Church of Lancaster v. Presbyterian Church of Lancaster*, GCCCE, KDLA.

45. *The Baptist Church at Lancaster v. The Presbyterian Church*, 57 Ky. 635, 639, Lexis 76 (1857).

46. Particular Baptist Society Deed, Davidson County Deed Books, vol. F, 53, Tennessee State Library and Archives, Nashville, TN (hereafter TSLA); emphasis added.

47. For instance, in June 1834, not long after a split with a Campbellite faction, Nashville's First Baptist Church clarified that the phrase "The Lord's supper is to be administered to orderly Christians only," which appeared in its church constitution, referred to only "Christians of our denomination." See Records of First Baptist Church of Nashville, June 7, 1834, SBLA.

48. "Exhibit #1," *Bennett et al. v. Curd et al.*, folder 2, CJWCC, KDLA; underlining in original.

49. "Deposition of Robert Adams," in *Bennett et al. v. Curd et al.*, folder 2, CJWCC, KDLA.

50. Others disagreed, contending that the subscription paper was never "designed to exclude . . . as it was built on Republican principles." See "Deposition of Daniel J. Williams" and "Deposition of Alexander Dunlaps," in *Bennett et al. v. Curd et al.*, folder 2, CJWCC, KDLA.

51. Paul G. Kauper and Stephen C. Ellis, "Religious Corporations and the Law," *Michigan Law Review* 71, no. 8 (August 1973): 1504–1507.

52. Buckley, *Establishing Religious Freedom*, 67–68.

53. Buckley, *Establishing Religious Freedom*, 83.

54. Buckley, *Establishing Religious Freedom*, 82–85. For a complete account of Virginia Baptists' quest against glebe lands, see Buckley, *Establishing Religious Freedom*, 92–115, and Buckley, "Evangelicals Triumphant: The Baptists' Assault on Virginia Glebes, 1786–1801," *William and Mary Quarterly* 45, no. 1 (January 1988): 33–69. Buckley argues that victory in the glebe contest gave the Baptists the political tools and outside support necessary to pursue later legislative goals and laid the groundwork for them to push their cultural values upon the

wider American society. Baptists were also instrumental in crafting church-state relations in New England. Johann N. Neem claims that Baptists, in their effort to combat state interference in their religious matters, used arguments that proved "invaluable to defending the rights of associations, thus creating an ideological foundation for an autonomous civil society"; Neem, "The Elusive Common Good: Religion and Civil Society in Massachusetts, 1780–1833," *Journal of the Early Republic* 24, no. 3 (Autumn 2004): 390.

55. Buckley, *Establishing Religious Freedom*, 132–134; for quote, see p. 128.

56. See, in general, Thomas E. Buckley, "After Disestablishment: Thomas Jefferson's Wall of Separation in Antebellum Virginia," *Journal of Southern History* 61, no. 3 (August 1995): 445–480; for quote, see p. 452.

57. William J. Novak, "The American Law of Association: The Legal-Political Construction of Civil Society," *Studies in American Political Development* 15 (Fall 2001): 180. On religious groups seeking incorporation in the post-Revolutionary period, see also Chris Beneke, "The Free Market and the Founders' Approach to Church-State Relations," *Journal of Church and State* 52, no. 2 (July 2010): 332; McGarvie, *One Nation under Law*, 3.

58. *Journal of the House of Representatives of the Commonwealth of Kentucky, 1813* (Frankfort, KY: Gerrard and Berry Printers, 1813), 105.

59. *Journal of the House of Representatives, KY*, 141–142.

60. *Journal of the House of Representatives, KY*, 239–241. For actions taken by the joint committee and amendments, see *Journal of the Senate of the Commonwealth of Kentucky, 1813* (Frankfort, KY, 1814), 142, 149–150, 172, 205.

61. *Acts Passed at the First Session of the Twenty Second General Assembly, for the Commonwealth of Kentucky: Begun and Held in the Town of Frankfort, on Monday the Sixth Day of December, One Thousand Eight Hundred and Thirteen, and of the Commonwealth the Twenty-Second* (Frankfort, KY: Gerard & Berry—Printers for the Commonwealth, 1814), 211–212. The act also stipulated that "the quantity of real estate hereafter acquired by any religious society and vested in trustees and their successors . . . shall not exceed four acres of land." Two decades later, the Kentucky Court of Appeals ruled in *Gass*, 184, that the 1814 act does not limit religious groups from acquiring more than four acres; rather, "it only restrains the application of the benefit of its own provisions, to an acquisition not exceeding four acres." *Gass v. Wilhite* 32 Ky. 170, 203, Lexis 55 (1834). Section 3 of the 1852 Revised Statutes provided that religious societies could acquire up to fifty acres of land "for the purpose of erecting thereon houses of public worship, public instruction, a parsonage, a grave yard, and a horse pound." See C. A. Wickliffe, S. Turner, and S. Nicholas, *The Revised Statutes of Kentucky: Approved and Adopted by the General Assembly, 1851 and 1852* (Frankfort, KY: A.G. Hodges, 1852), chap. 14, sec. 3.

62. Preston S. Loughborough, *A Digest of the Statute Laws of Kentucky, of a Public and Permanent Nature, Passed since 1834* [. . .] (Frankfort, KY: Albert G. Hodges, 1842), 499.

63. Wickliffe, Turner, and Nicholas, *The Revised Statutes of Kentucky*, chap. 14, sec. 3, proviso 5.

64. Bryan's Station Baptist Church Records, March 1811, September 1812, KHS; South Elkhorn Baptist Church Records, 1822–1857, March 1822, KHS. For the appointment of trustees to the Mount Vernon meetinghouse by Curd's faction, see "Copy Order & Record," *Bennett et al. v. Curd et al.*, folder 2, CJWCC, KDLA.

65. See Berryman's note in *Baptist Education Society v. Berryman* (1846), Owen Circuit Court Case Files, Courts of Justice (hereafter OCCCF), box 31, bundle 74, KDLA.

66. "Bill of Exceptions" and "Jury Decision," *Baptist Education Society v. Berryman*, OCCCF, KDLA.

67. *Shannon et al. v. Frost et al.*, 42 Ky. 253 (1842).

68. *Alexander v. Slavens*, 46 Ky. 351, 353, Lexis 34 (1847). For the 1817 act, see R. L. Caruthers and A. O. P. Nicholson, *A Compilation of the Statutes of Tennessee, of a General and*

Permanent Nature, From the Commencement of Government to the Present Time (Nashville: 1836), 559.

69. United Baptist Church of Nashville, Davidson County Deed Books, vol. O, 193, TSLA. For actions taken by the church, see Howell, *A Memorial of the First Baptist Church,* especially chap. 3, SBLA.

70. Howell, *A Memorial of the First Baptist Church*, 68.

71. Records of the First Baptist Church of Nashville, vol. 1, p. 1, SBLA; Howell, *A Memorial of the First Baptist Church,* 67, SBLA.

72. Records of the First Baptist Church of Nashville, vol. 1, February 13, 1836, SBLA. Article X of the church constitution states, "If at any time a majority of the Church should depart from the principles embodied in the annexed Declaration of Faith, the property of the Church shall belong to the minority, however small, who adhere to those principles. Or, should at any time, even all the members depart from the present doctrines, the property shall still be held by the Trustees subject to the use and occupancy for religious worship, if any others in this city, or Davidson County, or both, or, if there be none here, any from any part of the Country who may come here to reside, and may now profess or hereafter embrace, the present principles of the Church."

73. Cedar Creek Baptist Church Deed, Wilson County Deed Books, vol. I, 471, TSLA.

74. Union Baptist Church Deed, Wilson County Deed Books, vol. P, 158, TSLA.

75. Antioch Baptist Church Deed, Davidson County Deed Books, vol. O, 32–33, TSLA.

76. Spring Creek Church Deed, Robertson County Deed Books, vol. M, 261–265, TSLA.

77. Little Cedar Lick Baptist Church Records, June–July 1837, June 1838, SBLA.

78. Spencer's Creek Baptist Church Deed, Wilson County Deed Books, vol. R, 369, TSLA.

79. Ridge Church of United Baptists Deed, Wilson County Deed Books, vol. R, 454, TSLA; emphasis added.

80. Concord Baptist Church Records, Brentwood, Tennessee, 1804–1901, September 1835–May 1836, SBLA.

81. Concord Baptist Church Records, December 1843, February 1844, SBLA.

82. Concord Baptist Church Records, June 1844, SBLA.

83. Concord Baptist Church Deed, Williamson County Deed Books, vol. S, 7, TSLA.

84. Howell, *A Memorial of the First Baptist Church*, 33, 66, SBLA.

85. Randolph A. Roth, *The Democratic Dilemma: Religion, Reform, and the Social Order in the Connecticut River Valley of Vermont* (New York: Cambridge University Press, 1987), 72–73.

86. Gordon, "The Landscape of Faith," 30. For the two cases, see *Town of Pawlet v. Clark*, 13 U.S. 292, Lexis 392 (1815) and *Society for the Propagation of the Gospel v. New Haven*, 21 U.S. 464, Lexis 291 (1823).

87. Gordon, "The First Disestablishment," 358n261.

88. In *Terrett v. Taylor*, 13 U.S. 43, Lexis 366 (1815)—a case involving Alexandria glebe lands that Virginia had ceded to the District of Columbia—Supreme Court justice Joseph Story claimed the 1802 Glebe Act was unconstitutional. However, as historian Sarah Barringer Gordon writes, "The case had little practical value outside the District of Columbia, because the Supreme Court's writ did not extend to land law outside the bounds of federal territories." See Gordon, "The Landscape of Faith," 27.

89. Buckley, *Establishing Religious Freedom*, 114.

90. Buckley, *Establishing Religious Freedom*, 115.

91. *Gass v. Wilhite*, 32 Ky. 170, Lexis 55 (1834). Judge Underwood filed a dissent.

92. *Gass v. Wilhite*, 32 Ky. 170–172, Lexis 55. In contrast, Underwood's dissent warned of tying property rights to religious creeds. "Under such convictions, they brought their property . . . into the society. But an individual member changes his faith; new views and opinions are embraced, and he now believes, that it is as inconsistent with the will of God to

continue in the society, as he formerly thought it was his duty. Under such a change, he abandons the society, and claims a share of the property. I think it ought to be decreed to him; because, as to him, all the purposes for which the partnership was entered into have ceased; and because, it was entered into for an indefinite period." See *Gass*, Lexis 55, 199–200.

93. "Bill," in *Trustees of African Church v. Welcher Breckinridge* (1833), Fayette Circuit Case Files, Courts of Justice (hereafter FCCCJ), box 100, drawer 894 (no case number), KDLA.

94. John Taylor, *History of Clear Creek Church and Campbellism Exposed*, 2nd ed. (Frankfort: A.G. Hodges, Commentator Office, 1830), 5–6, 36.

95. Minutes of the Floyd's Fork Baptist Church (Fishersville, KY), December 1834–January 1835, SBTL. For a similar example, see Harrod's Creek Baptist Church Records, Crestwood, KY, vol. 1, January/August 1841, December 1845, SBTL.

96. John Curd, "Lexington, Ky., Oct. 4, 1834," *Millennial Harbinger*, 1st ser., 5 (1834): 573–574; James Challen, "Lexington, Ky., June 14, 1834," *Millennial Harbinger*, 1st ser., 5 (1834): 333–334.

97. Note, "Judicial Intervention in Disputes over the Use of Church Property," *Harvard Law Review* 75, no. 6 (April 1962): 1152n57. In Tennessee, where the legislature failed to pass a nearly identical law in 1827 and where disagreements over doctrine and church governance similarly divided churches, there do not appear to have been any cases that reached the state supreme court. For Tennessee's failed bill, see "A Bill to secure religious society's [*sic*] & congregations in the peaceable & uninterrupted enjoyment & possession of their houses and tenements appropriated to the purposes of worship & devotion," 17th General Assembly, box 100, folder 9, TSLA. It does not appear that any other state passed a similar statute during the antebellum period. See William Henry Roberts, *Laws Relating to Religious Corporations: being a collection of the general statutes of the several states and territories for the incorporation and management of churches, religious societies, presbyteries, synods, etc.* (Philadelphia: Presbyterian Board of Publican and Sabbath-School Word, 1896); see also R. H. Tyler, *American Ecclesiastical Law: The Law of Religious Societies, Church Government and Creeds, Disturbing Religious Meetings, and the Law of Burial Grounds in the United States with Practical Forms* (Albany, NY: William Gould, Law Bookseller and Publisher, 1866). One problem with Tyler's work, however, is that he does not even mention the 1814 act or the similar measure retained in the 1852 Revised Statutes. Some state courts in the region did address church property and schism. The Ohio Supreme Court ruled in *Methodist Episcopal Church of Cincinnati v. John Wood*, 5 Ohio 283, Lexis 159 (1831), that seceding members from an organized church did not retain rights to the property of the church from which they departed. Likewise, three years later, that court ruled in *Keyser v. Stansifer*, 6 Ohio 363, Lexis 86 (1834), that a church majority that held property in fee simple could not be deprived of its control because of their supposed adoption of doctrinal error. Neither, however, could the church expel the minority, their "fellow-corporators," from the property's use. The minority's claim for sole use was denied. Judge Lane, writing for the court, declared that Baptists, as independent bodies, had control over their theological course. "The opinions of such a body cannot but change," he wrote. "To fix their fleeting wherries; to anchor them immovably in the stream of time is beyond human power; for the mind, at least, is free; ranging by its inherent strength through the boundless fields of knowledge, molding its belief according to its apprehension of the trust, and incapable of fixedness until the day when all truth shall be made known. And if it were possible, it was wrong; to limit activity of mind is to set boundaries to human knowledge" (pp. 365–366). The Illinois Supreme Court, in *Ferraria v. Vasconcelles*, 23 Ill. 403, Lexis 246 (1860), pointing to a number of Kentucky cases—including, *Shannon*, *Curd*, *Gibson*, and *Hadden*—ruled that in case of schism, the property should remain with the church that adheres to the tenets of discipline and organization to which was the property was originally dedicated.

98. See, for example, *Curd et al. v. Wallace et al.* (1838) 37 Ky. 190; *Shannon et al. v. Frost et al.* (1842) 42 Ky. 253; *Gibson et al. v. Armstrong* (1847) 46 Ky. 481; *Hadden et al. v. Chorn &c.* (1847) 47 Ky. 70; *Scott &c. v. Curle &c.* (1848) 48 Ky. 17; *Berryman v. Reese &c.* (1850) 50 Ky. 287.

99. "Deposition of James Fishback," pp. 25, 28–29, in *Bennett et al. v. Curd et al.*, folder 1, CJWCC, KDLA.

100. *Curd et al. v. Wallace et al.*, 191–192, Lexis 118.

101. *Curd et al. v. Wallace et al.* 190–198, Lexis 118; "Deposition of James Fishback," 3, in *Bennett et al. v. Curd et al.*, folder 1, CJWCC, KDLA. Fishback quotes the "Webster Dict."; underlining in original.

102. A Spectator, "To the friends of good order," *Baptist Banner*, December 12, 1835. "A Spectator" was probably James Fishback or someone closely connected with Fishback's church since some of the language mirrors Fishback's own writings and the article's appearance coincided with the trustees' filing of the suit at the circuit court; italics in original.

103. Unsigned, untitled article, *Baptist Banner*, December 12, 1835.

104. James Whitsitt, "Article 3—No Title," *Nashville Republican*, July 25, 1835, 3.

105. *Curd et al. v. Wallace et al.*, 196.

106. *Curd et al. v. Wallace et al.*, 197.

107. Some of these cases, such as *Scott &c. v. Curle &c.*, involved the 1835 act.

108. *Shannon et al. v. Frost et al.*, 42 Ky. 253 (1842).

109. *Watson v. Jones* 80 U.S. 679 (1871). In this case the Supreme Court points to *Gibson v. Armstrong*, 46 Ky. 481 (1847), among other cases, when discussing the deference rule; *Berryman v. Reese &c.* 50 Ky. 287 (1850).

110. See "Deposition of Robert Risk," in *Bennett et al. v. Curd et al.*, folder 1, CJWCC, KDLA. There was much debate over whether changing the name of the church body from "Baptist" to "Church of Christ" in some way lessened that body's affiliation with the Baptist denomination, weakening their potential claim to sole use of the meetinghouse. See "Deposition of William Poindexter." The quote about "Baptist" as a sectarian term is pulled from a question from the defendants to Poindexter about whether he had heard Fishback making such statements, to which Poindexter answered, "I have."

111. "Deposition of James McConnell," in *Bennett et al. v. Curd et al.*, folder 2, CJWCC, KDLA.

112. For Fishback's doctrinal leanings, see Curd, Steele, and Redd "Answers," folder 1, and "Deposition of James McConnell," folder 2, in *Bennett et al. v. Curd et al.*, CJWCC, KDLA.

113. See, for example, "Deposition of Thomas P Dudley," in *Garland Biggers & others v. Oliver Cahill & others* (1846), NCCCF, KDLA.

114. For an example of a church schism resulting from one faction's adoption of Particular Baptist principles, see Bryan's Station Church Record Book, March 1811 / December 1812, KHS. See also the opening pages of the South Elkhorn Baptist Church Records, 1822–1857, KHS. For division in a governing association, see "Minutes of the Elkhorn Baptist Association, 1812," accessed October 7, 2014, http://baptisthistoryhomepage.com/1812.ky.elkhn.lick.bry.st.html.

115. *Scott, &c. V. Curle, &c.*, 48 Ky. 17 (1848). In some instances courts had good reason to disregard clauses in land deeds. In *Curle*, for instance, the Reformed Church had sole use of the building for nearly a decade until a group of nearby Baptists, knowing that the house had been deeded for that denomination's use, organized a new church and pushed to gain control over the property. In that case the court looked to continued use rather than the doctrinal stipulations of the land deed.

116. *Watson v. Jones*, 723.

117. *Harper v. Straws*, 53 Ky. 39, Lexis 14 (1853).

118. *Gartin v. Penick*, 68 Ky. 110, Lexis 236 (1868).

119. *Watson v. Jones* 80 U.S. 679 (1871); see also Ronald W. Eades, *Watson v. Jones: The Walnut Street Presbyterian Church and the First Amendment* (Lynnville, TN: Archer Editions Press, 1982).

120. Recently church property disputes have found new life due to the cultural politics of gay marriage. See, for example, Michelle Boorstein, "After Prolonged Legal Battle, Virginia Episcopalians Prepare to Reclaim Property," *Washington Post,* February 11, 2012, accessed August 26, 2014, http://www.washingtonpost.com/local/after-prolonged-legal-battle-virginia-episcopalians-prepare-to-reclaim-property/2012/02/08/gIQAhfJI7Q_story.html.

Conclusion

1. For quotes, see Carlo Angerer, "Bobby Jindal Says West Allows Muslims to Set Up 'No-Go Zones,'" NBC News, January 19, 2015, accessed January 20, 2015, http://www.nbcnews.com/news/world/bobby-jindal-says-west-allows-muslims-set-no-go-zones-n289011; Associated Press, "Jindal: Muslims Form 'No-Go Zones' outside Civic Control," *New York Times*, January 19, 2015, accessed January 20, 2015, https://www.timesfreepress.com/news/national/political/story/2015/jan/19/jindal-muslims-form-no-go-zones-outside-civic/283493/. On recent statutes against sharia law, see Kimberly Karseboom, "Sharia Law and America: The Constitutionality of Prohibiting the Consideration of Sharia Law in American Courts," *Georgetown Journal of Law and Public Policy* 10, no. 2 (Summer 2012): 663–680. For the quote that opens this conclusion, see Minutes of the Franklin Association of Baptists, 1837, p. 5, Archives and Special Collections, James P. Boyce Centennial Library, Southern Baptist Theological Library, Louisville, KY (hereafter SBTL).

2. Christine Leigh Heyrman, *Southern Cross: The Beginnings of the Bible Belt* (Chapel Hill: University of North Carolina Press, 1997), 15–22.

3. Jewel L. Spangler, *Virginians Reborn: Anglican Monopoly, Evangelical Dissent, and the Rise of the Baptists in the Late Eighteenth Century* (Charlottesville: University of Virginia Press, 2008), 77–78, 81–83, 105.

4. Quoted in Rhys Isaac, *The Transformation of Virginia, 1740–1790* (Chapel Hill: University of North Carolina Press, 1982), 175.

5. James M. Pendleton, "The Condition of the Baptist Cause in Kentucky in 1837," Baptist History Homepage, accessed May 8, 2017, http://baptisthistoryhomepage.com/ky.bapt.in.1837.pendleton.html.

6. Minutes of the Franklin Association of Baptists 1837, pp. 5 and 7, SBTL.

7. Mark A. Noll, "Protestants, Money, and the Market, 1790–1860," in *God and Mammon*, ed. Mark A. Noll (New York: Oxford University Press, 2001), 270.

INDEX

Lightning Source UK Ltd.
Milton Keynes UK
UKHW010043210622
404705UK00001B/4/J

9 781421 443072